INTELLECTUALS IN LABOR UNIONS

INTELLECTUALS
IN
LABOR UNIONS

ORGANIZATIONAL PRESSURES
ON PROFESSIONAL ROLES

by Harold L. Wilensky

THE FREE PRESS, PUBLISHERS
GLENCOE, ILLINOIS

For JEANNE

PREFACE

THIS IS A STUDY of the relation of the "man of knowledge" to the "man of power" in the national headquarters of the American trade union—an appraisal of the functions, influence and role orientations of organized Labor's hired brains. These men are variously labeled "experts," "technicians," "specialists"; most of them are or once were "intellectuals." They have a variety of titles: legal counsel, research and education director, statistician, editor, publicity director, community relations man, engineer, pension and insurance expert, legislative representative.

The criteria for identifying an "expert" are: (1) he is a hired staff man responsible to elected officials and working full time in the headquarters of a national or international union; (2) he is a "man of knowledge" in the sense that he brings to the problem at hand a body of specialized information and skill acquired through formal education and/or training on the job. In general he is distinguished from the elected or appointed line officer (e.g., President, Regional Director, "International Representative," Business Agent, or Organizer) by virtue of the absence of formal executive authority. As an intelligence agent he is further distinguished from staff men on the "housekeeping" side of union functioning (e.g., administrative assistants, bookkeepers, most auditors).

The central problem of the study is the role of the expert in the decision-making process in unions. This is approached both from the "objective" side (the amount and direction of his influence in various areas of union decision), and the "subjective" side (the work experience of the expert and his conception of his role).

My aim is to describe the activities of various types of experts, identify some of the variables affecting their influence, and to do this in a way that will tell us something about the interaction of organization and person in the large-scale private association.

The problem of the staff expert could be studied in many types of organization. I chose the large national trade union for three reasons. First, the great rapidity with which the American trade union has changed from protest movement to complex established organization makes it a good place to analyze an important sociological problem: the effects of the growing division of labor on the exercise of power and influence, or, put another way, the process of bureaucratization. Second, as an instance of a successful (i.e., institutionalized) social movement, the modern American labor movement is one good place to study the role of the man of knowledge in social change—how the "intellectual" is attracted to or recruited by, shapes and is shaped by, a movement on the make. The third reason for my choice of the trade union is that I am more intimately acquainted with it than with other organizations, which has obvious advantages.

It is my hope that the questions explored and generalizations made in this study apply beyond the large trade union. The study is designed to treat the union as an instance of the class, "large-scale private association with democratic formal structure"; and to treat the persons studied as an instance of the class, "man of knowledge in large-scale organization." There are, further, some similarities between the situation of the intelligence agent in "authoritatively" structured organizations (e.g., military organizations or business enterprises) and "democratically" structured organizations (e.g., unions, many occupational, fraternal, and political associations). These points of similarity will be indicated where relevant.

In planning and doing this study I have drawn on a rich store of literature and advice. The written sources from which I have consciously borrowed are, I hope, all acknowledged in the text. Among the persons who helped, I would especially like to thank a group of my former teachers and colleagues at the University of Chicago:

Frederick H. Harbison for constant encouragement, the time

to complete the analysis, and many helpful suggestions.

Herbert Blumer and Everett C. Hughes for general sociological guidance and inspiration; and the late Louis Wirth for stimulating my interest in the sociology of intellectual life.

Economist Albert Rees and sociologist Erving Goffman for their characteristically penetrating advice at several stages of the study, and for critical readings of an earlier draft of the manuscript.

Joel Seidman, Kermit Eby and A. A. Liveright for their help in lining up interviews, and for many hours of fruitful discussion about specific cases and unions.

A grant from the Harry A. Millis Research Fellowship Committee at the University of Chicago in 1950-51 made it possible to gather the interview data. Thanks are due also to: Daniel Bell for access to the files of *Fortune* on some of the union staff experts; Raymond L. Gordon of Antioch College for constructive comment on Part III; my colleague Guy E. Swanson of the University of Michigan for a careful last-minute reading of the final draft and his valuable suggestions. For the brutal but nonviolent removal of 170 manuscript pages, the reader can be grateful to Jeremiah Kaplan's insistence and Malcolm W. Roemer's editorial assistance. Mr. Roemer also compiled the index. Mrs. Caroline Weichlein and Mrs. Courtney Adams typed the manuscript with an accuracy and at a sustained pace I have never seen before.

I owe a large debt to the many perceptive union people and labor relations specialists who gave so much time and intellectual effort to spell out their insights into the expert-officer relationship —an effort that was often embarrassing to me in its generosity. To some of these admirable union people, this book may occasionally seem out of harmony with union interests and ideology. For them I want to record my conviction that (1) any sociological analysis of the inner workings of any organization will seem anti-organization to the practitioner (it is not the role of the academic man to be as innocuous as possible); and (2) all social organizations, no matter how different in time, place or purpose, show some things in common, just because they are all examples of organized human effort in which people take account of one another. If the non-union reader thinks organizational life in trade union headquarters is a bit seamy, let him look to his own organization with a critical eye, and the labor movement by and large will come out pretty well.

I wish finally to acknowledge the valuable assistance of my wife, Jeanne. Without her vast fund of patience and good cheer, large-scale clerical-editorial help and general morale-building effort, the study would never have been completed.

University of Michigan
December, 1954

Contents

List of Tables

PART I

THE AREA OF STUDY

CHAPTER I

THE AMERICAN TRADE UNION

THE NATIONAL TRADE UNION in the United States is a good testing ground for some important propositions of sociology. This chapter will examine the nature of this testing ground. The next chapter will discuss the sociological problems and propositions to be explored.

Growth and Structure

The labor movement in America, though it dates back to Colonial days, did not take firm root until the 1880's with the creation of the American Federation of Labor (AFL). Even then, union membership remained a fluctuating, tiny fraction of the organizable workers. With the Great Depression of the thirties, however, the picture suddenly and dramatically changed. In only fifteen years, between 1934 and the late forties, union membership increased 10.5 million, from 3.6 million (fewer than one in ten of the nonagricultural wage and salary employees) to 14.1 million (about one in three of the organizable). After this spectacular boom, the labor movement has in the past few years stabilized at around 14 or 15 million.[1] Unions are now planted solidly in

1. The estimates are based on Leo Wolman, "Concentration of Union Membership," in Industrial Relations Research Association, *Proceedings of the Fifth Annual Meeting* (Chicago, Dec. 28-29, 1952), pp. 214-19. Canadian members are excluded.

3

every major industry—from manufacturing to utilities and services.
Union members are typically organized into local workplace
or geographical units. These local unions are in turn organized
into national unions (often called "international" because of some
membership in Canada). Most of the national unions are affiliated with one of the two major federations, the AFL or the CIO
(which have recently merged). The national trade union is the
main seat of power in the American labor movement today; and
it is with the national union, not the local, not the federation,
that this study mainly deals.

The Trade Union
as a Private Association

Any analysis of the role of the staff expert in the national
trade union or in any large-scale organization must begin and
end with analysis of the role and the problems of the executive
in that organization. Without the leader, the expert would not
get into the act; there would be no question of his influence and
outlook.

Executive processes are best described in terms of the nature
of the organization in which they arise.[2] To deal with the American
trade union is to deal with a voluntary private association, whose
formal organization is democratic.[3] The private association is a

---

2. Cf. Chester I. Barnard, *The Functions of the Executive* (Cambridge,
Massachusetts: Harvard University Press, 1938). Other leads for generic
treatment of the trade union in urban industrial society are in Bernard
Barber, "Participation and Mass Apathy in Associations," in *Studies in
Leadership*, ed. Alvin W. Gouldner (New York: Harper and Bros., 1950),
pp. 477-504; Robin M. Williams, Jr., *American Society* (New York: Alfred
A. Knopf, 1951), pp. 455-79; Arthur M. Ross, *Trade Union Wage Policy*
(Berkeley: University of California Press, 1948), pp. 21-44.

3. It is "voluntary" in a relative sense: though provisions for some form
of compulsory membership are found in contracts covering over ten million workers, the worker is not born into the trade union as he is into the
family, clan, tribe, nation, or sometimes the church. It is "democratic" in
the sense of a formal commitment to certain values (members should participate in selection of leaders and determination of the ends of the organization) and the specification of channels for such participation in a formal
constitution.

form of organization characteristic of American society. What are its characteristics as a type of social group, and how are these features expressed in the trade union?

(1) The association always pursues specific and explicit interests. The formal rationale of the union is to augment the workplace welfare of its members by establishing collective bargaining relations with employers.

(2) But every association develops multiple purposes. Its officials are faced with a wide variety of tasks which may be quite removed from the simple, formal purpose of the association as originally conceived. The best single lead for an understanding of union operations is to recognize that the union becomes an end in itself. "By a universally applicable social law," wrote Michels, "every organ of the collectivity, brought into existence through the need for the division of labour, creates for itself, as soon as it becomes consolidated, interests peculiar to itself."[4]

(3) The private association typically has a democratic formal organization—a written constitution, a set of office-holders chosen by the members and charged with carrying out the explicit purposes of the association.

(4) Yet, at the same time, it is typically controlled by an active minority. Applied to the trade union case, this is expressed in a shift in power away from the local and toward a centralization of policy control at the top of the national organization, accompanied by a growing chasm between the leader and the rank and file. Many students of labor have in a general way noted this tendency toward centralization and bureaucratization of the union movement.[5]

---

4. Robert Michels, *Political Parties: A Sociological Study of the Oligarchical Tendencies of Modern Democracy* (Glencoe, Ill.: The Free Press, 1949), p. 389. Cf. p. 373. Cf. A. M. Ross, *op. cit.*, p. 23.
5. See C. Wright Mills, *The New Men of Power* (New York: Harcourt, Brace & Co., 1948), pp. 52, 64. Joseph Shister, "Trade Union Government: A Formal Analysis," *Quarterly Journal of Economics*, 60 (Nov., 1945), 110-11. Cf. Shister, "The Locus of Union Control in Collective Bargaining," *Quarterly Journal of Economics*, 60 (August, 1946), 513-45; Will Herberg, "Bureaucracy and Democracy in Labor Unions," *Antioch Review*, 3 (Fall, 1943), 405-17; J. Barbash, *Labor Unions in Action* (New York: Harper and Bros., 1948), p. 63; Philip Taft, "Opposition to Union Officers in Elections," *Quarterly Journal of Economics*, 58 (Feb., 1944), 247, 249-50.

Perhaps the best way to understand the way these universal features of the private association are expressed in trade unions, as well as the characteristics unique to the union, is to examine the union leadership role with particular focus on the nature of the union's collective bargaining function. Control of the labor movement is increasingly in the hands of the national unions. And control of the national unions is increasingly in the hands of their top functionaries. What are the pressures working on the top leader and how does he assess them? What kinds of decisions must he make?

The union leader is continually faced with a battery of political pressures from various agencies and interest groups that want to help him define the function of the union. The major pressures are from (1) the rank and file and the officials at lower levels of his organization; (2) other unions—mainly rivals; (3) labor's "outside friends"—the church, liberal organizations, radical political parties, the Communists, etc.; (4) the government—legislatures, administrative agencies, political parties—both federal and local; and (5) employers and employer associations.

Areas of Union Decision

Relations with Employers: Collective Bargaining.—The formal purpose of a trade union is to bargain with the employer on wages, hours, and working conditions. Other purposes emerge, but the relation with management remains the core function of the union.

Collective bargaining is a process of accommodation of conflicting interests. Here is the first and crucial "decision-making area" for the union leader: the problems arising from this clash of union and management interests in collective bargaining. A vast literature on collective bargaining relationships permits us to sift out points of conflict derived from the aims of each party:[6]

1. *Survival and expansion of the organization.* The union

---

6. See, e.g., F. H. Harbison and J. R. Coleman, *Goals and Strategy in Collective Bargaining* (New York: Harper & Bros., 1951); E. W. Bakke and C. Kerr, *Unions, Management and the Public* (New York: Harcourt, Brace & Co., 1948); Harry Millis *et al.*, *How Collective Bargaining Works* (New York: Twentieth Century Fund, 1942).

aims for more members; union security; increased prestige as main go-between of management and workers, stronger treasury, more power to shut the plant down if necessary, etc. The employer aims for labor peace so he can plan ahead; loyalty of workers, prestige in eyes of customers, stockholders and community; strength to resist strikes, etc.

2. *Union control over jobs vs. retention of managerial rights.* For the union, seniority rules; apprentice rules; a voice in firing, layoff and recall, promotion and demotion, work standards, etc. For the employer, freedom to assign work, fix work standards, discipline workers, use machinery, plant and property as company sees fit, etc.

3. *More pay for less working-time vs. more profits, lower costs.* For the union, higher wage rates, shorter hours, premium pay, vacation and holiday pay, welfare programs and a host of other "fringe wage benefits." For the employer, more production per worker per hour, less lost time, etc.

4. *Increased responsiveness of government to union or management pressure* (to better chances of reaching above goals).

5. *Personal gains for union or management functionaries* (increased job security, prestige, power, income, etc.). This tends to be identified with survival and expansion of the organization.

The very existence of collective bargaining signifies a basic core of conflicting interests. Many employers and union leaders are realistic when they view collective bargaining as little more than a way to decide how many rights should be taken away from the employer, how much authority he should share with the union.[7] Employers complain that there seems to be no stopping point in this process. They quite naturally see it as an attack on their interest in (1) survival and expansion of the corporation and with it the prestige and authority of the management group; (2) fulfilling their legal obligation to maximize return to the stockholders. The logic of their position compels them to resist

---

7. For management and union views of the controversy over managerial prerogatives, cf. L. H. Hill and C. R. Hook, Jr., *Management at the Bargaining Table* (New York: McGraw Hill Book Co., Inc., 1945); E. W. Bakke, *Mutual Survival* (New Haven: Labor and Management Center, Yale University, 1946); Neil W. Chamberlain, *The Union Challenge to Management Control* (New York: Harper and Bros., 1948).

union encroachment on their authority to manage in such a way as to promote these goals.

The conflict that stems from these clashing interests is carried on through a battery of pressure tactics in industry. In the union's arsenal we find the basic weapon of the strike, as well as picketing (persuasive and otherwise), slowdown, the boycott, union label, anti-business propaganda and, infrequently, destruction of property and use of violence. The weapons in management's arsenal include the lockout, use of discharge, discipline and other means to discriminate against active unionists, encouragement of individual bargaining, exploitation of union rivalries to favor a relatively passive "company union," anti-union propaganda, and, infrequently, use of violence, strikebreakers, labor spies and bribery. Through the years government has been forced to define the limits on the use of many of these weapons. As a result the parties have long looked at government itself as a major weapon in their struggles against each other.

Relations with Government.—Here is a second major decision-making area for the union leader: the problems arising from his relations with political parties and with executive, legislative and judicial agencies of federal, state and local governments.

Political action for labor is nothing new (unions have backed candidates and legislative programs since the days of criminal conspiracy).[8] Political action for management also has a long history (since the days of the first protective tariff). But it has only been in recent years that the major battles have begun to shift fully into the political arena. Legislative history from NRA through Taft-Hartley shows each side devoting increasing energy and money to the political aspect of their struggle. Why?

First, there are *advantages to be gained in bargaining position.* Because of its growing importance in industry and possible impact on the nation's political economy, collective bargaining is carried on increasingly in a goldfish bowl, with both parties addressing their arguments more to the general public than to their opponents and organizing their strategy with an eye to mobilizing

---

8. See Henry David, "One Hundred Years of Labor in Politics" in *House of Labor,* ed. J. B. S. Hardman and Maurice F. Neufeld (New York: Prentice-Hall, Inc., 1951), pp. 90-112.

community and government support. Since relative bargaining power is a central determinant of collective bargaining outcomes, and government action can greatly strengthen the position of either side, the parties turn to politics for bargaining advantage. This is seen on many levels.

Direct legislative attacks on the institutional privileges of the other side are the most obvious form. To reduce the arsenal of legitimate weapons by law, to make certain demands or bargaining practices "unfair labor practices"—these are ways to get protection that cannot be won at the bargaining table.

The political search for bargaining advantage is also seen in crisis situations where government intervention is probable. An example is union use of a friendly administration and its fact-finding board to mobilize a series of pressures against basic steel in the 1949 negotiations.

Pressure on local courts, city administrations, state legislatures, government agencies, etc., to secure bargaining advantage is also common.

A second reason for the expansion of union-management conflict into the political arena lies in the *limitations of collective bargaining for the achievement of the broader purposes of the parties.* The union through its own lobbyists and identification with a federation, the corporation through its own lobbyists and membership in various manufacturers' associations, press for implementation of their own versions of the American Way of Life.

As the segments of the economy have become more interdependent, as unions have grown in political strength and have consolidated their in-plant gains, they have begun to recognize some of the limitations of bargaining (e.g., wage negotiations in an inflationary period). They have begun to see the possibilities of full-scale political action directed not only to the straight trade union issues, not only to protection of their institutional privileges, but to the entire range of government action. This "broad view" is easy to exaggerate (see Chapter IX). But there is little doubt that the last two decades have made union leaders more and more eager to pronounce upon a variety of issues of public policy, from taxation and trade to price control and public power.

Relations with Rank and File and Officials at Lower Levels.—

The third major decision-making area for the top leader stems
from internal pressures: the expectations, aspirations and problems of officials and activists down the line and the mass of members below.

What does the trend toward bureaucratization and centralization of the labor movement imply for the role of the rank-and-file
workers who are organized into local units? It means that the
bulk of the membership of unions, as in other private associations
(e.g., members of the American Legion, American Medical Association, etc.), are relatively passive and indifferent, willing to
entrust much decision-making to the officials. It means that day-
to-day participation in union affairs is, with rare exceptions,
confined to a small core of active members. It means, moreover,
that small splinters of the active core at a local level may upset
control of that local (since so few participate in control). Factionalism is often prominent in the affairs of the local, despite centralization of authority higher up.

The first survival dilemma facing the district or international
official, then, is to overcome rank-and-file apathy when a display
of unity and militancy is needed, yet at the same time prevent
that militancy from being directed against his own authority by
local union factions.[9] The result: most union leaders, while they
want membership participation in the sense of ritual affirmation
of solidarity and support of union policy, tend not to be overly
eager for widespread rank-and-file activity in policy-making. The
latter type of participation raises two problems for the union
leader: it encourages instability and makes quick decision and
action difficult. "Democracy in the union, like competition in the
product market, is universally the object of reverence, but is not
especially enjoyable to those who must reckon with it."[10] Especially in the upper regions of the hierarchy is it necessary to

9. Note the contrast in the corporation manager's problem. It is much
easier to mobilize and retain control of an official hierarchy built from the
top down by executive appointment than it is to balance forces and maintain stability in a hierarchy built from the bottom by election. To control the
enfranchised mass is a complicated job.

10. A. M. Ross, *op. cit.*, p. 31; cf. pp. 21 ff., esp. pp. 37-43. This is the best
analysis of the leader-member relationship as it is expressed in the operating
decisions which officials have to make in the course of wage negotiations.
Cf. Michels, *op. cit.*, p. 103: "The two gravest defects of genuine democracy,
its lack of stability . . . and its difficulty of mobilization, are dependent on

construct insulation from annoying rank-and-file pressures—so that
the official can get on with the business of efficient bargaining
and administration. The elaborate formal procedures designed to
insure rank-and-file control of policy are, therefore, manipulated
to insure control of the rank and file itself. For example, in wage
negotiations the membership is dependent on the officials for
guidance on what is equitable, obtainable, and acceptable, as well
as for the tactical wisdom that will make the employer come
across. Rank-and-file dependence on the top leaders seems to be
growing as the scope of bargaining widens and government say-so
grows. Bargaining on technical matters—such as job evaluation,
wage incentives, pensions, wage and work guarantees—requires
more top-level experience and advice. Government intervention
means the union appears before more government boards and
courts; technical help the local cannot provide comes from international and federation. Finally, a wage dispute often boils down
to the question, "Shall the international office subsidize a strike?";
therefore top leaders increasingly reserve for themselves the right
to decide when a strike is legitimate.

This is not to say that rank-and-file pressures are unimportant
in the calculations of the top official. He must rule, it is true,
and to this end he builds his machine and to some extent "manipu-
lates" the mass. But he must also deliver—"more here and now."
The winning of gains from the employer in the short run is a
union leadership imperative, whether the tactics be militant, con-
ciliatory, or collusive and whether the style be that of the demo-
crat or the autocrat. In the end, he is *accountable* to the rank and
file, and must constantly assess their sentiments and dispositions.

Pressures from Fellow Union Officials.—Another portion of
the decision-making area I have labeled Internal Union Control
and Organization is rooted in the fact that the union leader tends
to become enclosed by a circle of other leaders within his own
organization. The top leader cannot maintain face-to-face contact
with the thousands of little leaders in his organization. He has to
depend on his lieutenants for contact work. And they in turn are
judged for promotion on the basis of their loyalty to their superiors
in that contact work. The top officer has to make continual de-

the recognized right of the sovereign masses to take part in the management
of their own affairs." These defects are intensified in conflict groups.

cisions affecting the assignments and careers of officials down the line. The character of his relations with these other leaders must be considered when assessing the pressures on him.

Relations with Other Unions (especially rivals).—A fourth major decision-making area arises from one of the chief characteristics of the American labor movement: the rivalries, splits and divisions within it. The pressures generated out of these divisions between unions are not limited to the pressure of the traditional jurisdictional quarrel. A list of the types of division will illustrate the great range of internal conflict: (1) autonomous and competing internationals; (2) competition bewteen unions for certain kinds of work and for jurisdiction over certain groups of workers; (3) political and/or ideological rivalries—conflicting views on the proper relation of government to business and unions, on the relation of American labor to world-wide labor movements, and on the place of unions in politics; (4) racial or ethnic rivalries —conflict over the proper place of minority groups in unions.[11]

Relations with Labor's "Outside Friends" and the "Public."— As the union becomes an institution with multiple functions reaching out into many phases of community life, it seeks the approval and support of various amenable publics. The need for continued reinterpretation of the union's meaning and value to both the community and the rank and file gives rise to a final decision-making area: public relations. This is a two-way street: the union wants to make friends; friends want to use the union. The efforts of Communist Party operatives, radical political parties, liberal groups like Americans for Democratic Action, added to the less obvious influence of The Association of Catholic Trade Unionists and other Catholic groups, furnish ready examples.[12]

---

11. See W. Galenson, *Rival Unionism in the United States* (New York: American Council on Public Affairs, 1940); Bakke and Kerr, *op. cit.;* Fay Calkins, *The CIO and the Democratic Party* (Chicago: The University of Chicago Press, 1952); David C. Williams, "International Labor Relations," in G. W. Brooks *et al., Interpreting the Labor Movement* (Industrial Relations Research Association Publication No. 9, Dec., 1952), pp. 192-207; W. A. Kornhauser, "Labor Unions and Race Relations (Unpublished M.A. Thesis, University of Chicago, 1950).

12. For interesting documentation of Communist Party influence on leadership decisions, see Joel Seidman, "Labor Policy of the Communist Party during World War II," *Industrial and Labor Relations Review*, 4 (Oct., 1950), 55-69; Philip Selznick, *Organizational Weapon* (New York: McGraw

To understand the top officials' problems and the resulting areas of union decision is a first step toward understanding what the national labor union does and what prompts the call for specialized knowledge and skill.

Hill Book Co., Inc., 1952). For material on Catholic groups, see "Catholic Social Action and the Labor Movement" (Unpublished manuscript, mimeographed, distributed by Kermit Eby). Cf. P. Taft, "The Association of Catholic Trade Unionists," *Industrial and Labor Relations Review*, 2 (Jan., 1949), 219-18. J. Weinberg, "Priests, Workers and Communists: What Happened in a New York Transit Workers Union," *Harpers*, 197 (Nov., 1948), 49-56.

CHAPTER II

THEORY, PROBLEM AND METHOD

UNIONS ARE INTERESTING in their own right, and an accurate description of their workings would be useful without further ado. But unions are also interesting as a testing ground for some live ideas in social science. It is the main purpose of this study to describe the operations of trade unions and the job of the staff expert in a way that will contribute to our knowledge of organizational life in general.

The Theory and the Problem

Three interrelated bodies of thought about the development of modern urban industrial society furnish the questions and working hypotheses for this study. They are: (1) theories of bureaucratization; (2) theories of the rise to power of various skill groups; (3) theories of the changing role of the intellectual. All stem from a concern with the consequences of the growing division of labor in modern society. This increasing division of labor—a process which fascinated writers as diverse as Adam Smith, Marx, Toennies, Weber, Durkheim, Simmel, Park and Mannheim—has brought much speculation about the rise of the "expert" or the "intellectual" and his place in the social order.

The work of Max Weber sharply poses one issue in this speculation. Analyzing the development of rational bureaucratic organizations in the modern world, Weber speaks of "the complete depersonalization of administrative management by bureaucracy" and pictures the individual professional bureaucrat as "only a single cog in an ever-moving mechanism which prescribes to him an essentially fixed route of march." He is "chained to his activity by his entire material and ideal existence."[1] This mechanism, Weber points out, "is easily made to work for anybody who knows how to gain control over it."[2] The modern professionalized bureaucrat, in Weber's view, is ready to support any party or faction that has power—and this holds whether he be in government, business, industry, religion, the military or some other sphere of organizational life.

While professionalization thus makes the modern bureaucracy a subservient tool, at the same time its superior efficiency, based on technical knowledge, makes it indispensable—gives it a "monopoly of skill."[3] This means the development of considerable administrative autonomy. Weber thought of the emergence of the expert (autonomous within his sphere of competence) as the epitome of the bureaucratic trend.[4] While he recognizes that "the ever-increasing 'indispensability' of the officialdom" with their technical expertness is no true measure of their social and political power position, he nevertheless states that "under normal conditions the power position of a fully developed bureaucracy is always over-towering. The 'political master' finds himself in the position of the 'dilettante' who stands opposite the 'expert,' facing the trained official who stands within the management of administration." This holds, adds Weber, whether the master is an aristocratic, self-appointed colleague group or a popularly elected president. As for the absolute monarch, he is "powerless

---

1. *From Max Weber: Essays in Sociology*, ed. H. H. Gerth and C. Wright Mills (New York: Oxford University Press, 1946), pp. 239, 228. Cf. Karl Mannheim, *Man and Society in an Age of Reconstruction* (London: Routledge and Kegan Paul, Ltd., 1940), pp. 319-26.

2. Gerth and Mills (eds.), *op. cit.*, p. 229.

3. Cf. Reinhard Bendix' interpretation of bureaucracy in "The Public Servant in a Democracy: A Study of the Social Origins and Careers of Higher Federal Administrators" (Unpublished Ph.D. Dissertation, Department of Sociology, University of Chicago, June, 1947), pp. 20-35, 37.

4. Max Weber, "The Routinization of Charisma and Its Consequences" in *The Theory of Social and Economic Organization*, ed. and trans. A. M. Henderson and T. Parsons (New York: Oxford University Press, 1947), p. 339. Cf. Gerth and Mills (eds.) *op. cit.*, p. 235.

opposite the superior knowledge of the bureaucratic expert. . . ."[5]

Many writers, as C. Wright Mills suggests,[6] have apparently assumed a magic leap from occupational function and indispensability to political power (an assumption Weber explicitly rules out but in some places implicitly adopts). Among others, Veblen, Lasswell, Laski, De Man, Burnham single out various technical specialists or intellectuals as groups or strata rising to power.

These writers vary in their precise specifications of the new men of power—ranging from Veblen's "engineers,"[7] Laski's "experts,"[8] or Burnham's "managers"[9] to Lasswell's "propagandists" (allied with or identical to lawyers).[10] These writers also vary in their depiction of the generating forces. But they all have two things in common: (1) they all point to a group or groups of functionaries in large-scale organizations who possess specialized knowledge and skills as the indispensables in the modern world; (2) they all assume the correspondence of indispensability and power. Those writers in this group who speak of the "intellectual" as the new man of power see him as a prime mover in radical social change. Schumpeter, for example, holds that intellectuals (the "people who wield the power of the spoken and the written word" but who have no "direct responsibility for practical affairs") "impress their mentality on almost everything that is being done."

5. *Ibid.*, pp. 232-34.

6. C. Wright Mills, *op. cit.*, p. 280.

7. Thorstein Veblen, *The Engineers and the Price System* (New York: The Viking Press, 1921).

8. Harold J. Laski, *The Limitations of the Expert* (Fabian Tract No. 235, London: The Fabian Society, Feb., 1931).

9. James Burnham, *The Managerial Revolution* (New York: John Day, 1941).

10. H. D. Lasswell, *The Analysis of Political Behavior* (London: Routledge and Kegan Paul, Ltd., 1948), pp. 176, 26-27, 143. Cf. Lasswell, "World Politics and Personal Insecurity" in *A Study of Power* (Glencoe, Ill.: The Free Press, 1950), pp. 6-7. More recently the Lasswell group has interpreted the revolution of our time as a shift in influence from "specialists in bargaining" to intellectuals ("symbol specialists" or "masters of persuasion") to "specialists in violence" or to those with "administrative and police skills." These rather loose distinctions confuse the problem of locating the ruling groups with the problem of analyzing the means of control and styles of leadership available to any ruling group. H. D. Lasswell, Daniel Lerner, and C. E. Rothwell, *The Comparative Study of Elites* (Stanford: Stanford University Press, 1952), esp. pp. 16-18, 31 ff.

He applies this specifically to intellectuals who invade the labor movement as staff people and supply theories and slogans for it. He says these men of critical mind eventually impart "revolutionary bias to the most bourgeois trade-union practices," and work the movement up "into something that differs substantially from what it would be without them."[11] De Man goes further:

. . . the working masses are the dough, whereas the ideas of non-proletarian intellectuals are the yeast. . . . Were it not for the influence of the motives of intellectuals, the labour movement would be nothing more than a representation of interests, aiming at the transformation of the proletariat into a new bourgeoisie.

This is because "the manual worker who rises in the social scale . . . can be embourgoised far more readily than the socialist intellectual in like circumstances."[12]

A second group of writers have, in contrast, seen the intellectuals, technicians, experts, as powerless, impotent, helpless by-standers in the main drift. Znaniecki, for instance, emphasizes the complete dependence of what he calls the "technological expert" on the man of power ("technological leader").[13] The knowledge of the former is tapped at will for whatever purposes the latter has at hand. The man of knowledge here is a passive tool. Mills offers a similar formulation: he points to the emergence of the "sophisticated conservatives" who may make junior partners of labor leaders in a merging of military, state, industrial, and labor bureaucracies—with the intellectuals and experts falling in line, serving any master.[14] This plight of the intellectual Mills traces to

11. Joseph A. Schumpeter, *Capitalism, Socialism, and Democracy* (2d ed.; New York: Harper and Bros., 1947), pp. 143-55. Cf. Eric Hoffer, *The True Believer* (New York: Harper and Bros., 1951), pp. 129-30, 137-39. Cf. Karl Mannheim, *Ideology and Utopia* (New York: Harcourt, Brace and Co., 1946), pp. 138-39, 142.

12. Henry De Man, *The Psychology of Socialism*, trans. Eden and Cedar Paul (2d ed.; New York: Henry Holt & Co., 1927), pp. 28, 234-35. Cf. Michels, *op. cit.*, esp. pp. 316-29; and Max Nomad, *Rebels and Renegades* (New York: The Macmillan Co., 1932). Other references on this point are cited in *Socialism and American Life*, ed. D. D. Egbert *et al.* (Princeton, N. J.: Princeton University Press, 1952), II, pp. 217-22.

13. Florian Znaniecki, *The Social Role of the Man of Knowledge* (New York: Columbia University Press, 1940), pp. 47, 55, 72-75, 170.

14. See C. Wright Mills, *White Collar* (New York: Oxford University Press, 1951), and *New Men of Power, op. cit.* Mills states: "Perhaps . . .

(1) the social developments centered upon the rise of the new bureaucracies of state and business, of party and voluntary association; and (2) the ideological developments centered upon the continual demands for new justifications among competing power groups. More and more the men of knowledge "are becoming dependent salaried workers who spend the most alert hours of their lives being told what to do."[15]

Robert K. Merton's more careful articulation of the same theme leads him to advance the hypothesis that "bureaucracies provoke gradual transformations of the alienated intellectual into the a-political technician, whose role is to serve whatever strata happen to be in power."[16] "Typically," Merton adds, "the bureaucratic intellectual finds himself in a position where he is called upon to provide information for alternative or specific policies which have already been formulated by policy-makers." He "is implicitly lending his skills and knowledge to the preservation of a given type of institutional arrangement." The pressure to be "practical," "realistic" means that "he comes increasingly to think in technical and instrumental terms. . . ."[17]

This vast body of speculation about the indispensability, the power, the influence and the direction of influence of various groups of knowledgeable people in the organizational machinery of modern society raises several large questions which the present study in a small way seeks to clarify:

---

intellectuals have at all times been drawn into line with either popular mentality or ruling class, and away from the urge to be detached; but now . . . the recoil from detachment and the falling into line seem more organized, more solidly rooted in the centralization of power and its rationalization of modern society as a whole." The intellectual, he says "is becoming a technician, and idea-man, rather than one who resists the environment . . . and defends himself from death-by-adaptation." Mills, *White Collar, op. cit.*, pp. 155, 157. Cf. Hans H. Gerth and C. W. Mills, "A Marx for the Managers," *Ethics,* LII (1941-42), 200-15. Randolph Bourne earlier complained that "our intellectuals have failed us as value-creators, even as value-emphasizers." (*Untimely Papers* [New York: B. W. Huebsch, 1919], p. 136). And there was Lenin's contemptuous dismissal of intellectuals as "prostitutes."

15. Mills, *White Collar, op. cit.*, pp. 152-56.

16. *Social Theory and Social Structure* (Glencoe, Ill.: The Free Press, 1949), p. 167. Cf. Weber, *op. cit.*

17. *Ibid.*, pp. 169, 171-72. Cf. Kurt Reitzler, "On the Psychology of the Modern Revolution," *Social Research,* 10 (Sept., 1943), 320-36.

1. Just *who* is it who is alleged to be important or unimportant, active agent or passive tool, coming to power or not?

2. *How indispensable* are these people, from whose point of view, and what are the *sources of their indispensability?* What are they expert in?

3. *How influential* and powerful are they, in what kinds of social structures, under what conditions, and with respect to what kinds of decisions?

4. What is the probable *direction of their influence*—the nature of the bias introduced by their presence, if any?

5. What is the nature of the *impact of the large-scale organization on the man of knowledge?* Is it a transformation from alienated intellectual to apolitical technician, or something else? What are the identifications and job orientations of experts entering the big organizations and how do these change?

Through an application to the trade union case, I attempt to explore these questions.[18]

---

18. The speculation about intellectuals in modern "mass" society has often been applied to trade unions in Europe and America with much the same picture emerging. On the one hand, the intellectual or the expert is the prime mover; on the other, he is a tool. Mills, *New Men* . . . , *op. cit.*, pp. 281-82, claims that "professionally-trained intellectuals" used as staff assistants in American unions have no power, no status, and with rare exceptions and brief periods of time never did have. Selig Perlman, on the other hand, argues that unionism could never establish itself until it had shaken off the hold of the outside intellectual on its policies. (*A Theory of the Labor Movement* [New York: Augustus M. Kelley, 1949], pp. 5, 9, 68, 105, 136.) Sidney and Beatrice Webb made an early prediction that the centralized union of the future would be "served by an expert official staff of its own"— a class of "expert civil servants." (*Industrial Democracy* [1920 ed.; London: Longmans, Green and Co., Ltd., 1897], pp. 833-49, esp. pp. 834, 844.) Michels, looking at Continental trade unions, co-operative societies, and political parties, observes, The "technical specialization that inevitably results from all extensive organization renders necessary what is called expert leadership." (*Op. cit.*, p. 31.) More recently Maurice Neufeld invokes Michels' "iron law" of oligarchy and concludes, "certainly by mid-century, the managerial revolution has already engulfed labor organizations as well as those of industry and government. . . . Even more than business and industrial concerns, a union must be prepared to deal immediately and expertly with almost perpetual crises." This, he continues, has meant the emergence of "managerial unionism"—the dominance of the full-time executive, flanked by his indispensable experts. (Hardman and Neufeld, *op. cit.*, pp. 16-18.)

Defining the Expert and
Selecting the Unions

Answers to the question of who is an expert and who is not (and where to find him) had to come both as a prerequisite to field work and as a product of it. The sampling problem for this study was complicated by two basic facts:

(1) The size of the universe was uncertain: no complete list for any type of union staff technician was in existence at the beginning of the study; for some types no names at all were in print.

(2) The nature of the universe was uncertain—even if a list of "Research Directors," "industrial engineers," etc., were available—because the problem of defining the "expert" in part had to await what turned up in the field. To delineate types of experts was an aim of the study and could not be done *a priori*.

Classification and Selection of Unions.—To tackle the problem of locating our experts and estimating the size of the universe, I sampled not experts, but unions.

The study is confined first to international headquarters of unions with 50,000 members or more. Two assumptions justify this: (1) the character of the American labor movement is determined by the character of its large and essentially autonomous national unions; (2) the most important decisions (in terms of impact on the nation's political economy) are made by the top officials of these unions. It is their use of staff experts I am concerned with.

There are about 209 national or international unions in the United States.[19] Eliminating those with membership below 50,000 leaves about 71 unions. To cut the field work to manageable proportions and to permit more intensive analysis, I chose 30 of these 71 unions. The following criteria were judged to be most relevant for the purposes of this study (extremes of each criterion were included): (1) kind and amount of use of staff experts; (2) traditions and social-political orientation of top leadership; (3) kinds of industries dealt with; (4) degree of union control

---

19. U.S. Department of Labor, B. L. S., *Directory of Labor Unions in the United States, 1950*, Bul. No. 980 (Washington, D. C.: U.S. Government Printing Office, 1950). This was used as a guide in selecting unions.

over the union's jurisdiction; (5) impact on the nation's political economy (hence involvement with the federal government); and, where other things were equal, (6) accessibility.

The 30 unions were chosen to represent the likely range of variation (in expert functions, influence, role orientations and conditions of work) among the large unions which employ staff experts. This was necessary to gain a cross-union perspective, to permit analysis of which aspects of the expert-boss relationship depend on the unique circumstances of the particular union's development and which aspects can be generalized.

While I aimed for a cross-cut picture to capture the range of the phenomena under study, I also had to meet the practical limits of time and money, and attain reasonable reliability in the data. I therefore arranged the 30 unions by priority and divided them into two groups of 15, with major field work effort going to the top group. Saturation interviewing was accomplished with 11 of the first priority unions (all top experts, some of their assistants, and, where possible, the top officers and/or their administrative assistants, heads of operating departments, and some ex-experts). Interviewing effort shaded off into interviews with several, down to one or two key people in the rest of the unions. (Six of these unions, I found, employed only one expert within my definition; two employed none.) An attempt was made to gather questionnaire data for all 30 unions—both in person and by mail.

As a check on the analysis of the expert's functions in the unions where one finds him, I added a third group of six unions where one does not find him—unions which make no use of full-time staff experts. In three of these expertless unions I interviewed the chief executive; in three I interviewed at least one key person in a position to describe its administration (e.g., its legal counsel). The attempt here was to elicit reasons for not using full-time staff experts.

Thus, *there are three groups of unions in my sample: (1) 15 first priority unions; (2) 13 second priority unions (two of the original 15 were shifted to the no-expert category); and (3) six expertless unions—a contrast group. The staff experts in the 28 unions in groups one and two constitute what I hereafter refer to as the "Questionnaire Sample" (or "Q Sample").*

A distribution of unions contacted by size shows that I covered all but two of the 19 American unions with 200,000 or more members, six of the 16 in the 100,000 to 199,000 group, and 11 of the 36 in the 50,000 to 99,999 group—reflecting a bias toward large size, where other factors were equal. Appendix B contains further information (for each union) on structural characteristics, the number of experts employed, the number of experts in my Questionnaire Sample, the number of people interviewed, the number on which I have Questionnaire data, etc., plus a general discussion of representativeness and the criteria for selection of unions. In Chapter X the significance of structural variations is considered with reference to the competences of union leaders.

Defining the Expert.—After the unions were selected, there was still the problem of finding the experts, and pegging the nature of their expertise. I began with these criteria for identifying the "expert": (1) he is a hired staff man, responsible to elected officials, working full-time in the headquarters of a national or international union; (2) he is a "man of knowledge" in the sense that he brings to the problem at hand a body of specialized information and skill.

It was thought (and the data confirmed this) that the employees fitting this description were distinguishable from other people on the union payroll. The distinction from routine clerical and stenographic workers is obvious. The experts are distinct from union officers because the latter are elected and have formal executive authority. They are distinct from "International Representatives," Organizers, Directors of Organization, line negotiators and administrators and the like because these are primarily politicians representing a bloc of rank-and-file votes and they, too, have executive authority. Moreover, the latter have usually made their way up the union ladder from the plant via election, then appointment;[20] only a few of the staff experts have taken that route.

Implicit in the second criterion (specialized knowledge) was the idea of "preparation for the role." It was found, however, that this could not be spelled out rigidly without doing damage to the

20. Cf. data in C. W. Mills, "Leaders of the Unions," in Hardman and Neufeld, *op. cit.*, p. 33. My interview data, plus common knowledge, confirm this picture of occupational origins of top union officials. Some exceptions are noted below, Ch. XI.

concept "expert" (e.g., I could not say an expert is a college graduate whose major field of study was relevant to his job function).
Save for the labor lawyers and perhaps the pension experts and
a few of the industrial engineers, the degree of professionalization
is low: there are no codes of professional ethics, no institutional
means for training, licensing and disciplining the practicing economists, statisticians, publicists, lobbyists, workers' education specialists, race relations specialists, political experts, etc. In terms of
knowledge and skill possessed, work performed, and relationship
to the line officials, however, many staff functionaries with little
formal training clearly qualified as experts. After preliminary interviews in two unions, I added to the phrase "specialized information and skill" the qualification "acquired through federal education and/or formal or informal training on the job."

In practice, of course, the application of these criteria produced
many borderline cases, and excluded many people it is possible
to define as expert. Moreover, in the analysis that follows I use
different samples for different purposes.

1. *The total count.* The total count of staff experts *at all levels*
in headquarters hierarchies of these 28 unions comes to 298 (see
Appendix B).

2. *The Questionnaire Sample.* This includes:

(a) All those within the definition of staff expert who worked
six months or more during the period September 1, 1950 to September 1, 1951 (my major field work period) in the national
headquarters of one of the 28 unions on the list, and who were
directly responsible to the top officer(s).

(b) All lawyers, engineers, pension and insurance experts and
Washington lobbyists within my definition—whether associates, assistants or department heads. (It was possible to compile complete
lists here, and it was assumed that these groups have sufficient
contact with line officials to warrant inclusion, even if their formal
position in the hierarchy is below the experts directly responsible
to top officials.) The sample, of course, includes all department
heads in other occupational groups who fit the above criteria (e.g.,
Research, Publicity, etc.).

(c) Three ex-experts. Where a change was just made at the
time of contact, and data were available on both the man leaving

and his successor, I used the respondent who was leaving (data were more reliable and complete, as was their knowledge of the organization).

The Questionnaire Sample adds up to 175 staff experts in the 28 unions. These constitute a group of reasonable homogeneity fitting our definition of expert. These are the top staff experts who fulfill the intelligence function in large American trade unions.

There were usable questionnaire returns—covering job descriptions, social characteristics, occupational history, associations, salary, job offers, father's occupation, predecessors' occupations, etc., —on 123 cases. (See Table 7 in Appendix A.) Similar information on background and job content was obtained from interviews or secondary sources for 31 of the 52 non-returns—making a total of 154 of the 175 cases, or 88 per cent of the Questionnaire Sample, for which I have such data.[21]

One hundred and eighteen of the 175 experts in the Questionnaire Sample were interviewed at least once. In all, there are 306 interviews with 250 people—in and out of the Questionnaire Sample.[22] The people include 37 union executives and administrators; six housekeeping functionaries other than administrators; 170 incumbent experts, professional assistants, and private consultants; 21 former staff experts ("ex-experts"); and 16 outsiders with broad labor contacts.

3. *The "Main Sample."* Adequate data were available from all sources to type 129 cases by function. It was possible to assign influence ratings to 128 of the 129 cases typed by function. I shall refer to the 128 cases for which I have complete data—function,

----

21. Two cases from two "extra" unions not in the Questionnaire Sample are nevertheless included in the analysis as substitutes. They are scarce types which proved difficult to contact in one union within the Q Sample, but less difficult in the comparable "extras." Their inclusion brings the total in Q Sample tables to 156.

22. In the following chapters the numbers following interview quotations designate the interview number and page number of the source (e.g., 121-4). A "G" preceding a number means "Group Interview" (more than one person's comments recorded); I have 17 of these. "N" means "brief notes" (less than two single-spaced pages recorded); I have 47 of these. An "a," "b," etc., following an interview number (121a-4) designates the first repeat interview, the second repeat interview, etc. I have 56 repeat interviews. "D10-2" refers to document number 10, page 2. Where documents can be identified fully, the standard references appear in footnotes.

influence, social characteristics and the like—as the "Main Sample."

It was possible to type 121 staff experts in the Main Sample (plus five administrative assistants who began as staff experts) by present role orientation. Of these 126 cases, 122 could be typed by past role orientation ("career theme").

The cases for which I have data on all the major variables to be considered—function, past and present role orientation, influence—include representation from all first priority unions and seven second priority unions (making a total of 22 of the 28 unions in the Questionnaire Sample); plus two cases in two "extra" unions.

When I generalize about any phenomenon where the data cover fewer or more than the 175 cases (154 "returns") in the Questionnaire Sample, or the 128 cases in the Main Sample, I will be specific as to nonresponse to given questions or missing areas of interview content. Keep in mind, however, that whatever the representativeness of the data, the study probably covers the range of variation—for this was sought not only in the selection of cases and unions, but also in the extensive use of knowledgeable outsiders, ex-experts, and independent consultants with broad labor contacts or clientele.

The sources of data, the interview situation and procedure, the interview guides and the questionnaire are described in detail or duplicated in Appendix A. The kinds of union functionaries excluded from this analysis of the staff expert are listed in Appendix B. The methods of analysis and the problem of reliability are also discussed below in the various chapters and appendices. In general, the large number and length of interviews (focused on a small number of top staff experts), the use where possible of ex-experts before approaching the incumbents, as well as the supplementary use of questionnaires, documents and first-hand observation, permitted (1) some cross-checking for reliability; (2) the necessary pre-interview grasp of the structure and problems of each organization. (See Appendices A, C, D.) Limited internal checks of validity could also be attempted—e.g., the use of objective data on salary level, salary transition, intergenerational mobility, affiliations, occupational history, etc., as a check on typologies based on qualitative analysis of interview verbalization.

Recent Expansion of the Intelligence Function in the Modern Trade Union

The presence of intellectuals and experts in and around the labor movement is nothing new. A procession of labor intellectuals marches across the scene of labor's nineteenth century struggles: ideologues who for brief moments captured labor power (F. A. Sorge, Daniel De Leon, Eugene Debs), uplift reformers (Robert Dale Owen, Frances Wright, Horace Greeley, Henry George), and other friendly outsiders. These were men who, like their European counterparts, were hardly strangers to the world of ideas.[23]

The hostile environment of the nineteenth century—the repressive framework of labor law, the tenacity of employer resistance—not only gave the radical intellectual his chance in the unions, but it also nurtured a demand for the services of lawyers. The men who fought the early labor cases before the courts were among the first experts to advise the unions.

It was not until the 1900's, however, that it became common in America for men of specialized knowledge and professional training to serve the unions—lawyers and nonlawyers, in and out of court, on and off the staff, for the fee or for the love of it. Before World War I, unions on the railroads and in the needle trades had used legal-economic-statistical specialists, as well as

---

23. For a history of the nineteenth century operations of intellectuals in and around the labor movement, see Selig Perlman, *op. cit.*, pp. 176-82; and Egbert, *et al.*, *op. cit.*, Vol. I, pp. 175 ff., 228-67. In 1893, the Socialists, led by Morgan of the Machinists and Barnes of the Cigarmakers, came close to capturing the AFL. Three years later, when De Leon launched the dual Socialist Trades and Labor Alliance, AFL President Samuel Gompers let loose this scorching editorial polemic: "We note . . . that the work of union wrecking is being taken up by a wing of the so-called socialist party of New York, headed by a professor without a professorship, a shyster lawyer without a brief, and a statistician who furnishes figures to the republican, democratic and socialist parties. These three mountebanks, aided by a few unthinking but duped workers, recently launched, from a beer saloon, a brand new national organization, with the avowed purpose of crushing every trade union in the country." *American Federationist*, April, 1896, p. 33, quoted in Egbert, *op. cit.*, p. 253. It should be noted that the early leaders of the AFL—Adolph Strasser, P. J. McGuire, and Gompers himself—had all gone through the sectarian schools of nineteenth century socialism.

journalists. In the twenties several more unions began to put them on the staff full time. But having a few experts around all the time was an idea most American labor leaders took to only slowly. The few experts hired in these early years entered the picture where any or all of these conditions were present: (1) an economic crisis faced the industry (e.g., coal); (2) government imposed drastic regulation (World War I wage stabilization, or 1920 railroad reorganization); (3) the union got into the insurance business (railroads); (4) the leaders were socialist-oriented (needle trades before World War I); (5) the company used economic data in bargaining (railroads, bakeries, etc.).

The real push toward staff experts came with the emergence of the garrison state: World War II and after. Let us take the expert jobs in the Questionnaire Sample. When were these jobs created? First, we must drop ten jobs created in two unions started recently (so as not to bias the picture in favor of recent growth in the use of experts). Almost two-thirds of the staff expert positions in the remaining 26 unions were created in 1941 or after.[24] Forty-four per cent of the jobs were created as recently as the period 1945-51—which suggests that the trend toward union use of full-time staff experts has not slowed up with a declining rate of membership growth during the Cold War.

By 1951, the twenty-eight unions in the Questionnaire Sample employed 298 staff experts (175 of whom fall in the Questionnaire Sample). This, of course, understates the extent of total use. In 1951, there were in the Washington headquarters of two major federations about 50 staff experts (23 for CIO, 27 for AFL). These federation experts (excluded from my count) cover such fields as research and education, publicity, political action, lobbying, the law, world affairs, race relations, housing, etc.[25] Fifteen nonoperating railroad unions support *Labor*, an influential weekly

24. Based on answers to Question 8a: "How many years has somebody been working full time on the kind of work you now do for your union?" The date the title was created is often much later than the date on which I base the analysis.

25. Additional staff members more or less expert in international affairs represent the labor movement abroad either directly on union payrolls or as labor representatives in such government agencies as ECA (now ICA), AMG, and the State Department. At least a dozen of these are former union staff experts.

put out by five professional journalists; these unions either indi-
vidually or through the Railway Labor Executives' Association
also use economic and legal consultants. Moreover, many regional,
state, city, or local units in the labor movement employ staff experts. The Michigan CIO Council, for instance, in 1950 employed
five full-time and two part-time staff experts, in publicity, education, and politics (additional staff is added around election time).
The Amalgamated Clothing Workers had, in 1951, 18 regional education specialists. Many railroad unions have a legislative representative in every state and several Canadian provinces. Another
impressive example of regional and local use of experts is the
Teamsters, probably the world's largest union. Each of a dozen
regional units of the Teamsters has at least one research man.[26]
St. Louis Local 688 of this union alone employs four researchers,
one editor-education director, and a medical director (plus 47
doctors, nurses and technicians in its Labor Health Institute).

Above all, the figure of 298 experts in the 28 unions misses
the unions' wide use of private professional consultants of every
description. No union—even if without one expert on its staff—
can get along without lawyers. All unions contacted reported
frequent and extensive, albeit reluctant, use of legal consultants.[27]
All of them use auditing or accounting firms. Seventeen of the
28 Questionnaire Sample unions and four of the six expertless
unions report the use of consulting economists, statisticians, actu-

---

26. In his first policy statement, newly elected General President Dave
Beck said he planned to develop a "strong program of public relations" and
"a central economic and statistical service." Teamster officials, he indicated,
would have "immediately available top-flight economic and statistical experts" for collective bargaining and governmental relations. Bureau of National Affairs, *Daily Labor Report*, No. 238 (Dec. 5, 1952), A-9.

27. One General Counsel did a questionnaire survey of his union's use of
lawyers. He estimates that in the course of a year this union uses at least
350 local lawyers (including 25-30 on cases where the International is sued).
"Practically every medium sized local and all big city locals had a regular
attorney." (222-4.) Robert M. Segal estimates that out of 200,000 lawyers in
the U.S. about 500 spend at least 25 per cent of their time on labor law.
"Labor Union Lawyers: Professional Services of Lawyers to Organized
Labor," *Industrial and Labor Relations Review*, 5 (April, 1952), 346. The
AFL Teamsters used enough attorneys to warrant the establishment at the
1952 Convention of a "National Conference of Teamsters' Lawyers" with 17
lawyers as officers and board members. *The International Teamster*, 49, No.
11 (Nov. 1952), 51.

aries, or pension experts. Sixteen of the 28 and three of the six say they employ public relations firms, advertising agencies or free-lance writers. Many employ outside artists, cartoonists, radio or film specialists. A large number of AFL unions have their official magazines handled by a publishing firm which prints, mails, edits, and in some cases even gathers the news and writes the copy. One can grasp the vast range of outside expertise tapped by labor from this composite list of consultants hired by the six largest unions in the country—not counting experts and operating personnel in union-owned enterprises: Insurance and casualty firms, pension and insurance consultants, social security experts, health insurance experts, professors of actuarial mathematics, economics and labor relations; lawyers (e.g., tax specialists and "tax contacts" on tax reduction cases, law professors to prepare digests of arbitration cases, famous attorneys for big cases, etc.); advertising agencies to handle placement in the media; industrial hygienists; professors and teachers for leadership training institutes; safety engineers; industrial engineering firms; artists; photographers; speechwriters; recreation specialists to lead or train choral groups, dramatics, sewing, etc.

In addition, there are special experts for special needs unique to certain unions: The Communications Workers Union uses specialists wise in the ways of telephone rate hearing officers; the Mineworkers—which represents workers with a very high accident rate—uses many specialists in workmen's compensation; the railroad unions hire lawyers specializing in railroad retirement matters; the Transport Workers Union, CIO, hires consultants to represent members appearing before the N. Y. C. Civil Service Board or the N. Y. C. Transit Authority; the National Maritime Union hires translators to cope with special needs of its non-English-speaking members; and so on. Discussion of the influence and special position of the private consultant is in Chapter XI.

Final testimony to the fact that the labor movement has hit its managerial stride is in the vast administrative machinery it takes to run union-owned enterprises, and the size of headquarters' staffs on the housekeeping side of union functioning .

Unions in mining, the needle trades and auto manufacture run large health centers (the ILGWU-AFL has 12 of them), each with its own staff of doctors, nurses, technicians. The Amalgamated Clothing Workers of America, CIO, owns two banks (combined resources of close to 80 million dollars), a housing project, an investment company, and an insurance company. Besides its health centers, the ILGWU owns a summer resort, an office building, and before 1952 owned several FM radio stations. The UAW-CIO, when it had FM stations, employed some 20 radio "technicians"—engineers, announcers, bookkeepers, salesmen, etc. A battery of staff experts and white-collar workers assist the Chairman of the Mineworkers' Welfare and Retirement Fund.

Some of the union-owned, separately incorporated enterprises are operated for a profit: the Carpenters' Union owns the Adams Packing Company; the Brotherhood of Engineers owns several office buildings and an apartment hotel in Cleveland; the IBEW-AFL in 1951 was building a large apartment house, the Bricklayers' Union owns the Bowen building in Washington. Ownership of such properties (for profit or not) invites a new set of problems—and we see the unions looking to legal and other specialists in corporation law, finance, real estate, banking; to radio attorneys to handle relations with the FCC; real estate men and architects to handle the growing physical plant, etc.

The specialized managerial and white-collar cadres needed to administer the big modern union are not limited to staff experts and professional consultants. The housekeeping and service side of headquarters operations consumes the energies of hundreds more.

Thus, today, if one adds to the count of 298 staff experts (for twenty-eight large unions), the fifty or so employed in the federations, scores who work in regional, state, and local units, plus the many specialists (on and off the payroll) who run union-owned enterprises, plus hundreds of private consultants of every kind, an impressive picture of the expansion of the intelligence function in the labor movement emerges. At the end of the guaranteed annual wage negotiations of mid-1955, a banner headline of the *Detroit Times*, June 19, dramatized the trend: "From Brickbats to Briefcases: Ph.D.'s Do Bargaining for UAW-CIO."

The rest of this study will concentrate on the group of top staff experts designated as the Questionnaire Sample and the Main Sample.

PART II

A FUNCTIONAL TYPOLOGY
OF UNION STAFF EXPERTS

CHAPTER III

GENERAL FUNCTIONS

WHEN GROUPS ARE IN CONFLICT with one another over a long period of time, they are forced to develop some means of accommodation simply to sustain their relationship. Sustained conflict shapes both the internal and the external relations of an organization and creates a demand for specialists in accommodative techniques. As collective bargaining and the strike became institutionalized (legitimate and accepted) means of organizing and channeling labor protest, as unions grew in size and their internal administration became more complex, the unions developed or hired such specialists. Thus, the outside intellectuals and ideologues who once braintrusted for union leaders or themselves won power in the unsteady unions of the last century have been replaced by men of more specialized training and talent. The union leader has come to tolerate the man of knowledge as a permanent fixture; he has hired, among other specialists, the full-time staff experts. Once on the payroll, what do these experts do? What does the leader look to them for? What consequences does their presence in the union entail?

To explore these questions, a typology of staff experts was constructed which is based on three criteria: (1) *Distinctive job content*—their typical activities, knowledge and skills and the areas of union decision to which those skills give them entree—in so far as this is relevant to analysis of (2) their *functions*—manifest and latent—defined in terms of observable objective consequences for the maintenance of the trade union as a social structure and its adaptation to the complex of internal and external pressures working on the union leader;[1] and (3) the nature of the bias introduced by their presence—the likely *direction of their influence* in view of their functions.

There seem to be three major types of labor staff experts in terms of their activities and skills, functions and net effect: the Facts and Figures Man, the Contact Man, and the Internal Communications Specialist. This typology does not do justice either to every variation in work and skills or to the dynamics of the work situation. It singles out instead what is important in terms of the problem (the content of "expert," the character and sources of his indispensability, the likely direction of his influence) and seeks to present a cross-cut picture of the top staff experts in the central headquarters of the large unions studied in 1950-51. Later the types will be related to influence ratings to provide a clue to the kinds of skills and knowledge that carry most weight in the modern union. The typology also provides a necessary means for later analysis of the tensions between the meaning the expert assigns to his work and the objective nature and consequences of that work. How the types were constructed and the cases classified is described in Appendix E.[2]

Some activities, some skills, some functions are common to all the union staff experts. Before moving to the distinct types, these common features will be considered.

---

1. Cf. Robert K. Merton's discussion of the concept "function" in *Social Theory and Social Structure* (Glencoe, Ill.: The Free Press, 1949), pp. 22 ff. I recognize that (1) there may be "dysfunctional consequences" in the activities of the staff expert (consequences that lessen the adaptation of the union to these pressures) and that some of his activities may simply be irrelevant; (2) the expert and/or the officer may recognize and/or intend some of these consequences, others may be neither recognized nor intended; (3) in the absence of the expert a wide range of alternatives might fulfill the functions depicted. I neither try to itemize all the diverse activities of the staff expert nor imply all these "functions" are fulfilled by each and every expert. The "complex of internal and external pressures" referred to here is spelled out in Chapter I.

2. Examination of borderline cases suggests that this functional typology applies less well to staff experts of rank-and-file origin and to unions which are (1) new and engaged in vigorous organizing drives; (2) engaged in all-out factional war; and (3) small. In such cases the degree of specialization is low and the work of the Internal Communications Specialist is done by all. See Appendix E.

"Window Dressing"

The most general of the self-characterizations of the union experts—one often echoed among labor's outside friends—is summed up in the phrase "window dressing." Economists, publicists, editors, education directors, fair practice representatives and (less often) engineers, lawyers—all in their candid moments—define their functions or those of their colleagues as "just for the show," "just fashion," "we're there for front." "The union leader doesn't really know what the economist does for him," says a sympathetic observer of the labor scene. "He sees statistics and economic argument as window dressing." (905-1.) A former Research Director, commenting on his ex-colleagues' factual presentations, says: "That's window dressing—all window dressing. They have to do something to justify their existence." (903-6.) The story is told that on only two occasions in several years did one top officer use his research man: (1) to ask where he could buy the *Encyclopaedia Britannica* cheaply—he wanted it for display in his home; and (2) to ask how to set a sundial "scientifically." (17-3.)

But these stories and characterizations reveal more of the subjective experience of thwarted missionaries and hemmed-in professionals (to be discussed in Chapter VII) than of the objective consequences of their activities.

The phrase "window dressing" encompasses a set of functions common to all the experts: (1) A psychological function for the officer, who wants to feel he's as good as the employer and/or any other union leader and wants the world to know it. "You don't sit down with the company any more without bringing in all that stuff," says a top officer. "We have to match them." (21-2.) (2) A psychological function for the rank-and-file activists, who want to feel that their union is "doing something" and is "keeping up." ("I'm introduced as [Director of ———] to a local union meeting and that gives them a feeling that this union has got something—it's progressive, modern."[454-5.]) In its most general terms this is an index of a drive towards respectability which is apparent

from the top to the bottom of the union hierarchy.[3] The presence
of the staff expert shores up the self-esteem of the union agent;
he borrows prestige from his educated hireling.[4]

An activity common to all our experts—and a second phase of
this self-esteem component of "window dressing"—is "public relations." Whether the expert be in economics, insurance, lobbying,
or the law—some part of his job involves, with few exceptions,
the long-range effort to win friends for the union among the
publics that count in the eyes of the boss. One engineer, discussing
his (typical) affiliations with the learned societies, said: "I travel
around the country to various universities. . . . But I don't think
my first responsibility is public relations the way some of these
guys do." (460-2.) Several men whose formal titles and job responsibilities have little to do with public contact appear to spend
the bulk of their time with university, government, civic, political,
and other outside groups. Almost all cases in the Q Sample spend
some time "fronting" for the union. The number and kinds of
their associational memberships are one rough measure of this:
About two-thirds of them (96 cases) hold at least one membership in a "respectable" professional or nonprofessional association.
In some additional cases, staff expert membership in a few of the
"Miscellaneous" or "Missionary" Organizations may also be a
source of prestige for the union.[5] At least part of the affiliation

---

3. Cf. David Riesman's observation on new motives for business entre-
preneurship: ". . . and the aim becomes not so much dollars as the possession of those appurtenances which an up-to-date company is supposed to
have. We see a succession of demi-intellectuals added to the staff: industrial relations directors, training directors, safety directors." *The Lonely
Crowd* (New Haven: Yale University Press, 1950), pp. 138-39.

4. This phenomenon is further analyzed in Chapter XIII, which includes
discussion of the social psychological content of the officer-expert relationship.

5. Only eighteen of 154 cases in the Q sample said they held no memberships at all (twelve more were not asked). A vast variety of respectable
professional and nonprofessional associations are represented among the
affiliated—well above 100 different organizations. The "Missionary" category includes such organizations as League for Industrial Democracy, American Civil Liberties Union, Socialist Party, Workers Alliance, National Association for Advancement of Colored People, etc. The "Miscellaneous" category consists of "respectable" organizations, membership in which indicates
neither professional nor missionary identification (e.g., local community
tenants' council, nonmilitant tolerance organizations, art appreciation society,
co-op society, trade unions, etc.).

picture can be attributed to the public relations activity of all functional types.

Verbalization

The "window dressing" and the public relations functions put a premium on the skill and function of symbolic manipulation. If any talent of our experts is universal, it lies in the field of verbalization. Be able to write, speak, present ideas quickly and easily —experts of all types stress this as one of the keys to success on the job.[6] A typical comment: "You need someone who can write English—simply, clearly. That's not funny. It's a job of communication—not like a Ph.D. thesis. Most Ph.D.'s couldn't qualify." (704-7.) The union experts need this word-processing skill to write speeches and resolutions, by-laws and contracts, to give testimony, edit papers, articulate policy, prepare legal or economic briefs, deal with the rank and file, speak in conference or mass meeting, contact community groups, and more. This is the craft skill that forms a partial basis for the expert's entree to the union, whatever his specialty. This is his most general function: to supply the verbal environment, create and sustain the symbolic atmosphere of the union world.

"Taking the Heat"

Another function experts of all types fulfill on occasion is variously labeled "taking the heat," "acting as fall guy," "getting him off the hook," etc. A lobbyist puts it this way:

They can use me for a fall guy. They can let me extend myself in a situation. Then if we find it means trouble, they can repudiate me—say that "———'s statement was unauthorized, made without our knowledge."

---

6. Almost half the 116 staff experts cases in the Main Sample on which data are available mentioned skills in writing and speaking on an open-end question about what it takes to make good. These responses were well distributed among all functional types (with some concentration in the Contact Man and Internal Communications types).

I'm a decoy. If subsequent judgment is that the line I'm pursuing is a tough one to stick with, they'll dump it. I understand, so it doesn't bother me. (704-3.)

A research man, discussing the joys of political "stability" in a union, says such stability gives him a chance to build the officers' prestige without getting into trouble, and this in turn promotes stability:

SE: If I see a chance to . . . build them up, well o.k. If I see a chance to take the heat off them, I do it. If it's a little dirty job, o.k.

HLW: How do you mean, a little dirty job? What's the dirty work on this job?

SE: Well, on this [issue] I could come out and make a statement, "You better come off it." If it turns out bad, then they could blame me.

HLW: It's a prearranged understanding that you have that you're to take the heat off them? Be the scapegoat, so to speak?

SE: No, there's no understanding. I just feel it's better that they keep me as the scapegoat. It's o.k., though, they insulate you. And they make it a policy to say that it was on the advice of good authority that we took that position and all that kind of thing. (301-7.)

Contributing to the self-esteem of the union officer at all levels of the organization by lending him prestige and "fronting" for the union with various publics, "taking the heat" when mistakes are made (which avoids injury to the reputation of the officer), and, in general, creating the verbal environment of the union world—these are universal functions of our experts.

Of course, the various trade union staff experts do not perform the same work, nor do all activities have the same consequences. Analysis of the distinctive activities, talents, functions and net effects of each functional type will yield a more meaningful classification.

CHAPTER IV

THE FACTS AND FIGURES MAN

Skills and Job Content

ONE GROUP of staff experts are distinguished by their relatively specialized professional training and background in the law, the social sciences (especially economics, industrial relations, statistics) and engineering. They have a primary concern with and skill in manipulating facts, figures, documents, records and arguments; their human relations skills tend to be less prominent. They are the men who furnish technical-economic-legal intelligence—the "ammunition"—to build the union's "case."[1] Their activities and talents give them entree directly and primarily to the areas of collective bargaining and governmental relations; secondarily to the area of public relations; indirectly to the areas of internal control and organization, and rival union relations. They have relatively little personal contact with the "field" (rank-and-file activists, and lower echelons of the line organization). The Facts and Figures label applies to: almost all the researchers, economists, and arbitration-screeners (in so far as these are specialized and trained); many of the lawyers (only those who are confined largely to court litigation, case-building for negotiations, ar-

---

1. See Chapter IX for a full discussion of the place of technical-economic-legal intelligence in the decision-making process. Almost two-thirds of the seventy-five Facts and Figures Men in the Q Sample have had some graduate training, in contrast to about one-third of the experts in other categories. See Appendix E, Table 9.

bitration, drafting contract language and briefs, appearances before
NLRB and other administrative agencies, and housekeeping operations); and a few of the lobbyists (the few who are principally
Washington extensions of Research Departments). The industrial
engineers and the pension and insurance consultants constitute
subtypes of the Facts and Figures Man, by virtue of their unique
union relationships and job content; I shall consider them separately.

Despite a vast range of activities, analysis of job descriptions
shows a heavy concentration of the effort of the Facts and Figures
Man in certain directions. The bulk of his day-to-day work is routine—undramatic answers to commonplace requests from officers
and staff for information. For example, the hard core of the union
Research Department's activity—and the task by which it demonstrates its indispensability most clearly—is keeping records on and
analyzing (1) economic characteristics and conditions of the industries and companies with which the union deals—with particular
emphasis on ability to pay; (2) jobs, contracts, and wage structures
—with heavy attention to rate comparisons by occupation, area,
industry, subindustry, company, and other unions.[2] If there is any
formula expressing the style of wage negotiations in America today,
it is the union formula, "Here's what we want; this is what it will

---

2. All but five of the unions in our Questionnaire Sample report as a
major and time-consuming activity some sort of contract analysis and/or
wage rate analysis—ranging from the elaborate punch-card systems of the
IAM-AFL (which codes 120 clauses and records other facts from each of
more than 11,000 collective bargaining contracts), USA-CIO and UE-Ind.,
or the cross-filing system of the ILGWU-AFL (this union is recognized as the
nation's best single source of information about the ladies garment industry—
one to which management often turns) to more sporadic wage surveys and
contract breakdowns. The UAW-CIO Research Department records show
that ". . . it answered nearly 3,000 requests . . . during the period December
1, 1947, through May 25, 1949. A breakdown shows that 1,413 of these
requests were for financial information, 956 were on wage rates, and 499
concerned contract problems." Hardman and Neufeld, *op. cit.*, p. 252. The
IBEW-AFL reports "the bulk of our requests come from small locals in the
field . . . wanting wage rates and comparable contracts." The Steelworkers
report requests for financial data on companies representing about one-third
of the total under contract in the course of a year. TWUA-CIO notes an
increasing number of requests for financial information on individual companies. During a five-month period in 1948, routine reports on forty companies were prepared plus fuller analyses of whole industries, overall studies
of financial conditions, and a full financial history of a mill which closed.
(D4-12.)

cost; you can pay it; besides, look at all these other employers who
are paying it (not to mention these other unions that have it)."
This is reflected in the definition given to the Facts and Figures operation by union leaders at all levels. It accounts for the fact that
"long-term" or "basic" research in union parlance is apt to mean
projects that take more than a few days' time, or analysis of problems that will not become pressing or obvious till next year—and
in either case it must be squeezed in between the day-to-day
"servicing" of field staff and officers.[3]

So, too, with Facts and Figures lawyers. In or out of unions,
the staff lawyer usually gets his initial chance—his entree to the
places where organizational decisions are made—because of his
technical craft skills, underscored by his state-sanctioned license to
practice. Union leaders often hold the conviction that (as one staff
man put it) "the union is surrounded by laws" (301-12); they
sometimes share a common American reverence for the "mystery
of the law," and believe that it takes a lawyer to understand a
contract, or even the English language. The lawyer's mastery over
contracts, constitutions, statutes and deeds, his skill in the courtroom and the quasi-judicial conference cannot be ignored. The oft-
repeated phrase, "It's the lawyer who keeps us out of jail," testifies
to the importance of this knowledge and skill.[4]

---

3. Examples of the relatively rare long-term research job: a history of the
union; effect of a change in style, material, or product on employment and
job content; a poll of the membership on a possible bargaining issue; a study
of proposed government regulation of the industry.

4. Several unions in the Questionnaire Sample had no House Counsel
until the passage of the Taft-Hartley Act, whose complex provisions have
brought it the label "The Lawyer's Full Employment Act." Typical interview comments: "At one time there [in a strike in 1948] they had us tied
up with 30 million dollars in damage suits, 22 injunctions, 310 arrest cases,
plus 375 counts on contempt. . . . We had to hire seven additional lawyers
and keep them on about a year." (203-1.) A top officer: "The General
Counsel was hired in 1947 . . . to take care of legal affairs which has
mounted and mounted steadily. . . . We get all kinds of directives and
memorandums drafted by government lawyers that have to be interpreted.
. . . It's expensive, too." (21.1.) "Right now [our lawyer] is working day
and night defending our officers on contempt of Congress charges." (312-4.)
All unions contacted, including those who make no use of staff experts, employ lawyers, either on or off the staff, for these traditional purposes: litigation, legal review of intended union action, preparation of arbitration cases,
etc.

The bread-and-butter nucleus of the work of the Facts and Figures Man—lawyer or economist—puts a premium on his ingenuity. He becomes skilled in the production of quick and simple answers to complex questions. To act the general "Information Please" role, he has to develop friendly sources of data. Some of the ammunition he is asked to supply can be secured only through staff men in the many government agencies with which he deals (the BLS, the Bureau of Labor Standards, the ICC, the NLRB, Defense Department or various mobilization agencies). Some of the judgments he is asked to render require more leisurely study than he can give; a government expert who knows the intricacies of the problem can supply the answer (e.g., "What are the effects of the reciprocal trade agreement on X industry's employment and wages?"). The Facts and Figures Man develops the mentality of a sleuth: to uncover the profit position of a given company he must collect and piece together bits from the trade press, Dun and Bradstreet, the SEC, even his bank—and locate an inside dopester who can check his judgments;[5] to "get the goods" on a rival union, he must watch the daily and labor press, collect scraps of information and sample contracts from visiting representatives in the area, reserve a listening post on the grapevine. To get rate and contract information from within his own union, to prepare an NLRB case or an arbitration brief on a grievance, he must cultivate the co-operation of the field staff.

Functions

What are the distinctive functions of the Facts and Figures Man, the objectively observable consequences of all this activity for the maintenance of his trade union as a social structure and its adaptation to external and internal pressures?

---

5. Some researchers have "friendly channels" specializing in supplying data on the business condition of individual companies. These probably include investment counselors, brokers, industry economists, and other functionaries who may be in touch with the business world but attuned ideologically to Labor. We might hypothesize that some intelligence agents in all interest groups are sufficiently flexible in their allegiances to pass on information to the "enemy."

1. *He builds pressure on the employer in contract negotiations where the employer is concerned about "public opinion" and/or government, and he indicates the seriousness of the union demands.* The greater the impact a shutdown would have on the economy (local or national), the clearer the public stake in a peaceful outcome, and the greater likelihood that government agencies will intervene, the more important this function becomes. But it operates to some extent in and out of the "big leagues"—wherever the employer becomes convinced that he has a public relations problem. An officer, asked whether bargaining power isn't what counts in the end, comments:

It gets so that you're negotiating for the benefit of the local press, not to convince the company. . . . That happens when the company goes to the papers and says, "Here's why the union is so goddam wrong!" We have to come back. We say, "No, here's where we're so goddam right"—and we have to prove it with these facts and figures . . . especially if [we're] going to be forced to strike. (9-3.)

The image of an enraged public in a strike situation worries this union leader; that same image may operate to force an employer into line before it ever comes to a strike. "The stronger the case the union can build," explains one Facts and Figures Man, "the tougher the public relations problem of the company will be and hence the more willing they are to settle." (302-2.)

Thus, "research" operates as a means of communication by which the parties assess their positions in relation to possible or imagined public and state pressures.[6] The Facts and Figures Man sometimes serves a communication function in another sense: his research presentation can be interpreted as a ritual whose year-to-year variations indicate the seriousness of specific union (or company) demands. "Here's the kind of [off the record] statement we get from one of the shrewdest employers," explains a Facts and Figures Man. "'I don't think you're serious about this issue, because last year you had a whole brief prepared for it.' On [another issue where we had done a real job] he said, 'It looks like you guys are serious on

---

6. One angle of this "case-building" as a pressure in collective bargaining is the occasional union or company use of the Facts and Figures Man in negotiations for straight "stalling" purposes. Either party may need time while public or other pressures build up on the other party or an internal pressure of their own is dealt with. A research brief uses up time.

this thing.'" (305-4.) More commonly, this is never made explicit. The research presentation serves as one means of informing the other party of your intentions without explicitly tipping your hand. The point can be extended to a more general principle: in order to reach accommodation, each side must have some means of assessing the power and the willingness to use power of the other. Various means of communicating these facts about power and intent must therefore develop.[7] The Facts and Figures operation in union-management relations functions (with varying reliability) as one such means, especially in the period of negotiations before the eleventh hour is reached.[8]

2. *He persuades and impresses quasi-judicial boards, arbitrators, government hearing officers, and promotes a reorientation of the negotiators toward data.* As national and multi-employer bargaining grew, as unionism became entrenched in our key industries, as heavy state intervention in economic life became accepted and union-management relations "matured," unions found themselves dealing with an increasing number of fact-finders, mediators, arbitrators, hearing officers, joint councils, jurisdictional claims boards, etc.

When a tribunal is set up—whether it be a board of control in a nationalized industry in Britain or a Presidential Fact Finding Board in America—labor-management relations becomes a more self-conscious process. A board, after all, is supposed to operate according to principle, whether there are any agreed-on criteria or not.[9] These representative comments illustrate the point:

---

7. Cf. H. D. Lasswell's discussion of "measurability" and "visibility" as two of the conditions of a "balancing of power" process. "World Politics and Personal Insecurity" in *A Study of Power* (Glencoe, Ill.: The Free Press, 1950), pp. 57-58.

8. Obviously, other possibly more important means exist; e.g., the intervention of the government conciliator and mediator, the private conference of the legal counsel on each side, etc.

9. Apparently, both here and in Britain, the criterion which these boards embrace most typically is "existing inequities." Wage stabilization in America has always left room for adjustment of "gross inequities," "substandard" wages and the like. See G. W. Taylor, *Government Regulation of Industrial Relations* (New York: Prentice-Hall, Inc., 1948), pp. 177 ff. Cf. lecture by Barbara Wooton at the University of Chicago, January 15, 1951. This accentuates the attention union Facts and Figures Men give to comparable rates and contracts, noted above on p. 40.

A railroad researcher: If the dispute is ultimately going to be settled before a fact finding or arbitration board, you want to make a record pointing toward the Board. . . . It's true [in steel and coal], too—except there's more expectation on the Railroads. The basic industries are all on their way to fact finding and arbitration, but they're not as far along as the public utilities. (912-2.)

An ex-expert from a multi-industrial union: He used research to make a point with the WLB—to impress academic people like ———. (N913-1.)

A building trades researcher: When top officers would appear before a wage body of the government or the [Industry Council—joint Labor-Management body empowered to settle disputes] we supplied advice and facts—just as the lawyer would accompany his client to a court of law, so the Research man would go along with the officer to a hearing. (910-3.)

A few staff men and officers in the Railroad Brotherhoods, after years of experience with the three-cornered collective bargaining routine, remain cynical about the use of facts and figures; they point to national economic and political pressures as the real determinants. Nevertheless, even they become reoriented in their bargaining attitudes:

A top union executive: We have a going wage case—it's been brought up-to-date every so often since 1921! It's something we can prepare a year before and put the last page together the day of the hearing. . . . We'll show that manufacturing got an increase; we're farther behind. It don't influence the bargain too much. It must have *some* influence, though. The Board certainly has to consider it. (303-2.)

A staff man: There were 150 exhibits. One took us five days to prepare. It was 150 pages. How they can read it I don't know! [HLW: "Then why bother?"] You can't do it without statistics. You have to present arguments; it's like it was before a court. (111-1.)

These men doubt that the Boards are impressed by anything but political pressures. But they are not quite sure: On the one hand, "Truman is what counts"; on the other, "You have to have proof." Even the cynics, like their colleagues in unions more convinced of the desirability and workability of the government's dispute-settlement machinery, become concerned with the assembly of impressive arguments, trend exhibits, mountains of data. Similarly, the union official who is persuaded that "lawyers are a menace," that games, especially legal games, are made to be beaten, can nevertheless become concerned with the assembly of impressive legal briefs, the citation of precedent, the letter and the spirit of the law.

3. *He strengthens the morale of the union committee and in turn the rank and file; this boosts the bargaining power of the union in negotiations, and in general enhances the leaders' control over the members.*

(a) The arguments of the Facts and Figures Man serve to give the negotiators the conviction and sense of moral rectitude they need to hold out for their demands in the face of opposition. One Facts and Figures Man spelled out the internal two-step flow of argument:

> . . . the . . . purpose of our research presentation is to give encouragement to our own people. Our negotiators need to feel they have a good case, that their demands are just and reasonable. The morale of the union representatives is strengthened by a well-prepared case. And to the extent that they pick up our arguments and carry them back to the rank and file, the morale of the membership is strengthened, too. That can be important both as pressure on the company and in the success of a strike if that should develop. These arguments do get around the shop, to some extent at least. A story like the one about management's refusal to answer a question "is a wage increase ever justified"—a story like that will get around. (302-2,3.)[10]

After the bargain is made (by officers whose hand has been strengthened by conviction), this indirect function of internal union control and morale-building comes into play. It is often made explicit:

> These . . . people take their job seriously (even though they're in the background when actual settlements are being reached). When they go home they want to understand so they can explain it to their local committees and local meetings. (316-5.)

(b) A second aspect of this internal control function of the Facts and Figures Man is seen in his attention in many unions to

---

10. Cf. the flow of campaign ammunition from the mass media to opinion leaders to rank-and-file voters, noted in the study of the 1940 Presidential election campaign in Erie County. P. F. Lazarsfeld, B. Berelson, H. Gaudet, *The People's Choice* (2d. ed.; New York: Columbia University Press, 1948), pp. 151-52. Compare this description of the purpose of the extensive research and planning of the Facts and Figures Men in the Ford Motor Co.: "The value of all that preparation was readily apparent during bargaining. . . . Our negotiators were *prepared.* They had *confidence* in their ability to meet any question, any problem or situation within reason, and their attitude reflected that confidence." Mel B. Lindquist, "Preparation for Collective Bargaining," address before American Trucking Associations, Inc., First Annual National Forum, Jan. 30, 31, 1950 (text in Bureau of National Affairs *Daily Labor Report* No. 21:D-5, Jan. 31, 1950).

the activities of rivals. Union policy is often determined in light of rival unions' policies. If the IUE and UAW are for joint administration of pension plans, the UE is against it. If the AFL Pulp, Sulphite and Paper Mill Workers get ten cents, the CIO Paperworkers try for twelve cents. Moreover, in the crazy-quilt pattern of jurisdictional lines characterizing the modern labor movement, few unions escape the necessity of staving off or carrying out rival union raids. Thus, a large part of the Facts and Figures operation in some unions is devoted to reading the labor press, collecting rivals' contracts, sleuthing to uncover damaging facts about other unions and "expose" them.

(c) To fulfill this morale-building and control function— in dealing both with management and union rivals—a union has to act dramatically, as well as deliver the goods. The excitement of the "investigation" and "exposure" helps sustain membership loyalties and at rare moments makes the Facts and Figures Man very dear to the hearts of the union officialdom. One line official describes this entry of a Facts and Figures Man into negotiations:

It was a day when the morale of our committee was real low. He was obnoxious, completely obnoxious to the company. He gave them hell. He'd pull out this [college] textbook, and then another, and he'd tell them they didn't know their ass from a hole in the ground. It brought a complete change in our bargaining committee. (Doc. 21.)

As for the rank-and-file response to this drama: "The company will bring some hotshot in to give us some double-talk. You'll hear the rank and file say, 'We ought to hire some guy and go in there and out-talk the sunnuvabitch.' Bringing the outsiders in hasn't created a problem, it's solved one. Before, our guys would tell me, 'The company had all their legal brains in there; who the hell did you have?'" (9-5.)

(d) This conviction that the union has to "match" the company, out-talk its experts, is widespread. Most of the union officials interviewed who were using Facts and Figures Men gave as one (unsolicited) reason that the company hired them first. Many of the union experts also use this argument to support requests for expansion or maintenance of staff. It is, therefore, interesting to note the comment of the Ford Motor Company's Assistant Director of Labor Relations. He says the union started the whole thing:

Another conviction that we hold strongly—one that is basic—is that there should be careful, thorough preparation for collective bargaining. I don't know of any company, however fortunate it may be in its labor relations, which can afford to "play by ear" at the bargaining table. . . . Unions have long recognized the necessity for this preparation. Many of the large unions like the UAW spend a great deal of time and money in research work—far more than many companies can afford to spend. This . . . makes it possible for the union to throw an almost endless array of facts and figures at smaller companies—and even the big ones—on a uniform basis, which (sic) each company must dig up its own statistics. The advantage enjoyed by the union on this score is obvious.[11]

Whether in given cases management or the union initiates the use of experts (or whether either side enjoys an advantage in their use), the process, once begun, perpetuates itself. The dialectic of "experting" in industrial relations is a reflection of a larger process that goes on wherever organized groups become involved in a conflict of interests. "Intellectuals," as Lasswell observes, "have elaborated symbols on behalf of nations, races, classes, religions, and all other collective entities . . . their struggles with one another . . . multiply the opportunities in society for this kind of activity."[12] The existence of a Facts and Figures Man—on the company or the union payroll—tends to provoke a like response from the other party. Both sides, however reluctant, become convinced of the necessity of matching the other argument for argument, fact for fact, expert for expert.[13]

I have suggested that the principal functions of the Facts and Figures Man are to (1) build pressure on the employer in contract negotiations by permitting him to assess his position with respect to real or imagined public or state pressures, and to size up the seriousness of various union demands; (2) persuade and impress

11. Mel B. Lindquist, op. cit., p. D-2. Lindquist details the operation of the Planning and Analysis Department of Ford's Industrial Relations Division. It appears to be similar in focus and function to union Facts and Figures operations, but much wider in scope and more closely integrated with policy levels.

12. Op. cit., p. 112.

13. Cf. Simmel, who notes that the secret society through formalism and hierarchical organization ". . . makes itself into a sort of counter image of the official world, to which it places itself in contrast." He sees this as an instance of a general sociological law. ". . . structures which resist larger encompassing structures through opposition and separation, nevertheless themselves repeat the form of these structures." The Sociology of Georg Simmel, ed. Kurt H. Wolff (Glencoe, Ill.: The Free Press, 1950), p. 360.

quasi-judicial boards, arbitrators, government hearing officers; (3) strengthen the conviction and the morale of the union committee and in turn the rank and file.

Before analyzing the probable bias inherent in these Facts and Figures functions, I shall deal briefly with the engineers and the pension and insurance consultants. They constitute subtypes of the Facts and Figures category. But important aspects of their work, their contact with lower echelons of the union, and their relations with employers, mark them off enough from other Facts and Figures Men to warrant separate treatment.

The Pension, Insurance, and Engineering Experts: Facts and Figures Subtypes.—Pension and welfare plans became popular as collective bargaining issues only in the past few years. As recently as 1942, health, welfare and retirement benefit plans were rarely included in collective bargaining agreements.[14] But by 1954 such provisions in union contracts covered more than eleven million workers.[15]

Also in the past few years, the techniques of industrial engineering have been widely applied and bargained over in unionized plants.[16] These include: (1) time study of production standards; (2) design and administration of wage-incentive payment plans; (3) job evaluation; (4) merit rating; and (5) the installation of work simplification techniques through motion study.[17]

These relatively new issues in collective bargaining have meant the entry of two sets of experts into the union headquarters and their rapid rise to indispensability, and (within their spheres of competence) even to high influence: the management engineers, and the pension and insurance experts.

Few unions have as yet employed full-time staff experts to deal with these new issues. Three unions employ more or less trained pension and insurance experts: twelve in UAW-CIO, one in USA-CIO, one in TWUA-CIO. Four unions employ more or less professional engineers: six in ILGWU-AFL, three or four in USA-CIO,

---

14. BLS Bulletin No. 686, *Union Agreement Provisions* (*1942*), pp. 198-201.

15. BLS, *Monthly Labor Review*, 78 (April, 1955), 424.

16. See Solomon Barkin, "The Technical Engineering Service of an American Trade Union," *International Labour Review*, LXI (June, 1950), 1-9.

17. Gomberg, in Hardman and Neufeld, *op. cit.*, p. 256.

two or three in TWUA-CIO, and three in UAW-CIO. But several
other unions use the advice of Facts and Figures Men not specializing on these issues or assign organizers and staff men who have
little special training; most of the unions in our Questionnaire
Sample have used outside consultants in one or both of these areas.
(During its 1950 negotiations, the Steelworkers, e.g., used eleven
pension and insurance consultants on a temporary full-time basis.)

The experts hired to deal with these issues include both the
most highly trained of the functionaries in the labor movement
and the least trained but most politically astute. This is explained
by two aspects of their work that distinguish them from other
Facts and Figures Men. First, there is the high degree of technical
complexity (or at least conceptual elaboration). This is discussed
in detail in Chapter IX. Second, there is the necessity of frequent
field contact.

Both engineers and pension and insurance experts—in contrast
to the other Facts and Figures Men—are likely to spend much time
in personal contact with officers and staff in the lower echelons; this
gives their work an "operational" (their word for "political")
flavor.[18]

Facts and Figures Men with much direct field contact (like the
Internal Communications Specialists discussed later) are in a position to strengthen or weaken loyalties to the union administration.
This is especially true of the engineer, who enters the local as a
trouble-shooter to settle job grievances going to the heart of the
union's functioning. One Facts and Figures Man discusses this
unique feature of the engineer's job:

> On the workload problem he goes to the root of unionism—the work-
> er's job. He can choose in any given case whether he'll act tough and
> tell the management: "You sunnuvabitch, pushing our guys around that
> way: we'll take it to arbitration"—and then when the arbitrator turns

18. See below, footnote 6, p. 188, for the pension and insurance expert's entree to the locals during negotiations. Another group of Facts and
Figures Men who come close to the subtype we are discussing are the compensation experts (who enter the local to advise members of their rights in
unemployment compensation and/or workmen's compensation cases and as
liaison with administrative agencies enforcing these laws); and the safety
experts (who enter the local as advisers on members' rights under state
safety codes and as trouble-shooters where accidents occur).

him down, say, "That sunnuvabitchin' arbitrator—he and the company
are ganging up on us, but we'll never stop fighting." Or, on the other
hand, [the engineer] is in a position to make [the top officer] look
weak. He can go in and tell the local, "Sorry, boys, much as I'd like to
fight your just case, the contract here makes it look pretty bad—and besides, you know how it is, my hands are tied by [the administration].
(N902-1.)

Where an internal factional situation exists—and both sides are vy-
ing with one another to see who can get the most militant reputation on the workload problem—the "operational" aspects of this
Facts and Figures function loom large. Where relative stability exists within the union, the engineer and the pension and insurance
expert are in a position to be more "responsible," i.e., pay more
attention to the "facts" in dealing with management. It is here that
another unique feature of this subtype is apparent: the engineer
often finds himself mediating between conflicting management and
worker points of view; and both the engineer and the pension-
insurance expert often act as adviser to management as well as
union. Two pension experts explain:

A pension plan goes into great detail on how claims will be determined. The employer may get a suggestion from an actuary or an insurance company; I've found that in a good number of cases I can get
them to change their views. You see, often it's not a dollars and cents
argument—it's the efficiency of administering the plan. . . . there are
theoretical and sound reasons why the employer should not deduct
payments with respect to different kinds of risks. (224-4.)

Company negotiators listened to me with astonishment as I started
talking about facts. Sometimes as I told a union man he's unreasonable,
the companies were shocked. I don't see why offering advice to both
sides is not legitimate. (911.)

The engineers report a similar experience: (1) the company, as
well as the union, calls them in, accepts (within limits) their integrity and impartiality; (2) this often leads to rank-and-file suspicion. A typical comment:

I've actually been named as impartial umpire in four or five contracts. I don't like it. . . . It puts you in an uncomfortable position.
. . . It's a job trying to get our people to agree to my findings—even
if it helps them they often balk! But they come around. . . . we have
so much experience they listen. . . . We act more as arbitrators. . . .

I thought management would look at us as biased. But they don't. They trust [our] honesty and integrity. Management accepts us as impartial. (453-2,3.)

The possible dysfunctional consequences of this conflict in roles (union advocate vs. impartial mediator) are plain: the engineer may act to mystify and alienate the rank and file and lower leadership, create opposition and instability, and loosen the top leaders' control over them.[19] Balanced against that are the functions previously discussed: (1) he "takes the heat"; (2) he demonstrates that the union is interested in servicing the local and can "match" management; (3) he talks the company into making concessions, improving efficiency, i.e., his technical competence on these issues means tangible gains in the long or even short run.

Net Effects

I have now traced the distinctive skills, work and functions of a series of experts labeled "Facts and Figures Man," including the subtypes exemplified by the engineer and the pension-insurance expert. What is the net effect of his work? What is the probable direction of his influence, the nature of the bias he introduces into the union's operations, considering all the activity and functions we have discussed?

To get at this difficult problem I shall trace the changing styles of negotiation and union administration and note the role in which the Facts and Figures Man enters. Two kinds of data are especially relevant: the recollections of union leaders, now using Facts and Figures Men, of the days before they felt the need for them; and the explanations of union functionaries in unions who today do not use experts.

From Table-Pounding to Facts and Figures.—The historical re-

------

19. It should be noted that all of those experts involved in the engineering operation are aware of this possibility, and, depending upon their role orientations, resist it in varying degrees. Several point the finger of scorn at their colleagues among the professionals, or at the laymen who fulfill the same functions in other unions: "They take their time study seriously. They miss the whole point. They don't know the fundamental deficiencies of this stuff."

constructions of officer and staff are usually put in terms of a shift from "table-pounding," "bluff," "rule of thumb" and the ready use of force—both in collective bargaining and organizing—to the (usually reluctant) resort to Facts and Figures Men. "In those days [thirties]," a former organizer recalls, "if we didn't like what management was doing, we didn't call in a time study man; we shut the plant down." (460-2.) "It isn't like it was in the old days," a top officer recalls. ". . . You don't organize with brickbats any more; you have to be prepared to cite instances and quote laws and know your agreements. . . . You have to come in with arguments. People are getting enlightened, including employers." (17-1,3,4.)

These reminiscences of a bygone table-pounding era are matched by a living reality in some sections of today's labor movement. As far as my data show, the unions which have the necessary financial resources but make little or no use of Facts and Figures Men fall into three categories: (1) unions with much "militancy" in industries characterized by frequent resort to force (e.g., UMW); (2) unions whose "maturity" in some places borders on collusive collective bargaining relations (e.g., Bricklayers and Carpenters); (3) unions whose job control is so great that for all practical purposes they legislate working rules and even wage rates unilaterally for large sections of their membership (e.g., Musicians and ITU).

An officer in the first nonuser category—militant, strike-prone—puts it succinctly:

All the facts that all the statisticians in the world could get you, all the arguments of the best economists, all the skill in presenting it don't mean a damn thing when the chips are down. . . . The arguments roll off the [employers] just like water off a duck's back. There's just one thing they understand and that's the power of the union. There's no argument—it's "How much are you gonna pay." . . . We know the facts don't mean anything to them; and they know it, too, when they argue with us. . . . Through years of experience we've learned that you'll get only what you take away from them. . . . What can an actuary [that is, researcher] do for us? What could an actuary say to a [representative of this industry]? (19-5,6,3.)

Union people in the "mature but collusive" category (and informants with first-hand contact with them) stress the existence of "friendly relations," high wages, and the desire to avoid new problems—a general attachment to the status quo—as the reasons for not using experts. "We have high wages," observes one top officer. "Among the highest in [the industries we deal with]. We have friendly relations with employers . . . a minimum of strikes; we don't need technicians around here. We get along fine." (15-3.) Apparently, where monopoly powers exist, where employers have what one informant termed "quiet understandings" with the union, it is felt that the Facts and Figures Man would merely disrupt a good thing, and the functions he fulfills in other unions are not needed.

The third nonuser category—"legislators not bargainers"—is also satisfied, and there again no need for "research" is felt.[20]

Not only has there been a reorientation in the bargaining styles of officers (which is highlighted by contrasting research users with nonusers) but there has been a marked change in the kind of Facts and Figures Man hired. The most obvious change can be seen in the figures for our Questionnaire Sample on occupational and educational backgrounds of those who entered the Labor movement as staff experts before 1945 contrasted with those who entered in the postwar period 1945-51. The proportion with graduate training went up from 57 per cent to 70 per cent. The proportion whose occupational experience just prior to entry was clearly relevant to the Facts and Figures operation went up from about one-third to three-fifths. This indicates that the newer Facts and Figures Men the unions are hiring probably have more technical competence and their previous training and experience is more closely tied to their present job functions. Even some of the Facts and Figures Men who have been with the union many years report a change in their mode of dealing with the facts and figures: "We operated on a completely different basis," reports one. "We'd make a decision that productivity was on the increase and by God we'd prove it. We'd put the company in the position of saying, 'We didn't murder eight guys; we only murdered seven! You see what I mean? . . . [We] didn't do only an economic analysis, [we] did a job." (318-7.)

The contrast in the bargaining approaches of present nonusers

---

20. Note, however, that both the "mature but collusive" and the "legislator not bargainer" types may have sections of their membership in industries or trades where such relationships are not typical. In such cases, one or two Facts and Figures Men are typically employed.

with those of present users of Facts and Figures Men—coupled with the reminiscences of the latter of their transition from table-pounding to fact-finding—and the change in the training and background of the experts themselves, suggest the conclusion that the Facts and Figures Man tends to push the union towards a more "rational," "responsible" mode of operation. The previous delineation of his functions in collective bargaining would seem to support that general conclusion: he builds pressure on the employer via the state and the public—which tends to give the bargaining a "public responsibility" flavor; he acts as a channel of communication—which tends to prevent inaccurate assessment of union intentions; he sometimes convinces the employer of the soundness of union proposals; he persuades quasi-judicial boards—where, as we said, the whole process becomes more self-conscious and promotes a reorientation of the negotiators; and, finally, his presence on either side tends to convince the other party of the necessity of counter-argument, fact for fact.

The components of this "rational-responsible" bias and the process by which the Facts and Figures Man introduces it, require further elaboration. We deal with Facts and Figures lawyers first.

1. *The conviction that lawyers slow the union down.* "The first thing we do," wrote Shakespeare, "let's kill all the lawyers."[21] The modern Shakespeares are the writers of union contracts who insert the provision "no legal adviser of either party is to serve on any grievance committee." There is much antilawyer talk in my interview data (including lawyers' digs at their colleagues), most of it adding up to the complaint that the lawyer slows the union down:

Top officer: Some labor organizations lean on the lawyer heavily. That's a weakness in the labor leader. He gets involved with all the legal law [*sic*] and thinks his services as labor leader are minor—that all he's got to do is play it safe and keep his eye on the law. (21-3.)

Top officer: . . . I'll tell you my experiences with lawyers. They're always telling you what you can't do. That's the trouble with lawyers. . . . Tell me truthfully now. You're from up around Chicago. Don't you think that having a lawyer as President of the Packinghouse Workers has slowed 'em up? (5-4.)

House counsel: In the upper regions of the hierarchy there may be some resentment. This is natural—the lawyer will try to pitch it to de-

---

21. *Henry VI*, Part II, 4, 2. (Dick's remarks to Jack Cade.)

cided cases. They resist this. So there's a lot of by-play: "Aw, you lawyers are all the same; if we left it to you we'd have to go out of business." Basically there is reliance on the lawyer, though, despite the talk. (211-4.)

The lawyer here is pictured as a neutral technician throwing up legal barriers to scare the union leader and slow him down.[22] The respondents above are worried about the possible conservative impact of the lawyer. Some lawyers, as we shall see in Chapter VII, reveal a role conception that confirms such worries. For example:

> *Fee counsel: My* role is that of a "No-man." I try to assess the situation and point out alternatives and the limitations the law imposes on them. Now there are lawyers who are different. . . . (205-6.)

2. *Researchers and a "sense of reasonableness."* Not all lawyers are Facts and Figures Men, but the work of those who are has consequences very similar to the impact of the research men in the union. Matching one lawyer's observation that he introduces the concept of "higher-plane bargaining" is frequent comment from both officers and experts pointing in a general way to the "restraint," the more "civilized atmosphere" introduced by the presence of researchers: "We make for a sense of reasonableness . . . they like to have arguments—it's civilized . . . you throw economists at each other . . . you become reasonable." (320-4.) "Our work serves to sharpen issues and narrow the area of controversy." (322-2.) Thus do the experts speak. Their officers indicate the same drift (as their reminiscences above have already shown).[23]

This sense of reasonableness comes about because (1) the Facts

---

22. The story is told of a labor lawyer who had spent most of the day outlining to the Executive Board in learned terms how the union would create cases to test the Taft-Hartley Law at the very highest level, the Supreme Court. When he sat down, a top officer got up and made a five-minute speech to this effect: "I've always operated on the principle that the job of the XYZ Workers Union, like any other union, is to protect and defend the interests of the workers against the employer. I propose we go on with that great work. I am sure that the lawyers in our unions will also continue with their great task: to keep us out of jail while we're doing it!" (G22a-3,4.)

23. Compare the observations of a management spokesman: ". . . we believe a good deal of time and patience was saved simply by having the facts there at hand to refute any unreasonable statements. Having ready proof is one sure way to limit long-winded arguments." As he looks to the future—and the increasing use of Facts and Figures Men on both sides—he sees bargaining being put on a more "business-like basis." Imagine, he says ". . . how much time and effort would be saved if the traditional bargaining 'ritual' . . . all for the benefit of the 'boys' in the union . . . could be dis-

and Figures Man tends to be preoccupied with rational argument and criteria—and the criteria usually arise within the framework of management's value system or a set of laws rooted in that system; (2) his technical competence compels the employer to be more careful and/or honest in his use of facts.

The preoccupation of the Facts and Figures Man with rational argument is often noted by other types of experts. One Internal Communications Specialist expressed his concern over the alleged "conservative" influence of his colleagues (one an economist by training, the other a lawyer): "Here with these goddam statisticians and lawyers you don't say a goddam word that isn't proven. 'You can't say that,' the lawyer will tell you. Or [the economist] will say 'I can't support that.' . . . Always wanting evidence." (613-2,3.) Some typical opinions from the Facts and Figures Men themselves confirm the point:

> We're aware of the problem the company executive faces, we can honestly talk about profit position and not talk about what a sunnuvabitch the boss is. . . . We can honestly say what we believe; the officers can't. . . . (405-4,2.)
>
> We cry and yell about getting hurt. Somebody's going to get hurt. We should grow up and face the facts of life. . . . Conservative influence? Yes. Make them see the consequences of their decisions. (306a-1.)

Once such criteria as "ability to pay," "cost of living," "comparable rates," or "the pattern," "productivity," "real wages," etc., are introduced into the bargaining process, they are likely to become permanent fixtures. Moreover, all these arguments (depending on the times and the conditions) can serve either side equally well. As one expert said: "The fact that you're presenting a case—using data—introduces a certain restraint. If you feel wage gains are made on the basis of patterns, then the company is right when they say 'Ten cents is the pattern and that's all we'll give you.'" Another expert, asked where his impact on officer thinking and policy has been greatest, answered: ". . . overcoming in the minds of [our] people the fear of the cost-of-living argument—they're afraid it'll boomerang. But they've come to accept the idea that real wages *do* rise . . . and that should be the objective." (912-3.)

---

pensed with. More emphasis on preparation is not the whole answer, but perhaps it could cut down the opportunities for histrionics." Lindquist, *op. cit.*, p. D-5.

In accepting these concepts and criteria for bargaining purposes the union expert, whatever his motives and identifications, often finds that he is caught within a framework of norms that inevitably increases the rational-responsible bias of his activity. He finds himself "selling what's sounder"—adopting the cost-conscious, production-minded logic of the employer. A shrewd observer explained it this way:

To the extent our industrial engineers so called are involved in this monkey business, they feel called on to develop rational arguments. The relatively "intellectual" staff man—bright, he's read a book or two—when he's confronted with a guy making $2.00 an hour, $1.23 base, doing five hours of real work (loafing around the rest of the time) and he must justify this, he can't. The intellectual mind thinks in terms of criteria, of blueprints. In the [plant] the worker says, "What do you mean, my rate's too high?" (318-3.)

It should not be assumed from this discussion that, because the Facts and Figures Man introduces a rational-responsible bias, this necessarily means that the union takes less in its negotiations. It is true that Facts and Figures Men representing at least five unions report instances where the union leader changed, scaled down or abandoned given demands because his researcher advised him of negative employment effects, or of some possible injury to the union.[24] In other instances Facts and Figures lawyers invoked legal barriers to persuade the leader to play it safe, or go slow. But it is also true that much decision-making material indicates areas where Facts and Figures Men have influenced the choice of demands, encouraged last ditch fights on given issues, pointed to alternatives the union leader hadn't thought of, etc.[25] Moreover, as we have already seen, the Facts and Figures operation often serves to bolster union morale and the bargainers' sense of rectitude, thus increasing the union's power to "deliver the goods."[26]

Even where the Facts and Figures Man doesn't participate in negotiations, his mere presence on the union payroll—implying the threat of "exposure"—may strengthen the union's bargaining power,

---

24. See Chapter IX, pp. 189-190.

25. See Chapter IX, pp. 187 ff. For instance, a local bargaining situation where there was no "pattern" and a weak local would have taken less because of company allegation of inability to pay if expert hadn't stepped in. (304-1, 2.)

26. See above, pp. 46 ff.

as well as encourage reasonableness and a better enforcement of contract: as one expert said, "The employer is willing to deal with them instead of threatening arbitration or giving false data." (311-4.)

It is, therefore, not a conservative bias in the sense that the union leader becomes timid, or "sells out"; it is a rational-responsible bias in that there is a more conscious examination of alternatives, of relevant factors beyond power, and even in some cases of long-range consequences. Neither does the discussion imply that union leaders using experts are now making decisions with exclusive reference to technical-economic intelligence. The decision-making process involves a variety of pressures and intelligence agents having nothing at all to do with Facts and Figures Men. These are explored in chapters to follow.

In adding up his functions, and appraising their net effect for the maintenance and adaptation of the trade union as an institution, I have thus far focused on the difference the Facts and Figures Man makes in the collective bargaining process. My conclusion is that his presence there tends to introduce a rational-responsible bias. What about the direction of his influence in other areas of union decision—relations with the rank and file and with rival unions?

Here the task of analysis is more complex. On the one hand, as shown above, the Facts and Figures Man fulfills indirectly an internal control function (including control in the face of raids). This is seen in (1) his general enhancement of the prestige of the officer; (2) the morale-building effect of his arguments in bargaining; (3) his "heat-taking" work when mistakes are made (common to all the experts); and (4) his help in increasing the size and quality of the "take" (in the few areas where facts and figures in themselves *do* persuade the employer and/or government).

On the other hand, the Facts and Figures Man may act to weaken leadership control. This occurs to the extent that (1) the rational-responsible bias mystifies and alienates the rank and file and lower leadership (e.g., "What do you mean, my rate's too high?"); and (2) his work and advice lead the leader to settle for less in the short run (e.g., a lawyer cautions against a popular strike that the union might have won; a researcher estimates the company's financial condition to be weak). It is probable, however, that the functional consequences are more frequent and dramatic than the dysfunctional. "Responsibility" and "respectability," moreover, are qualities the rank and file and lower-level leadership aspire to, so the rational-responsible bias does not always alienate. Furthermore, the cases in which the expert would have to advise the lower echelons of the union to take less, be reasonable, go slow, etc., are few; and, where he deals with the top leadership in these terms, the members seldom know that the facts and figures have made any difference. Where the expert is in direct contact with rank and file and he exerts necessary restraint, he may at the same time act to relieve an embarrassed business agent and drain off hostility that would otherwise be directed against the administration. Suspicion of the expert is not necessarily suspicion of the top officer.

On balance it is, therefore, probable that on the internal control problem the functional consequences of the Facts and Figures operation are more frequent, important, and visible than the dysfunctional. Our conclusion that the net effect of this functional type is towards a more rational-responsible mode of operation in collective bargaining (including both employer and governmental relations) may be extended to other areas of union decision: he buttresses the union leader's ability to maintain internal discipline and cope with rival unions.[27]

---

27. If the Facts and Figure Man were as prominent in the trade union as his counterparts are in business and government, we might see a more clear-cut and direct influence on internal control: the extensive use of "morale inventories," special studies of human relations and "communications" problems, and periodic appraisals of the state of worker opinion. Such use of social science for control purposes in unions, however, is quite rare. Only six unions, to our knowledge, have undertaken in the past decade any thoroughgoing sociological or psychological studies of membership opinions or problems—three of them on minority group problems, two on "substandard" living conditions. One of them also sponsored a readership survey, a study of membership health and welfare problems, and a study of political orientation and voting behavior of its members. Add to this a few instances of postcard opinion surveys (e.g., one in World War II: what is your opinion of our no-strike pledge), some audience surveys by union-owned, separately incorporated radio stations, and the picture is probably complete. Only one officer mentioned the possibility of expansion in this direction; his comment may be taken as representing the model of the future: "I could use [attitude studies] to keep the membership in step—and to keep me in step with the membership, too. I'd like to get a technician to do a continuous study of our day-to-day operation—a very definite part of intelligent operation. [HLW: You actually mean you want a full-time social scientist to evaluate your performance?] Haven't got the money now, but I'd like to get someone eventually." (3-4.)

CHAPTER V

THE CONTACT MAN

Skills and Job Content

A SECOND GROUP of staff experts, despite marked heterogeneity of occupational, family, and educational background, share a primary concern and skill with facts about and techniques of manipulating the thoughts, feelings, and conduct of men. They are the experts who furnish the political-ideological intelligence the union leader needs to find his way around in bureaucratic society. Theirs is a skill in mediating the complex relationships between the union and the outside world. "Trouble-shooting," "keeping us out of trouble," "putting in the fix," "expediting"—these are typical phrases officers and experts alike use to describe their activities. "Knows the ropes," "realistic," "has connections," "is a helluva good handshaker"—thus are their talents characterized. These activities and talents involve the Contact Men in all union decision-making areas—primarily governmental relations, public relations, and collective bargaining, but with an occasional concentration on internal union control and relations with rival unions. The "Contact Man" label applies to ten of the twenty-five lawyers in our Main Sample; to all but one of the lobbyists, "Washington Representatives" and "Legislative Representatives" and to several of the public relations, community relations, and press relations specialists (those whose primary concern is not the production of a house organ). Their entree to union councils stems from a basic feature of modern society: the entanglements of diverse interest groups pursuing conflicting purposes and meeting at the level of the legislative, judicial and administrative agencies of government. The existence of these complex bureaucratic entanglements puts a premium on the human relations skills of the intermediary.

Of course, each of the union functionaries classified as "Contact Man" engages in some activities and possesses some skills unique to the particular job, union or time locus. The "Washington Representative" who came up from the ranks with a sixth-grade education via elective offices over a period of forty years and the "General Counsel" who arrived recently with a couple of Harvard degrees, *magna cum laude,* and several years of experience in a government labor agency are, at first glance, in sharp contrast. But the common core of their activity, the skills and knowledge for which they are valued, and the similar consequences of their presence on the union staff permit common treatment. A brief discussion of the main skills and activities of each major occupational group represented among the Contact Men underscores this similarity.

THE LAWYER

Many union lawyers, as we have seen in Chapter IV, remain craftsmen fulfilling Facts and Figures functions. They fit the orthodox descriptions of the legal profession which emphasize the lawyer's technical skills. But the most prominent and visible of the labor lawyers merit the Contact Man label. For the means of entree (in those cases where technical craft skills figure prominently in initial recruitment) is not identical with the means of ascension to position of high influence. The Contact Man "arrives" more through his skills in private consultation, negotiation, and mediation and his intimate knowledge of the workings of his union and of American society, than through his knowledge of contracts, constitutions, statutes, and deeds, or his skill in the courtroom.[1] "The

---

1. Ferdinand Lundberg, writing about this type of lawyer, accurately observes: "The lawyer comes to know society not as a tenant or owner knows a house but as the architect, building contractor, and repair men know it. And his knowledge of society extends beyond the knowledge these technicians have of any building, for he is intimately acquainted as well with the servants

best thing you can have" to make out as a labor lawyer, says one Contact Man, "is a general social science background. Most of what we do isn't connected with the law anyway. . . . A lot of it is public relations. You act as go-between." The skills are the skills of political realism, an ability to sense the attainable and do what it takes to reach it.

The range of the lawyer's activities as Contact Man is typically even greater than that of the Facts and Figures Man. And the overwhelming impression yielded from interview job descriptions is that the union lawyer as Contact Man concentrates his efforts and time outside the court, outside the legislative or administrative hearing, or even the arbitration conference.[2]

---

that staff the structure. He either knows all there is to know about judges, public officials, business leaders, bankers, professional politicians, labor leaders, newspaper publishers, leading clergymen, and the like, or through that informal clearing house of esoteric information, the bar association, can find out from colleagues. The lawyer is a vast reservoir of actual or potential information about the social and political topography. . . ."'The Legal Profession: A Social Phenomenon," *Harper's Magazine*, 178 (Dec., 1938), p. 10. Cf. the similar analysis by David Riesman, "Toward an Anthropological Science of Law and the Legal Profession," *The American Journal of Sociology*, LVII (Sept., 1951), 121-35.

2. No purpose would be served by a listing of all the things labor lawyers do. A study based on 213 mailed returns from a conservatively estimated universe of 500 lawyers who spend at least 25 per cent of their time in work for labor organizations concludes that their main activities are: "(a) regular appearances before administrative agencies; (b) court litigation; (c) approval and negotiation of collective bargaining agreements; (d) arbitration work; (e) drafting legislation and speeches; and (f) public relations work for the union; (g) . . . considerable free or extra work. . . ." Segal, *op. cit.*, p. 349. The picture of job content this Bar Association study presents contrasts sharply with my interview data on the Contact Men. Probable reasons: (1) only sixteen out of the fifty house attorneys I know of returned their questionnaires—the conclusions reflect the answers of lawyers with a diversification of clients who are more likely to be called on in the technician role; (2) the structured questions designed to get at job content would miss much of what is crucial in the lawyer's routine; (3) mailed questionnaires are not likely to yield accurate and detailed information on the unofficial "nonlegal" aspects of the union lawyer's work; (4) the returns are probably biased in favor of high professional identification. A more adequate approach to a job analysis is seen in Harold D. Lasswell and Myres S. McDougal, "Legal Education and Public Policy," in Lasswell, *op. cit.*, pp. 27-28. All of the activities listed here appear in my union lawyer data.

THE LOBBYIST

"Washington representation" has become a big, multi-million dollar industry. *Fortune* guesses there are at least 2,500 lawyers engaged in this sort of practice, plus ". . . thousands of lay practitioners—ex-officials with a smattering of law, resident manufacturers' representatives, salaried or retained lobbyists, ex-newspapermen and the like. . . ."[3] The union slice of this industry is small, indeed. No estimate of the full-time staff devoted to national representation of union interests puts the figure above 100. The Railroad Brotherhoods, who have the most highly developed lobbying operation on the union side, have only twelve full-time Washington staff men.

Unions vary greatly in their attention to the Washington scene. The Letter Carriers estimate that 75 per cent of the time of their staff of ten (all line officials) goes to national legislative activity—and much of the rest goes to grievances handled through government agencies. (19-4.) In the Carpenters' Union, in contrast, the time spent is negligible.

"Legislative activity" (lobbying) is typically a minor portion of the labor lobbyist's job. One lobbyist whose union is highly involved with government estimates that Congress takes less than one-third of his time. (704-1.) Over the years, agency contact and political intelligence tend to loom large in the concentration of job content—and here again the talents lie on the human relations side. As one Washington Representative said:

> It's not easy to take over a job like this. You build up a tremendous amount of personal relationships it's very difficult to transfer. My predecessor left me a phone book! . . . To know who in the Army can make a decision, where to go to get information on [the plans of a regulatory commission]—this doesn't require a Harvard Ph.D. (704-7.)

Like the lawyer, the lobbyist is generally valued for his "contacts," for his skill as intermediary, for his knowledge of the formula by which the bureaucratic machinery of modern society works.[4]

---

3. "Lawyers and Lobbyists," *Fortune*, XLV (Feb., 1952), 129.

4. All Washington Representatives interviewed stressed skill in personal contacts as a crucial part of the lobbyist's equipment. Compare these bits

Most union editors and "Public Relations Directors" can best be classified as "Internal Communications Specialists"; their public is the union membership. But an increasing number are broadening their functions in a way that justifies a Contact Man label.

Here, as with lawyers and lobbyists, technical craft skills may loom large in initial recruitment. Nine of the 11 public relations men in our Questionnaire Sample have backgrounds in journalism. All of them know the production end of the channels of mass communication. A typical answer to the question "What does it take to make out on this job, etc.": "To begin with you have to be a versatile newspaper, publicity and advertising man; know enough to get along in each." (515-3.) This versatility, of course, involves knowledge of style and deadline, printing and layout—a general skill in the technical side of writing and planting favorable content in the mass media, and avoiding the unfavorable. But it is much broader than that. Like the lawyer and the lobbyist, the successful labor public relations man is valued for his skill in dealing with people.

The labor publicist knows the individual quirks in the key papers covering his union; he has wide acquaintance among newsmen. He systematically "works" his personal contacts. "Why have a public relations man unless he knows somebody," says one labor publicist. "You got to have contacts. My contacts are with the Metropolitan Press. I have a good relationship with the reporters—a very informal pick-up-the-phone relationship with [he names reporters]. . . . There's complete mutual confidence." (504-7.)

---

from the *Fortune* study of business lobbyists—who apparently operate on the same principle, albeit on a grander scale: "A major facet of the Corcoran formula is, as he puts it, the finest intelligence service in Washington. He makes it his business to get around, picking up information from his friends and sharing his own information with them, and delivering the end product to his clients. . . . The sort of acquaintance displayed here—Clifford's friendship with the President [Truman], with Coy, Allen, Anderson, and Boyle, and Allen's ready access to the President and Coy—is the most precious commodity on the influence market. It and the general know-how that comes with it are what many of the businessmen and corporations involved with Big Government pay for." *Ibid.*, pp. 142, 149.

His contacts and knowledge go beyond the world of the media. Speech-writing, for example, is likely to be a frequent and time-consuming responsibility. This tests his ability to gauge reactions of a wide variety of audiences and requires intimate knowledge of the interests and prejudices of both audience and boss.[5] He can himself act as union spokesman if need be; at least he can make his boss more articulate and worldly-wise in the latter's new and increasingly public roles.

In sum: whether lawyer, lobbyist, or publicist, the Contact Man is called to union service because of the impact of union power on the interests of competing groups. The complicated entanglements of diverse private and public bureaucracies defending and promoting special interests generate a need for the knowledge and skills of human relations intermediaries. In the final analysis, it is the agencies of government that supervise the struggles of these bureaucracies, and it is government intervention in industrial relations that ultimately provides the Contact Man's entree to union councils. The more complicated the entanglements and struggles become, the wider the scope of government intervention, the more indispensable the resources of the Contact Man.[6]

---

5. Speech-writing sometimes comes close to a Facts and Figures operation—supplying the ammunition and little more. But since it typically involves an assessment of the political-social situation, an anticipation of people's responses, it is counted in Contact Man activity. As one top officer said, "Our research men have the information; the Publicity Department is needed to get it across." (13-2.) Sensitivity to audience is half the speech-writing task; knowing the boss' prejudices, strengths and weaknesses is the other half. A colleague of one publicist describes the speech-writing process in his union: "[The publicist] will go up and sit with [the top officer]. He's quick to grasp what is wanted—he's been here so long. [The officer] can talk in half sentences; [the publicist] will complete the thought for him without him saying it. There's a complete parallelism in the way they think and talk." (N509a-1.)

6. There is a widespread conviction among union people—supported by considerable evidence—that Contact Men (indeed, all staff experts) are needed only in conflict situations—to mediate, to "fix," to smooth the way to victory, to bail them out in defeat. As in the case of the Facts and Figures Man, little use is made of Contact Men in those unions whose bargaining relationships border on collusion. One officer who makes less use of lawyers than most says, "No lawyer is needed—there's been pleasant relations with employers and we have a better knowledge of the work in the industry than any lawyer has." (15-2.) Contrast this comment: "One of the important

The distinctive resources of the Contact Man consist primarily of (1) his knowledge of the political-social topography—the kind of "realistic" political intelligence that tells the union who can make what decisions at what time and how to reach him; (2) his "contacts"—contacts so well developed that they become nontransferable; and (3) his skills in "working" these contacts—social skills so typical of the "go-between" in the urban bureaucratic milieu that they lead to his categorization as a distinct personality type.[7] The occupational background of the Contact Man underscores his value as a fellow who knows his way around. The Contact Man is typically selling in the union bureaucracy knowledge and experience gained in other bureaucracies with which the union deals: the NLRB Regional Director becomes the union General Counsel; the reporter covering a labor beat on a commercial daily takes over the union's press relations job; the government staff technician, the liberal organization lobbyist, or the state politician moves into the Washington Representative spot. Eighteen of the thirty-four Contact Men in the Questionnaire Sample fit this picture; eight more have a background in union politics and/or lobbying in a state legislature (the other eight were private consultants, had jobs irrelevant to their present work, or their backgrounds are unknown).

That the knowledge and skills of the Contact Men put them in

---

things you need to organize in the South is to be a lawyer. . . . Every instance of violence brings a murder charge." (211-1.) An officer in the same union: "As employers accept unionism, they'll quit bringing lawyers in." (13-2.) An ex-expert summarizes the bargaining role of the lawyer: "[The officer and his lawyer] are both interested in the same thing—the enhancement and the exercise of power. They're joint adventurers in the business. If both go into negotiations and come out with a successful contract, they both share the credit and enjoy the pleasure. If the union loses, the lawyer is the apologist and defender; he covers the retreat—files Labor Board charges, gets a Congressional Committee to expose the wickedness of the employer, etc." (916-2.) As Lundberg says, "The very existence of a legal profession presupposes a society torn by conflicts. . . . "; *op. cit.*, p. 11. So, too, with the publicist. Without conflict he is needed neither to neutralize attacks on the union nor to rationalize the union's special interest in terms of the general.

7. Cf. C. W. Mills' "fixer" in "The Competitive Personality," *Partisan Review*, XIII (1946), 433; Fromm's "marketer"; and Riesman's "gladhanding" "other-directed" "inside dopester," *op. cit.*, pp. 199-207. All are types with a primary skill in smooth negotiation and a firm grasp of the limits of social action.

contrast to the Facts and Figures Man is emphasized by their comments about one another and top officer comments about both. Economists, statisticians, and Facts and Figures lawyers are viewed as a breed of men apart.

Top officer: The most difficult thing I find in research men is that ninety-nine out of a hundred can't work with anybody. There's a peculiarity among those people—you can't work together with them. I don't care whether they're geniuses. . . . I want a good high class man. . . . Some of these damn fools are prima donna types. (22-3.)

An ex-expert: [First describes close relation of lawyer and officer.] You have to like each other if you're going to sit at meals, stay up at nights with one another . . . sit together on all-day conferences. . . . That might explain why the economists and publicists [i.e., editors] . . . always remain employees. It's especially true of intellectuals, who don't have the confidence of the boss. They aren't liked. They're not rough and tough. They're not the same Joes. They don't like the same kind of women. The intellectual may be a cold individual who sublimates his emotion in intellectual pursuits. (916-2.)

The Facts and Figures Men frequently complain that the Contact Men are so busy "operating" that they let their technical skills waste away:

An economist: We can keep up on labor law maybe closer than an attorney. . . . In arbitration work its disgraceful . . . ridiculous. The majority of lawyers are so busy they get into the habit of not preparing themselves. (311-4.)

And the Contact Men, as might be expected, say the Facts and Figures boys "don't know the score." Contact Men who are lawyers often complain that their colleagues among the Facts and Figures Men are "too legalistic"!

A lawyer: [The lawyer] gets down to specifics with you earlier and faster than economists—aside from the importance of the legal phases. . . . The economist deals in the abstract or in the general. Take negotiations involving severance pay. The economist studies the overall picture. There are twenty companies in this industry who have severance pay. The lawyer will say, "Look, last year these fifty guys were fired here without a dime. What are you going to do about it?" . . . We're trained in the case system. That's what I mean by "the legal mind." . . . As a lawyer I've learned to deal with specifics realistically—deal down to earth. . . . Lawyers are like union leaders in this respect. (233-3, 4.)

As this respondent suggests, the knowledge and skills of the Contact

Man, distinct as they are from those of the Facts and Figures Man, typically border on those of the line official. It is true, as Henri De Man has said, that "there is no kind of regular political activity which does not need professional specialization."[8] And the Contact Men develop specialized skills, indeed. But the specialization is one common to all politician-executives, including union leaders. The identity of talents is underscored by two facts: (1) some of the Contact Men have backgrounds as elected union officials and their occupational and educational histories as a whole are quite varied (law, journalism, espionage, teaching, politics, religion, etc.)—which indicates that there is no one technical specialty that prepares one for a Contact Man role; and (2) at least one union (IAM-AFL) trains line men from the ranks as specialists to do the work Contact Man lawyers do in other unions, namely, preparation and presentation of cases before the NLRB.[9] Apparently, even on the technical craft side, the skills of the Contact Man merge with those of the union leader. This identity of talents in part explains why the Contact Man often conceives of himself as a "glorified business agent," a phenomenon to be examined below; it helps explain the position of high influence he has won (see Chapter XI).

Functions and Effect

I have analyzed the distinctive activities and talents of the Contact Man. What are his distinctive functions—objectively observable consequences of all this activity for the maintenance of the union as a social structure and its adaptation to the internal and external pressures outlined in Chapter I? What are the possible dysfunctional consequences of the political-ideological intelligence he feeds into the stream of union decision-making? What can be said about the net effect of his presence in the union?

---

8. *Op. cit.*, p. 200.

9. One lawyer explains how these lay experts in NLRB procedures win so many cases: "I've run into them both as clients and as opponents and I find that they frequently use this dodge, 'Now, I'm not a lawyer, so I can't etc.' or 'Oh, hell, these lawyers are always bringing in technicalities.' In that way they get away with murder. They act coy. The second thing is that the Board members are sympathetic to rank-and-file representation anyway and suspicious of the legalistic argument." (205-9. Cf. 915-1.)

This analysis involves a balancing off of two contradictory sets of functions symbolized in the phrases "playing it safe" and "making it look respectable," on the one hand; "beating the game," "cutting through the red tape," on the other. The Contact Man may move the union and its leaders in one direction at one moment, the other direction at another; he may even move the union in both directions at the same time. The task of assessing the likely direction of his influence is far more troublesome than it was with the Facts and Figures Man, who was seen to introduce a "rational-responsible" bias into union operations. First, consider the "beat the game" function.

1. *The Contact Man smooths the union leader's contacts with the nonunion world, helps him find his way around; this encourages a tendency to "political realism" already present in the leader's mentality—it strengthens his conviction that wherever there is a clash of interests some way can be found to mediate them, that whenever the union is attacked some way can be found to "put in the fix," bail the union out of trouble.* Previous discussion has dealt with some of this "smoothing" activity of the Contact Man. The lawyer—law degree aside—is valued for his skill in private negotiation, and operates largely outside the court or the formal hearing. The lobbyist gets his chance because of his ability to cut through the red tape; the publicist because of his ability to deal with a variety of publics, especially the press. All are valued primarily for their knowledge of the bureaucratic machinery of American society, their skills in "working" contacts. The talents of these men are not easy to define; their crucial activities are often hidden from view. Take skill and activity in "fixing"; what does "fixing" involve?

(a) THE DYNAMICS OF THE "FIX." Lasswell, pointing to skill in "fixing" as one basis for successful careers in the Italian fascist state, defines the fixer as "a negotiator who enhances his private income by exercising, or seeming to exercise, governmental and party influence."[10] This might be called "the fix proper," for the word is often used in a broader sense to encompass the simple securing of a hearing for the union representative, the private settlement between company and union lawyers of minor differences between their clients, and the like, and it often connotes no en-

---

10. "Analysis of Political Behavior," *op. cit.*, p. 168.

hancement of private income. Examples of "the fix proper" in my
union data usually concern interunion or governmental relations
confined to local situations:

A union officer describing a nonlawyer Contact Man: There's another
guy you might call a "technician" of a sort—we used him for one year—
gave him $1,000 for the year. He was a local politician with contacts.
You see, we need to find our way around that town. Members who get
tickets, arrests for disturbance of peace, picket line violence, we get
federal and local injunctions of all kinds. He knew his way around. He
was to protect us any way he could. He'd help on whether a case would
end up with a friendly judge or not. I don't know the judges down there.
He can simply tell us what to expect, where to turn, how to cut red
tape. I don't know whether you would call him a technician. . . . We
were leery of this arrangement, though—it bordered too much on bribery
—so we stopped it. (3-6.)

Same officer describing basis for recruitment of his lawyer: Now the
attorney we didn't hire on that basis [i.e., technical competence and
"labor philosophy"—his criteria for selection of his Facts and Figures
Men]. We needed him because he knew his way around the Teamsters.
(3-7.)

A local fee counsel: I call up the Teamsters for the XYZ Workers
whom I represent and say, "Look boys, don't cross the picket line, huh?"
(233-1.)

The broader use covers everything from the exercise of influence
based on "connections" to transact business, to the skillful but
routine exercise of judgment in the negotiation of a contract involving no "connections" at all. Examples of Contact Man operations on the fringes of "the fix":

A publicist describes the function of a public relations firm: Union
leaders hire guys whom they know—guys who can help them get along.
Like a fixer. Consultant or staff man, "Can the guy do something for
us?" X is important to [top union leader] because of his [political party]
connections. He was a big man in their publicity set-up before he went
into business for himself. He could get [the union leader] to Truman.
It's "Who do you know?" (504-7.)

A house counsel: Even some of the company lawyers in the bad
companies we deal with will often maintain friendly relations. Many's
the company lawyer who's called me up and wanted me to tell him how
to save face and back up from a position the company has taken. I'll
have lunch with them and talk it over. (203-6.)

A Contact Man describes another: During this whole thing . . . he
was assigned . . . as liaison between [the union] and "X" in the White

House—working behind the scenes. [The top officer] would tell him, "This is how far we'll go on this issue. Go tell 'X'. The government didn't want to get into this thing. . . . But public pressure was building up. . . ." "X" asked "How far will you go to keep us off your necks?" . . . [The Contact Man] comes in . . . as a trouble-shooter. . . . His job is to transmit messages back and forth between the White House and [the top officer]. (525-4.)

(b) THE CONVICTION THAT ANYTHING CAN BE "FIXED." The *Fortune* study of business lawyers and lobbyists concludes ". . . there is excellent evidence that the demand for venality in government, and for improper influence short of venality, exceeds the supply."[11] So, too, with Labor. The strength of the union officer's conviction that the Contact Man can "put in the fix"—or more generally "keep us [or get us] out of trouble"—often exceeds the latter's capabilities along that line. This conviction is not only strong, but widespread.

A *fee counsel in Washington practice:* Everybody thinks there's some way to beat the rules. The typical attitude is: "I want to do this; get it done—you must know somebody!" There's really no respect for the purpose of the law: . . . cut corners . . . "so it's not legal, so what?" You've got to have the sentiments of a prostitute to be a lawyer. . . . Most of it doesn't have much to do with the law. The lawyer is a guy who has connections. . . . If any union people come to me and say "We just negotiated X and think it fits Regulation No. 4, check on it," and I find it's no soap, I tell them and it stops them. The average lawyer will tell them what the chances are—"It's a small thing, the regulation isn't well enforced, there's a small risk, but it's possible to argue like this ——;" or "For Christ's sake, don't ask me about this, fellas." (G225-1,2.)

A *house counsel* (Contact Man): We're merely there to tell them [officers] *how* to do it. It's a great joke to say "You can't have a closed shop but we got the best lawyer in the business." (211-6.)

A *top officer:* We say to our counsel, "This is the way we want to operate. Tell us how to safeguard our interests legally while we do what we're going to do anyway." (18-6.)

This conviction that the union with the help of the Contact Man, can "beat the game" takes a slightly different form in the case of the publicist:

Union officer: We need a general public relations job done. We're a powerhouse. . . . We're selling a good package, but we need to adver-

11. *Op. cit.,* p. 128.

tise it. You can't permit your enemies to take away the credit and stymie the program. (3-4.)

Union officer [explaining why he hired a publicist]: It became so bad—the situation [on an issue important to the union] was becoming bad. So we had to do a job—not just a job, but a scientific job. I couldn't do it. (17-2.)

Other comments reveal a similar pattern: the officer looks to the publicist (1) to neutralize opposition to union programs and to furnish justifications of new powers; (2) for painless deodorization when he gets in a public relations jam—not just painless, but "scientific." The officer who shops around for a lawyer who will think of an angle to furnish possible legal sanction for his anticipated action is like the officer who says he needs a public relations man to do the job "scientifically." Both are going through a self-convincing, self-justifying ritual that functions to ease their own doubts and increase their sense of safety and well-being.[12]

(c) THE CONTACT MAN STRENGTHENS THIS "BEAT-THE-GAME, CUT-RED-TAPE" APPROACH." The belief that government red tape can be cut, trouble with rival unions, employers, the courts, the police, can be "fixed," and trouble with the press and other publics overcome —this is something the union officer as a participant in American society picks up from his experience with these agencies and groups. But the presence of the Contact Men acts to encourage a "beat-the-game" approach to union administration. This is because: (1) The Contact Man *tells* the officer he can do these things (". . . It isn't only what you *do* that counts," a union publicist advises, "but what people think you're doing"); (2) the Contact Man *is* often able to deliver on the "fix" and its variants; and (3) most Contact Men conceive of themselves not as professional specialists but as general "trouble-shooters," and they foster a leadership view of themselves as manipulators who "know the ropes."

I'm a *labor* lawyer, not a lawyer. . . . I try to be a glorified business agent. I keep away from legalisms. I talk their language in the shop. I know how to deal with them. The pure lawyer would be a menace—

12. It is noteworthy that even John L. Lewis, for many years his own best publicist, set up a News Bureau in 1947 to promote the UMW and its welfare programs and to neutralize attacks on John L. It is staffed by a professional newspaperman, the only nonminer on the headquarters staff outside of three lawyers and an editor.

that's what I meant when I said the lawyer shouldn't get mixed up too much in policy. I don't consider myself to be practicing law. . . . Negotiations—that's 50 per cent of my time. But "negotiations" doesn't describe the process. There are a lot of conferences at the top level that involve relations between Labor and Management. You run into a mess; you have a conference to ward off trouble. . . . I spend a lot of time conferring with the union representatives who call up or come in with their problems—any problems. I put in about 80 hours a week. . . . I spend ten per cent of my time on the phone—for example, on their organizational problems. This fellow who just called: "We got one main road to the plant . . . the cops say no." I handle that on the phone. . . . I pick arbitrators—they're unofficially cleared through this office. They don't think of me as a legal counsel. I've been living with this for [many] years. They call on me as they would a union representative who knows the ropes. They don't stop to think, "This is a legal problem, this isn't." (210-4,5.)

Even where the Contact Man's claims are modest, the officer has seen enough performance from him to get a sometimes exaggerated notion of his ability to put out fires or avoid the spark that lights them.

The professional identification of the Contact Man is likely to be low, and the amount and range of his influence great. These facts, which will be examined in Chapters X and XI, provide further support for the view that the Contact Man is likely to move the union toward a "beat-the-game" philosophy; they put him in sharp contrast to the Facts and Figures Man. An extreme statement from an ex-expert (who was bitter about Contact Men in general, but lawyers in particular) underscores this point:

It's all right for an economist to be in a policy-making position because by the nature of his profession he'll come out on the side of the gods, but the lawyer—why his very function is immoral and corrupting: The question he asks is, "What can we get away with?" For the economist the question is, "What are the facts?" (910-4.)

Alongside this picture of the functions of the Contact Man must be placed a somewhat contradictory picture:

2. *He interprets officer and union to important publics (including judges, government officials, employers, the press, etc.) and he interprets these publics to the officer; this acts to build an image of officer and union as "respectable" and "responsible" both in the eyes*

of the officer and in the eyes of his publics; the officer's new self-image tends to make him "play it safe" in order to cultivate the good-will of these (real or imagined) publics. Again, this set of consequences of Contact Man activity takes different forms among lawyers and among publicists.

(a) THE ALLEGED CONSERVATISM OF LAWYERS. Hostility to lawyers is widespread among union leaders. As suggested above, most of this antilawyer talk adds up to the complaint that lawyers slow the union down. Note, however, that (1) the lawyers complained about in these interviews are typically Facts and Figures types; (2) the officers who complain refer to the influence of lawyers on *other* officers, and they seldom refer to the house counsel employed on their own staff; and (3) the lawyers who complain about their colleagues ("the pure lawyer is a menace") usually refer to Facts and Figures types, especially fee or retainer counsel in private practice. It is, therefore, probable that the craft-minded lawyer (who is likely to be a Facts and Figures type) will introduce a "rational-responsible," even a "conservative take-less," bias into union operation, while only the lawyers I have classified as Contact Men will introduce a "beat-the-game" bias.

(b) THE CONTACT MAN'S EFFECT ON THE OFFICER'S SELF-CONCEPTION. A more impressive negation of the hypothesis that the main function of the Contact Man is to promote the "beat-the-game" approach are the data pointing to his possible encouragement of officer interest in wooing publics of varying shades of concreteness and specificity. Simmel has generalized the process most incisively:

> An open association [in contrast to a secret society], no matter how violently it fights against other associations within the same larger society, or against the general foundations of this society itself, must always maintain that the realization of its own ultimate purposes is to the advantage of the whole; *and the necessity of this outward assertion somewhat restricts the actual egoism of its actions.*[13]

How does this process work in the unions? Does attention to "the public" slow the union down?

Most of the job of rationalizing union actions in terms of the public interest falls to the Contact Man. He is often deeply concerned about the attacks his union is subject to; he is usually

---

13. K. H. Wolff, (ed.), *op. cit.*, p. 368. Italics mine.

enthusiastic about the possibilities of changing antilabor attitudes among the people that count in his own and/or the boss' eyes. He is likely to worry about the respectability of his union. A publicist, complaining about the bad English of convention resolutions, says "It makes the union look like a bunch of bums." (501-6.) Comments of other Contact Men reveal a similar solicitude for the union's reputation. The publicist is usually most optimistic about what can be accomplished. The growth of systematic, professional press coverage of labor news, the increase in the number of information-seekers who come *asking* for the union story (including magazine writers, authors, professors, radio forums)—these are the props for his optimism.

Sometimes the target is a bit vague: "We do not regard any person's opinion with contempt," says one public relations expert. "Even screwballs get courteous answers." (516.) "What strikes you," adds a colleague, "is the enormity of the job—there's almost unlimited public relations possibilities!" (515-3.) In huckster-like fashion, the public relations expert envisions a great sea of potential converts waiting to be guided into proper channels of action and attitude.

That union leaders often catch this enthusiasm is shown by (1) their increasing use of professional public relations men; (2) their use of these men for purposes beyond the production of a house organ; and (3) the "publicity hound" reputation of some top officers. Since 1941—besides adding many editors and editorial assistants who spend some time in press relations—the unions in our Questionnaire Sample increased employment of top staff publicists (Contact Man type) from four to eleven; the responsibilities of these men typically enlarged in the direction of press relations and other contact work. (See discussion of skills and job content, above.) By arranging public appearances and opportunities for friendly contact with big shots, the Contact Man (publicist, lawyer, lobbyist) further encourages the publicity hound tendencies of these new men of power.[14]

The public relations stance of the Contact Man and his boss is

---

14. For analysis of the union leader as an *arriviste* whose concern with "public opinion" and whose drive for respectability is likely to be well developed, see Chapter XIII.

basically a defensive one. Many labor leaders, having seen whole communities moved to a frenzy against them in the early thirties, were indelibly impressed by the power of the printed word and have since moved into public relations, calling on trained specialists to "make the pitch." The style of the Contact Man in making this pitch tends to be promotional and friendly, not agitational and aggressive (contrast the Internal Communications Specialist, Chapter VI). Inevitably this defensive concern with "the public" must, in Simmel's phrase, "somewhat restrict the actual egoism" of union action.

I'm hinting at a conservative bias introduced by the presence of lawyers—maybe of all technicians [says a Facts and Figures Man whose lawyer colleague is a Contact Man type]. They're concerned with getting things settled rather than strike, complying with laws and regulations, not stirring up the pot. They'll tell you don't blast management in the newspaper if there are violations of the law or the contract. . . . Inherently in the human relations angle there's a conservative bias and the lawyer is the man who mediates the situation. (305-1.)

The desire to avoid "stirring up the pot," to "mediate the situation" without alienating anyone, has been seen as constituting the substance of the main drift of American society. Riesman sloganizes the trend in such phrases as "from invisible hand to glad hand," "from craft skill to manipulative skill," "from free trade to fair trade," etc. He sees Contact Men on the business side as "self-convinced intellectuals" who frighten businessmen ". . . about what a host of amorphous publics, as likely to disappear on inspection as the Cheshire cat, might do to them or for them."[15] It is easy to exaggerate the "amorphous" nature of the publics the Contact Man invokes to scare the union leader. Typically, they are a great deal more concrete than the Cheshire cat: judges, legislators, government bureaucrats, arbitrators and college professors, newspaper editors and policemen. The relation of their good-will to the pursuit

15. *The Lonely Crowd, op. cit.*, pp. 252, 203, 130 ff. Compare Lundberg's and Riesman's categorization of public relations men and lawyers as men who profit from keeping their business and government clients "in a condition of permanent convalescence, always dependent upon the expensive advice of specialists in obscure, often nameless disorders, never thoroughly ill, never wholly cured." Lundberg, *op. cit.*, pp. 2, 7. Cf. Riesman, "Toward an Anthropological Science of Law . . . ," *op. cit.*, p. 131.

of (also tangible) union interests is often quite clear; every union leader can cite cases where this good-will paid off in a successful wage bargain, a strike won, an administrative regulation eased. Moreover, if the new preoccupation with these publics takes the form of merely dressing up union policy in acceptable verbiage, with no consideration to alterations in the policy itself, then the public relations operation cannot be said to slow the union down.

It is true that the union leader who captures a conception of himself as a statesman moving on a world stage (see Chapter X) may begin to play to a wider audience. The "public opinion" he worries about may consist of the lightly held opinions of masses of people who expose themselves to the mass media. As yet, however, concern with the Cheshire cat-like "public" has not developed so strongly in officer mentality that it can rank with concrete political and economic pressures as a major influence in the decision-making process. As will be seen in Chapter IX, there are few important union decisions where an imaginary "public" invoked by a Contact Man can be said to have been crucial, however well developed the "publicity hound" tendency of the top officer may be.

I have attempted to assess the net effect of the Contact Man's presence in the union. On the one hand, he smooths the union leader's contacts with the nonunion world, helps him find his way around; this promotes a "beat-the-game" mentality," and strengthens the officer's conviction that wherever there is a clash of interests some way can be found to mediate them.

Against this, another picture appears: the Contact Man interprets officer and union to important publics, and he interprets these publics to the officer; this acts to build an image of officer and union as "respectable" and "responsible" both in the eyes of the officer and in the eyes of his publics; the officer's new self-image tends to make him "play it safe" in order to cultivate the good-will of these (real or imagined) publics.

What of the dysfunctional consequences of the Contact Man's activity? In so far as the lawyer, for instance, encourages the view that "the union is surrounded by laws" and the officer should "play it safe" and in so far as this advice is "unrealistic" (i.e., unnecessary for the most efficient accomplishment of union goals); in so far as all sorts of Contact Men promote a preoccupation with the wooing of nonexistent publics and this acts to "slow the union down"— then the presence of this functional type lessens the officer's ability to cope with the pressures upon him, weakens internal control, and threatens the maintenance of union stability.

It has been suggested, however, that the extent to which these dysfunctional consequences are operative is quite limited. The lawyer as Contact Man learns not to take the law too seriously. Moreover, the publics the Contact Man invokes for union consideration are likely to be very real and very relevant. The tendency to cultivate the good-will of imaginary or amorphous publics, while apparent at times in the orientation of both expert and officer, is as yet embryonic.

It is, therefore, probable that the direction of the Contact Man's influence is, on balance, likely to be towards a "beat-the-game," "cut-red-tape" bias. The smoothing and fixing side of his operations remain paramount in all areas of union decision.[16]

---

16. I have not dealt separately with the functions of the Contact Man in the area of Internal Union Control; they parallel those I have discussed in relation to other areas of union decision (which are usually more prominent in the work of this functional type). Internal union affairs—membership discipline, factionalism, etc.—often have legal and public relations implications. Here again, the lawyer and publicist may, as in other areas, act to slow the union down. But—while data on this is limited to a few cases— the more typical role of Contact Men in internal affairs is probably that of the "glorified business agent" spoken of above. One public relations and lobbying specialist says "it's my job . . . to feel the pulse of the membership. I'll go up to [the key local involved] and talk to the men." (701-2.) One Facts and Figures Man describes a lawyer: "He does the . . . hatchet work in intra- and inter-union politics. . . . Plants stories about local leaders . . . we want to get rid of . . . becomes the administrator of the . . . local." (304-3, 4.) Such political intelligence and hatchet work—not uncommon among Contact Men—is likely to facilitate rather than impede the maintenance of internal unity and discipline.

CHAPTER VI

THE INTERNAL COMMUNICATIONS SPECIALIST

Skills and Job Content

A THIRD GROUP of staff experts are distinguished by their background in radical party politics and/or union politics and by a primary concern with and skill in manipulating the thoughts and feelings and conduct of union members. They are specialists who furnish political-ideological intelligence to buttress the union leader in his task of communication and control within the union. Their work, in contrast to that of the Facts and Figures Man, is characterized by a relatively high rate of interaction with active rank and file and lower leaders, and a focus on membership opinion and aspiration. Their skills in the arts of propaganda and group work, their highly ramified knowledge of the political complexion of the labor movement, place them closest to the Contact Man. The range of their operations, however, is restricted largely to two interrelated areas of union decision: internal control and organization, and dealing with rival unions. In contrast to the Contact Man, their participation in relations with employers and with government is quite limited. The label "Internal Communications Specialist" applies to almost all the education and recreation directors, political action specialists, and antidiscrimination representatives; to all the editors but six, and to a few of the auditors.

The internal pressures which stem from the expectations, aspirations and problems of officials and activists down the line and the mass of members below, occupy a large share of the energy and attention of the top union officer. Two basic facts about the industrial scene intensify these pressures and give the Internal Communications Specialist his chance to help the officer cope with them: (1) union membership doubled between 1935 and 1938, and quadrupled by 1945; (2) competition for worker loyalty and participation has enormously increased in recent years.

With the growth of the union, the problem of controlling the enfranchised mass becomes more and more complex. Size, of course, lengthens the lines of communication in any organization.

A top officer, explaining why the union hired an editor (in the forties): Well, we had no way of communicating with the rank and file. The bulletins from headquarters were not getting the message across. California didn't know what Texas was doing. We really didn't have a union; we had a scattering of locals. So we [established the paper]. (5-1.)

Here the growth of the union threatened its national integration. More important, however, are the special administrative problems posed by an influx of new members without trade union identification or experience and the shortage of competent leadership at lower levels. Many interview comments emphasize the problems of loyalty and leadership in a period when union gains were being consolidated:

A top officer, explaining why he invested money in an education department: We realized the younger people coming into our industry have to be educated and they're new to this business. They have to negotiate, have to compare their conditions with others, have to know what the union is about. We found by training them we get much better results. Servicing is better. . . . We want to train them in the responsibilities of business agents and secretaries, you might say. (17-1.)

A former organizer, now Internal Communications Specialist, explaining why his union set up an education program: That had always been part of the duties of organizers. [Here he lists the typical problems, including "steward training, living up to the constitution, parliamentary law," etc.]. . . . The organizer had to get 'em on the track. Teach 'em the job from the ground up. . . . The problem was not to educate but to *get* the membership. . . . We've grown from [a few thousand] to [hundreds of thousands]. . . . When we became established and overcame the serious threats to survival, then we were faced with the problem of making trade unionists out of them. . . . They're not labor conscious. . . . We had to reach them some way. (612-1.)

A top officer, speaking of possible expansion of the education program: It's the rank and file that needs it. In the old days, fifteen years ago, we didn't have to educate them to attend meetings. They didn't have any money to go to the movies or to buy television sets, but nowadays it's different. . . . They aren't union-minded. You have to make them union-minded. (5-4.)

"Making them union-minded" becomes more important as the competition of other organizations and the mass media intensifies and as employer concern with "morale" grows. If collective effort is to be sustained, a sense of participation must be fostered, and loyalty cultivated. The union officer sees the editor, the education director and allied functionaries as his chief weapons in this struggle. Here, as in the case of the Facts and Figures Men, he feels an urge to "match" the company and his other competitors, both in internal propaganda and in leadership training. The result: from an estimated sixty in 1840 the number of labor papers had climbed to at least eight hundred by 1949.[1] The expenditure on these union house organs is considerable: as a percentage of total expense the figure ranged from 2.2 per cent to 17 per cent for nine large national unions studied.[2] All of the unions in our Questionnaire Sample have at least one regular publication.[3] The figures for educational activity are less impressive, but tend in the same direction. Before 1935 only three unions—ACWA, the Hosiery Workers, and ILGWU—had hired full-time staff specialists to direct national pro-

1. Earlier estimate from Nora Piore, in Hardman and Neufeld, (eds.), *op. cit.*, p. 196; 1949 estimate based on Labor Department mailing list. Cf. Herbert Little, "800 Labor Journals on Government List," *Editor and Publisher* (Oct. 15, 1949). Other estimates go as high as nine hundred (650 weekly, 250 monthly). Cf. Hardman and Neufeld, *op. cit.*, p. 180. Compare the management effort: by 1953, there were from five thousand to six thousand five hundred "industrial internals" or company house organs in the United States and Canada (most of them published only ten years or less) with circulation figures estimated as high as seventy million copies monthly. Annual management expenditure on these "vital tools of communication" has been estimated by the International Council of Industrial Editors as more than $112,000,000. Cf. "The Industrial Publication Comes of Age," *Management Review*, 41 (Nov., 1952), 724; Garth Bentley, *Editing the Company Publication* (New York: Harper and Bros., 1953), pp. vii-viii.

2. Albert S. Epstein, "Union Records as Statistical Sources," Paper delivered at 108th annual meeting of the American Statistical Association, Dec. 29, 1948.

3. But four of these have their publication written or edited in part by an outside agency.

grams of education and/or recreation (though labor's outside friends had contributed much devoted effort to nurturing a workers' education movement before that time). By 1950, 48 (of a total of 209) national unions were listing education directors,[4] and both major federations now have Education Departments. Eleven of the unions in our Questionnaire Sample have full-time personnel whose principal assignment is education and/or recreation.[5]

The democratic ideology and formal structure of the trade union reinforces the leader's concern with winning the minds of his followers (and in a sense complicates the control problem): most leaders feel compelled to use persuasion and manipulation where possible, and coercion only where necessary. Here again, the Internal Communications Man—as specialist in persuasion and manipulation —gets his chance. He helps tend the elaborate democratic machinery that gives the interested member a sense of participation and keeps the union leader from hating himself when the imperatives of action and efficiency require departure from the democratic norm. He buttresses the union ideology and at the same time supplies the ready rationalizations that accompany deviations from it in practice.

The skills needed to man the union's machinery of communication and control are, like those of the Contact Man, difficult to define. Typical phrases in my interview data are: "a sense of organization," "know the workers and talk their language," "political sophistication," "understanding of the psychology of the top leaders and the politics of [the particular union]." The most frequent prerequisite to success mentioned by the thirty-six Internal Communications Specialists in the Main Sample (aside from standards of

---

4. In 27 cases, however, the same individual is both education and research director, and in several cases the activities of the person who has the title peg him as a Facts and Figures Man.

5. Compare the management effort. J. M. Tricket reports that specialized functionaries on and off the company staff to carry on formal training programs is a relatively new but growing phenomenon. He found that 30 per cent of 1,954 company respondents reported a plan of "management development." Cf. A Survey of Management Development (New York: American Management Association, 1954). See also D. F. Reeve and H. S. Belman, "A Survey of Duties and Responsibilities of Training Personnel in Business and Industry," The Journal of Industrial Training, 7 (Sept.-Oct., 1953), pp. 4-35. In addition to supervisory and executive training programs, of course, many companies have sizeable programs of education and recreation aimed at the rank and file.

job proficiency, such as writing ability) was knowledge and understanding of labor personalities, politics and policies. The editors
among our Internal Communications Specialists spend between 50
and 95 per cent of their working time, according to their estimates,
on gathering news, writing, editing and making up the union house
organ. All Internal Communications Specialists (including educational directors, editors and others) are skilled in writing propaganda, in gauging group reactions; in all cases they are careful
students of labor politics. The knowledge and talents of the Internal
Communications Specialist are typically won through long experience in the rough and tumble of radical party politics or trade
union organization. One indication of this is in the fact that three-
fifths of the forty-seven Internal Communications Specialists in our
Q Sample had "ideological" or "labor political" jobs just prior to
their first full-time, paid union job. Many others had such experience at some time earlier in thir background; some can be assumed
to have been evasive on this point.

In most cases, the relations of the Internal Communications
Specialist with the membership give his work an "operational," i.e.,
political, flavor. A fuller account of job content accompanies analysis of the functions of the Internal Communications Specialist below.

Functions

The Internal Communications Specialist acts primarily as a
channel for downward communication, transmitting union programs
and policies from leader to rank and file; he occasionally furnishes
political intelligence to the officer, based on field contacts with
local functionaries and members. His activity functions to (1) build
top officer prestige, enhance his control over members in internal
union affairs (and increasingly in American politics), and in general strengthen the leader's political machine; (2) maintain union
morale in crisis situations; and (3) allay minority group pressures
when they threaten stability. These functions are best seen through
an examination of (1) officer views of the work of the Internal
Communications Men; (2) the target and the content of their pro-

grams; and (3) the political aspects of these programs (e.g., their involvement in factionalism).

1. *The officer looks at education, recreation and publication.* All union leaders interviewed who commented on their education and publication programs spoke of them in terms of membership-control objectives. The union newspaper or magazine "makes 'em union-minded," "keeps 'em informed of policy." It lets the rank and file know what good work the officers are doing. The education department puts out pamphlets and trains local leaders, "builds the union." "We want to teach them trade union objectives and our rights under the laws." (22-2.) What problems indicated the need to set up an education department? "We were developing a great big union and local leaders didn't understand their jobs. We got to develop leadership." (22-2.) "What expert services would we expand first? Well, our biggest job is organizing [so] I'd want to expand Publicity first." (13-2.) "Sure it's costly. How do I know the paper does any good? Well, our editor shows me letters he gets from the membership—and, besides the officers down the line tell me they like it."

The loyalty-building, policy-selling function of the Internal Communications Specialist—as seen from above—is accented in a story labor intellectuals amuse themselves with when feeling the weight of their larger purposes pressing against the content and consequences of their work. A former education director who was interviewed claimed that this conversation between him and his boss took place when he was setting up classes for a workers education program:

Officer: And what will you teach?
Expert: We'll begin with some Labor History——
Officer: Good! The workers should know how we suffered to build the organization for them.
Expert: Then we'll go into collective bargaining and the grievance procedure——
Officer: Fine. They should learn to talk back to the employers.
Expert: And we'll put in something on government, citizenship and politics.
Officer: That's good, too—the workers should learn how to vote, the [X Party] and the [right faction], too. And what else?

Expert: Well, a little parliamentary procedure.
Officer: Look, my boy. You're a nice bright fella and I like you—but the
workers are making too many motions already! (905-7.)

2. *The officer accent on education and publication as internal
control mechanisms is reflected in program content.* Who is reached
with what in Labor's programs of education, in union house organs?

(a) THE TARGET. Even the most vigorous of the union education
departments, according to their own estimates, reach but a small,
active core of the total membership in regular group activities—2
to 10 per cent at most.[6] The education directors I interviewed were
extremely modest in their claims and tended to debunk any colleague pretense to a mass audience. Similarly, the labor editors
interviewed generally see their target as (1) the union hierarchy
down to the steward and/or (2) the active rank and file. The only
reliable study of union newspaper readership I know of makes
this target objective seem the only reasonable one. A "through-the-
book," item-by-item interview with a sample of the members of a
large union (whose newspaper is mailed to every member's home),
indicated that only 23 per cent had read anything at all in the issue
they were shown, and average readership for any one item was
10 per cent. Articles on wage policy were the most read type of item.
It is interesting that while only one out of four members to whom
the paper was sent read something in it, the average reader read
some or all of fifteen items—well over half of a possible twenty-
three.[7] As in the case of education programs, high saturation of a
small target is evidently both the aim and the performance.

(b) GOALS AND CONTENT OF WORKERS' EDUCATION PROGRAMS. The

6. See "Trade Union Education Survey" (Made for the Fund for Adult
Education under the direction of Mark Starr, June-August, 1951) in *Labor
and Nation,* VII, 4 (Fall, 1951), 57. Responses from 44 labor organizations
were analyzed.

7. This was a confidential survey conducted by the Columbia Bureau of
Applied Social Research for a private social action and research agency. The
sample of 334—taken from one large active local—was probably biased in
favor of the more active and militant portions of the total membership of
this union, so these figures may be high for the union as a whole. None of
the editors in my sample used readership surveys; one implied that a study
of his paper might show such low readership that it would end his job. This
respondent specifically mentioned the Columbia study, and said, "That was
used against me. Hell, this paper is expensive. . . . They said 'Who the hell
reads a labor paper anyway!'" (521-7.)

workers' education movement has often been seen as a dedicated attempt to strengthen union democracy, increase membership participation, broaden workers' social and political consciousness. Its leaders are men and women whose devotion to democratic ideals is apparent. Their programs, however, at least as carried out within the trade union setting, reveal a focus and a tone that point to the central function of internal control. These programs try mainly to (1) train leaders—officers, shop stewards, business agents and organizers, union counselors and others—to carry on union business; (2) train leaders for political and community action on Labor's behalf; (3) develop social, recreational and cultural activities to build activist loyalty; and (4) interpret unionism to new members. Successful union programs in this area have heavily stressed leadership training. They generally reach established functionaries already committed to union principles, policies, and even careers.[8]

The content of workers' education programs is the best clue to their functions. There is much discussion among workers' education practitioners as to the proper balance of "practical," "vocational" or "tool" subject matter (e.g., grievance procedure, collective bargaining, union administration, how to conduct a meeting, how to run a strike, how to get your rights under the workmen's compensation laws, how to persuade a nonmember to join, etc.) and subject matter conducive to a "broad view" of union functions, subjects that foster "social vision" (e.g., full employment, labor and politics, "human relations," labor's stake in world affairs, etc.). The union staff education expert as he faces his limited time and resources typically comes out on the side of the "tool" approach. Whatever the views of labor's outside friends in the workers' education movement, whatever the misgivings of the staff experts themselves, there has been an unmistakable decline in the missionary content of trade union education programs.

Workers' education specialists in unions disagree sharply on

---

8. Compare Michels' comment about similar programs in Europe: "It is undeniable that all these educational institutions for the officials of the party and of the labour organizations tend, above all, towards the artificial creation of an *elite* of the working-class, of a caste of cadets composed of persons who aspire to the command of the proletarian rank-and-file. Without wishing it, there is thus effected a continuous enlargement of the gulf which divides the leaders from the masses." *Op. cit.*, p. 31.

many aspects of their work and its proper goals; but if there is any
one thing they are unanimously convinced of, it is that the primary
effect of their activity *must* be to "build membership loyalty" and
"improve union administration." A conversation among four education directors representing a wide range of role orientations and
one other union functionary illustrates the point:

AA: Workers' education does not exist to make people think; it exists
    to make them loyal union members. It's confused thinking like
    yours that makes our union leadership believe the workers' edu-
    cation movement makes a lot of what they call "long hairs" who'll
    take management jobs.

BB: There were four cases of men at our summer schools who became
    foremen. We get a kickback from the officers on that.

AA: The function of workers' education is to so indoctrinate people that
    when management offers come, he (*sic*) refuses the job. We've
    all had opportunities to go over to supervision. . . . Our classes
    are free as any union. But let's not kid ourselves. It's a restricted
    freedom. We encourage the greatest degree of freedom within
    the limits of union policy. We believe in a limit on academic
    freedom where a worker's education program is concerned. . . .

CC: There are two ways of control: pick the subject or pick the per-
    sonnel. In [Union D's] set-up they pick the subjects; in [Union
    X] they pick the personnel!

DD: The idea [that education directors] are free agents is utter non-
    sense. . . . I may [get my personal values into my work] un-
    consciously, but my conscious effort is to conform to the require-
    ments of the hierarchy. We're all doomed if we don't avoid
    that. . . .

EE: An education program is no good unless it meets the needs of the
    union. . . .

AA: You sell workers' education only by showing the guys that educa-
    tion helps them get what they want. [Gives an example of special-
    ized leadership training activity.]

DD: Here's another example. [Describes a jurisdictional dispute his
    union is involved in.] When they see I can help them on *their*
    problem—then after that I can talk about anything I want—UN,
    any damn thing you name. But first, I have to show the officers
    concrete evidence that education helps them reach *their* immedi-
    ate goals. . . . It all boils down to this: the guy at the top must
    feel that everything you do enhances his prestige. If he feels
    what you're doing threatens him, you're licked. (D14-4,7.)

Not all union education directors are as blunt or unpretentious
as those quoted. A few have different notions of the degree to

which the education director must stress "indoctrination," the "requirements of the hierarchy," "loyalty" and the like. But even those whose larger purposes dominate their thinking concede much of the case. All keep the basic job of "training" in the forefront.

In short, the "vocational" character of the union education programs, the conviction of all staff practitioners (whatever their personal values and ultimate goals) that their activity must first and foremost build membership loyalty, leadership prestige and hence more efficient union administration—these facts point to a central function of internal communication and control.[9]

(c) GOALS AND CONTENT OF UNION PUBLICATIONS. Regular union publications parallel union education programs in every respect: the target reached is the small leadership-activist core, the main content leans towards the straight trade union side, and the central function is downward communication of union policies, programs and views, with the consequent enhancement of top leadership prestige and power.

The union editor—like the education director, and whatever his private purposes—is convinced that his paper must function to build membership loyalty and facilitate efficient administration. Comments from three editors who, while they differ sharply in their role conceptions and political orientation, face the same job pressures, emphasize this point:

1. The paper is the propaganda medium of the union and three-quarters of it is editorial. (G526-7.)

2. You trim your sails to suit the wind. You know the industry, you know what you're trying to sell the members—you repeat it over and over again. . . . We've even got the demands sloganized. We operate on the principle that management is a sunnuvabitch and the union is all right. It keeps life simple. (N528-1.)

---

9. I have left out all consideration of the very sizeable union educational effort that goes into vocational training in its strict sense—apprenticeship training programs, schools and courses designed to improve trade skills. Several of the building trades unions carry on extensive programs of this sort, sometimes jointly with management. The ITU-AFL Bureau of Education reports that "at the close of the fiscal year ending May 20, 1951, there were 5,131 students enrolled in the regular courses of the ITU Lessons in Printing. . . ." "Report of the Bureau of Education," *The Typographical Journal Supplement,* (July, 1951), p. 21. These programs are not usually thought of as part of the workers' education movement, and they are generally administered by line personnel.

3. I don't have any illusions that the editor is supposed to be a free agent. I don't have the idea that he's a free and fearless crusader fighting for the truth and all that hogwash. This is a house organ, designed to promote the interests of the union as an organization. There may be some who think that it's the editor's job to take the part of the workers against the union administration. I say it's none of the editor's damn business. Just like any newspaper, the publisher owns and controls and sets down policy and the editor follows policy. The trick is to find out what the policy is and go ahead and follow it. (501-3,4.)

The content of the national union house organ, like the content of the education program, offers a further clue to its function. A study of 100 labor papers appearing in August, 1948, showed this topical space consumption: economic issues (including collective bargaining negotiations and settlements), 23 per cent; internal union affairs and inter-union matters (including educational and inspirational items), 22 per cent; political issues, 25 per cent; "frivolous" matters or subjects in the lighter vein, covering cartoons, humor, household tips, etc., 30 per cent.[10] This puts straight trade union subjects near the halfway mark. The figure for "practical," "vocational" content goes higher if one confines the analysis to national union house organs and refines the categories a bit. Four issues (one each for 1946, 1947, 1949, 1950) of each of twelve different union papers were measured in terms of inches of printed matter (exclusive of display heads, etc.) and averaged. In all, news of the union and the industry is by far the largest category. At least half to two-thirds the content of these publications points toward the internal communication and control function.[11]

(d) POLITICAL AND LEGISLATIVE AFFAIRS CONTENT AS AN ASPECT OF THE PROBLEM OF COMMUNICATION AND CONTROL. The fact that both studies of labor press content showed a sizeable portion devoted to politics and public affairs (25 per cent in the 100-paper study and

---

10. Content analysis by Martin Dodge of Dodge and Mugridge, labor and public relations counsels, in *DM Digest—Gist of the Labor, Leftwing and Group Press*, (Oct. 11, 1948), reported in Hardman and Neufeld, (eds.), *op. cit.*, p. 213.

11. Based on a study by Nora Piore, "Reading Matter for 15 Million Unionists," *Ibid.*, p. 199. The unions represented were: Teamsters, IBEW-AFL, ILGWU-AFL, ITU-AFL, UAW-CIO, NMU-CIO, Woodworkers-CIO, ACWA-CIO, USA-CIO. The three Independents were listed as the Carpenters, Mineworkers and Machinists.

from 12 to 17 per cent for the 12 national house organs) calls attention to the increasing involvement of unions in national politics. The
problem of maintaining membership, unity and discipline—always
prominent in internal union affairs, collective bargaining, and rival
union relations—is becoming a problem in community and political
action as well. Hence an impressive amount of newspaper space and
education program time goes to general political agitation. In an
election post-mortem reminiscent of the December, 1950, and
December, 1952, issues of many labor journals, an article reporting
a conference of 150 labor press representatives concludes:

> Political tacticians of the labor movement agreed that where the rank
> and file did not follow the leadership, it was because the leadership
> did not spell out the [national legislative] issues; that it is not just
> enough to tell the rank and file; that you have to explain. And that's
> where the labor press comes in. Evidently, the labor press did not ex-
> plain enough.[12]

The education specialists also easily adapt their tools and techniques to operation in the political arena. The training of shop
stewards to handle grievances becomes the training of "political
stewards" to collect voluntary contributions, register voters, and
"talk up" union-backed candidates. One reason for this adaptability
of the Internal Communications Specialist is the "contact," "trouble-
shooting" aspects of his work and his experience and background
in politics, union or otherwise.

---

12. "Labor Editors Pan Themselves," *The Butcher Workman*, XXXVII,
2 (Feb., 1951), 27. Editorial agitation on national legislative issues—so great
a part of this "explaining"—typically accepts the hostile environment motif:
Reactionary Big Business and its antilabor politicians are trying to destroy the
union and all our hard-won gains. This defensive stance and agitational
tone sometimes presents a sharp contrast to the rest of the journal's content.
For example, a recent issue of one union house organ headlined its lead
story, p. 1: "Fastest Growing Union: IAM. Membership Tops 708,000; Up
25% Last Year Hayes Reports." But on p. 8 of the same issue, where the
editorial dealt with the legislative situation (the Taft-Hartley Law), it was
a different story: "Organization has been slowed down. Millions of dollars
are being spent in law suits. Our members have been locked out and forced
to strike. Our enemies are able to checkmate almost every move we make
by using this legislation which was passed by our enemies for this very
purpose." *The Machinist*, VI, 44 (Jan. 17, 1952). The necessity of simul-
taneously proclaiming that the union has accomplished wonders and that
the union is stymied by its enemies at every turn, is a source of role conflict among some labor editors. See below, Chapter VII, pp. 129 ff.

3. *Contact work, morale-building and political intelligence.* The Internal Communications Specialist typically spends much time in contact with lower leaders and rank-and-file activists. Estimates of time in the field as a percentage of total working time range from a low of 10 per cent up to 50 per cent. Much of this consists of trouble-shooting and morale-building in emergency situations: strikes, drastic changes in local leadership, local deviations from national policy, union shop or bargaining elections, organizing campaigns, rival union fights, etc.

This sort of organizational trouble-shooting sometimes puts the Internal Communications Specialist in a position to gather important information about middle and lower leadership performance, membership sentiment, and the local political situation. Accordingly—though this is less prominent in his work than the transmission of policy downward—he becomes a source of political intelligence for the top leadership. The education director or the editor recently back from a field trip may sit in on Executive Board or other policy conferences to report on rank-and-file morale with respect to a projected wage move. Occasionally, even auditors—who in at least one union spend as much as 90 per cent of their time in the field—become a vital source of political intelligence. One top officer explained the advantage an auditor may have over a line functionary in the role of political sleuth:

> I had no time to do that work myself and politically speaking it's easier for an auditor to go into a local and nose around than it would be for me. If I go in, they always want to know what the hell's the matter. But it's routine for an auditor to go in. (5-6.)

In another union: "We have a huge staff of people who go out of the international office to check on the books of locals and every one of them does field work for 'Y' [top officer]." (506-4.) In a third: "Once an auditor refuses to sign, it can finish a local man [i.e., incumbent officer]." (110-9.)[13]

---

13. That the skills required here parallel those of the education director, editor, and other Internal Communications Specialists can be inferred from this description by a chief auditor of his traveling staff: "At the beginning they're looked at with suspicion—the local people figure they're out there to find out something bad against them. They've got to overcome that feeling. . . . We have one guy who's famous for that—he can find out more about what's going on in a local in a few days that I could in a year. . . . The

4. *The Internal Communications Specialist and the political machine.* With his relatively high rate of interaction with active union people, and his function of morale maintenance and troubleshooting in crisis situations, it is not surprising that the Internal Communications Specialist sometimes becomes involved in union factionalism (typically as part of the incumbent machine). Neither is it surprising that he becomes highly sensitive to the political implications of his routine job activity. This involvement in intra-union politics and the top officers' political machine takes somewhat different forms in the case of editors, education directors, and a series of miscellaneous functionaries, though the consequences are the same, i.e., the officers' positions are strengthened.

(a) EDITORS. All labor editors face the problem of how to report the political life of the union. "The paper is a showcase," said one editor, "and every guy wants to display his wares." (G509-4). Who gets how much space and with what slant? The answer depends largely on the factional state of the union.

In stable, tightly controlled unions with little organized opposition to the administration, political content may be minimized, or it consists of self-congratulatory propaganda for the incumbent administration. At the same time, the paper may very accurately mirror the relative importance of various economic interest groups within the membership.

In moderately factionalized unions with a vigorous internal political life where the administration has clear control of the national office, but maintains it through assimilation of the discontented, the paper may give news made by opposition forces considerable space, even objective treatment, though the function of shoring up the incumbent political machine remains apparent. An editor in this type of union describes his policy:

> Nobody gets overplayed because we don't have space. . . . Each faction is played straight on its news value. There've been no kickbacks yet. They'd be gunning for elimination of the paper if we ignored the people unfriendly to [the President]. So we play it straight—all interests get a play, so everybody likes it. (521-7.)

---

field auditor has to be a careful man. He has to go back there year after year. He's got to understand the politics of the thing. . . . The psychology of *trade union* auditing is different." (850-5, 6, 9.) The union auditor apparently audits more than the books.

In unions in which all-out war for full control is going on, with extermination of the opposition the announced objective of both sides, the editor plays a fully political role on the side of the officer who hired him. There is no case I have been able to discover where an editor was able to remain neutral through the entire course of such a fight; there are several cases where political activity on the wrong (i.e., losing) side or failure to follow administration policy was cause for dismissal. There are a few apparent exceptions to the rule against editor neutrality in an all-out war—exceptions, however, which offer further evidence of the inevitable machine-supporting function of the labor editor. In recent years, equal space and equal treatment were given to anti-administration candidates, or relatively neutral news treatment accorded them for at least a short period, in the publications of the National Maritime Union, the American Newspaper Guild, the International Typographical Union, and to a lesser degree, the UAW-CIO and the TWUA-CIO. At the time of "neutral" treatment in the UAW, NMU, and to some extent the TWUA, however, both factions were in power in the national office at the same time. It is in situations like this that running a labor paper is, in the words of Oscar Ameringer, "like feeding melting butter on the end of a hot awl to an infuriated wildcat."[14] An editor in UAW-CIO describes the editor's problem in that union during 1946 (when both Reuther and anti-Reuther forces were in power, and, though Reuther men staffed the paper, they were unable to use it as a factional instument):

. . . UAW editor Frank Winn and, to a lesser extent, myself were buffeted about by labor politics. We were caught between our desire to publicize democratic unionism [i.e., the Reuther caucus] and the demands of the belligerent Addes caucus for space in our paper. The hostile "mechanical majority" had created an editorial committee of three, composed of Reuther, Addes, and Leonard. Reuther was hopelessly outnumbered on this body. But by a constant process of give and take, we managed to keep both sides pretty well satisfied for a while.[15]

---

14. Oscar Ameringer, *If You Don't Weaken* (New York: Henry Holt & Co., 1940), p. 182. Cf. Clayton Fountain, *Union Guy* (New York: The Viking Press, 1949), p. 201. This book contains useful descriptions of the political role of the Public Relations Dept., Fair Practices Dept. and Education Dept. of UAW. See especially pp. 166-69, 199-202, 211.

15. *Ibid.*, p. 201.

As the battle was joined, however, and the ascendant faction began to consolidate its strength, the editors' propaganda skills were pressed into service for the boss and his machine, both in the official journal and (as before) writing caucus literature, etc. In NMU, where the Communist faction was eliminated and where there was a tradition of equal space and equal treatment and in TWUA, where the Rieve-Baldanzi fight ended in secession, the drift towards partisanship finally ran its full course. The Newspaper Guild and the Typographical Union—both characterized by high leadership turnover and a practice of allowing dissent and opposition a place in the pages of their official journals—remain the only negative instances for the hypothesis that the editor in an all-out fight invariably becomes a factional tool of his boss. But even here, the negation is not final. The ITU, at least, with its unique, institutionalized party system (of which the long tradition of equal space and equal treatment is a part) shows signs of departing from its permissive policy. A recent article in the labor press, euphemistically entitled "Typographical Union Keeping Abreast of the Times" reports on this development:

An officer of the Typographical Union says that anything used to go in the news department, and there was no limit to the number of words. Local officers used to express themselves on any and all controversies—national and within the union. Likewise, international officers argued their differences in the *Journal*. But it seems that such a policy led nowhere except to an enormous printing bill. Now the editor, Secretary-Treasurer Don Hurd, announces to correspondents:

"Items submitted must be non-political and of general interest to the membership of the International Typographical Union. They must be written in a factual manner without editorial comment and devoid of any controversial matters, local or national, and may not impugn the motives or reflect on the honesty of any member. Personal items, which are of interest in the local union only, should not be included."[16]

This sort of depoliticalization of journal content inevitably works in favor of the incumbent administration, whose leaders maintain their "report to the membership" pages as well as a dominant place in the news. In a deviant union with exceptional traditions of freedom, this development underscores the machine-supporting function of the labor editor.

---

16. *The Butcher Workman*, XXXVII, 3 (March, 1951), 10.

(b) THE EDUCATION DIRECTOR. Again, education and publication are parallel in their relation to internal machine politics.

In stable, tightly controlled unions, either there is no educational activity or what there is tends to have a recreational and cultural emphasis.[17] When political content seeps in, it is in the form of "selling" union policy and union personalities in places where they are badly understood, or where they are under attack by rival unions.

In moderately factionalized unions where one faction is in control of national offices, the education director is likely to be denied entry to opposition locals and regions, and the bulk of his work goes to training of leadership within the administration machine. In any case, the education director, like the editor, is careful to avoid any reflection on the policies and performance of his boss when in contact with leaders and potential leaders in the lower reaches of the hierarchy.

Finally, in unions where either secession or extermination of the opposition is in prospect (and these seem historically to be the two outcomes of all-out war), the education department is typically, even if reluctantly, compelled to play a fully political role as part of the boss' machine. Again, in the early stages when both sides are in an uneasy balance of power, the education director may try to stay on the sidelines. In one such case, the education director reports,

If you're working on a voluntary activity like education and any kind of internal fight happens then you're accused of reaching out and have to convince both sides you're no threat to them. (602-5.)

As the recent factional battle in TWUA-CIO increased in bitterness, more than fifteen of the educational and political action staff specialists whose sympathies lay with the opposition were fired. The choice put to these people was: be actively for the administration or be neutral. The top staff experts in education and political action became administration partisans and stayed. Similarly, the Education Department in UAW-CIO during the turbulent factional

17. One education specialist comments: "In many areas the emphasis is on cultural and recreational activities—mainly because this attracts more people. . . . There's a value in dance and music and knowing the union gives them that they'll look to the union for other things." (N608-1.)

history of that union became the political tool of first one and then another of the contending groups.

In all of this machine-building effort, whether he works in the context of all-out war or rock-like unity, a skillful education director is in a unique position to drain off hostility potentially dangerous to his boss. "I'm a different kind of union representative," explained one.

They know that I'm not there to give them a line . . . about the accomplishments of the International. . . . You'll see guys in every local who have a chip on their shoulder: they don't like the International Officers, they don't like this policy or that. But I'll listen to them, they can air their views, get it off their chest, hear the answers from their fellow members. I'm not selling any bill of goods. You'd be surprised how many of these guys come around after you let them sound off. (603a.)[18]

(c) MISCELLANEOUS INTERNAL COMMUNICATIONS SPECIALISTS. The function of enhancing and protecting leadership power against membership pressures and rival leaders, actual or potential, is partly fulfilled in some unions by a unique set of Internal Communications Specialists—those whose job involves a central focus on minority groups within the union. By 1951, at least eight

---

18. Compare the function of the internal human relations expert in industry: " 'The counselor . . . is in a neutral position . . . he is not the type of representative to which the employees are accustomed. The counselor does not defend management, or take the Company's stand with regard to layoffs; but rather he gives the employee the opportunity to talk, complain, criticize, ridicule or whatever he chooses, both management and the layoff situation . . . ,' " thus promoting a satisfactory adjustment to the needs of the enterprise. J. L. and H. L. Wilensky, "Personnel Counseling: The Hawthorne Case," *American Journal of Sociology*, LVII (November, 1951), 273 ff. The phenomenon may tentatively be generalized: all large-scale organizations—with their necessary systems of authority and discipline—generate hostility and resistance among the masses of people they control. As a condition of continued existence such organizations must prevent this hostility from undermining the system of authority. One universal way of taking care of this hostility is to drain it off through the development of local nodules of power, officials in the lower reaches of the hierarchy, or troubleshooters working out of central headquarters, who fulfill the main function of heat-taking. This is seen in the work of company counselors, lead men or gang leaders, union stewards, and the Internal Communications Specialists discussed above. In the Soviet Union, where the need for channeling mass hostility is especially acute, special sets of functionaries in and out of the Party have been developed to deal with the problem. See, e.g., J. Barrington Moore, *Soviet Politics: The Dilemma of Power* (Cambridge: Harvard University Press, 1950).

unions had what is known as an "Anti-Discrimination Committee"
or a "Civil Rights Committee."[19] There are now at least eleven staff
specialists in the labor movement assigned full time to minority
group problems.[20] In addition, technical staff jobs are occasionally
created to deal with questions raised by a militant minority based
on occupation rather than race, ethnicity or sex.

While the manifest function of these specialists for the minority
group involved is to represent their special interests in the union
and improve their occupational and union leadership opportunities,
their manifest function for the top officers is typically to allay
minority group pressures and neutralize potentially dangerous opposition. An example is the Anti-Prohibition Department in the Hotel
and Restaurant Workers. ". . . At the 1947 Convention," says one
observer,

some bartenders offered a resolution to appropriate $75,000 to set up
an Anti-Prohibition Department. It was passed as a sop to the bartenders.
It's like being against the flag to be against a resolution like that. . . . But
nobody in the organization gives one goddam about prohibition. The
department was set up so they [top officers] could tell the Convention
they'd done as told. (522-4.)

The same pattern appears in the case of the anti-discrimination
committees: (1) the minority group (Negro activists within the
union) agitates in private conference and on the convention floor
for representation in the form of appointed and elected offices
and/or a special committee; (2) the top officers assure the Negroes
that they will get their share of union jobs and something will be
done about protecting contractual rights of Negro members; (3)
convention resolutions are adopted; (4) a Negro staff man and/or
an interracial committee is eventually appointed in the national

---

19. Rubberworkers, CIO; Packinghouse Workers, CIO; International Union
of Electrical Workers, CIO; United Autoworkers, CIO; Textile Workers,
CIO; Newspaper Guild, CIO; Steelworkers, CIO; American Federation of
Teachers, AFL. In addition, both major federations have set up anti-discrimination committees. All the Committees are interracial, except the Steelworkers'.

20. On in Rubber, one in Packing House, two in Steel, three in Auto,
three in the new AFL-CIO, and one in the New Jersey State CIO Council.
This does not count the woman UAW-CIO has assigned to represent the interests and problems of the female minority in that union. Several other union
functionaries spend part time in minority group problems.

office; (5) the agitation subsides, though speeches continue to be made at the convention complaining about the slow progress— with Negro delegates both defending and attacking the administration. The Negro race relations functionary serves as symbol of the top officers' good intentions, acts as trouble-shooter wherever Negro militancy is directed against the dominant white machine, and becomes a cautious if sometimes persistent lobbyist for Negro interests at national headquarters.[21]

The utility of the propaganda and group-work skills of the Internal Communications Specialist, his involvement in factionalism, and his function of enhancing top officer prestige and power were all dramatically illustrated in the struggle for control of UAW-CIO, 1946-47. The choices of technical staff services made by the winning faction are significant for this thesis. With the Reuther caucus in control of the Presidency, and an opposition coalition in control of a majority of the Executive Board (March 31, 1946 to November 9, 1947), the battle was more or less deadlocked and some trades had to be made—on the jobs of the staff experts as well as on other issues. The ascendant Reuther group took the Publicity Department (editor of house organ and staff), the Education Department, and the Fair Practices and Anti-Discrimination Department, leaving to the losing faction the Legal Department, Research Department, and Radio Department and the Washington Office.[22] In other words, the side that came out on top in an all-out internal war controlled the Internal Communications Specialists; the side that lost had the Facts and Figures

---

21. Cf. W. F. Kornhauser's similar analysis of the "symbolic" and "liaison" functions of Negro line officers. "The Negro Union Official: A Study of Sponsorship and Control," *The American Journal of Sociology*, LVII (1952), 443-52. Similar observations about the functions of Negro personnel men and Negro officers in the Communist Party appear in Everett Hughes, "Queries Concerning Industry and Society," *American Sociological Review*, XIV (April, 1949), 218; and Wilson Record, *The Negro and The Communist Party* (Chapel Hill: University of North Carolina Press, 1951), p. 180. The functions of the miscellaneous staff experts we have discussed in this section constitutes an aspect of "window dressing"—broadly treated in Chapter III—unique to the Internal Communications Specialist.

22. Fountain states that President Reuther traded off a line organization with a large number of organizing jobs (the Competitive Shops Dept.), for two staff departments, Education, and Publicity. *Op. cit.*, pp. 199-200.

Men and Contact Men. Several informants give major credit for
the Reuther victory at the 1947 Convention to the machine-building
activity of these Internal Communications Specialists.   ,

Possible Dysfunctional Consequences and Net Effects

Through an examination of officers' comments on their work,
the target and content of their programs, and the trouble-shooting
aspects of their activity, we have seen that the Internal Communications Specialists act primarily as channels for downward communication, transmitting union programs and policies from leader
to rank and file, and that they sometimes constitute a source of
political intelligence. Their central functions, we said, are: (1) to
build top officer prestige, enhance his control over members in
internal union affairs (and increasingly in American politics as
well), and strengthen the leader's political machine; (2) to maintain union morale in crisis situations; and (3) to allay minority-
group pressures when they threaten stability.

What are the possible dysfunctional consequences of the Internal
Communications Specialist's activity? What can we say about the
net effect of his presence in the union?

Some of his activity may make the maintenance of the union
as a social structure more difficult; it may lessen the leader's adaptation to external and internal pressures. Among the possibilities: (1)
he may nurture new ideas, new leadership, and thus subvert established authority; (2) he may drain the energies and scatter the
attention of the top officers with his promotion of the broad view
of union functions.

It is true that the Internal Communications Specialist occasionally plants ideas about the way the union should be run in the
minds of potential opposition (ambitious leaders on lower levels).
An education director may nurture a sentiment for good union
government and promote fuller citizenship participation. An editor
may have a similar effect through his reiteration of the rhetoric of
democracy in the columns of the union journal. Both may encour-

age new leadership to rise. But this seldom gets out of hand. As we have seen, Internal Communications Specialists representing a wide range of role orientations agree on their primary responsibilities.

Both officers and experts are aware of the possibilities of the Internal Communications Specialists getting out of line in their contacts with lower levels of the organization, and both are on guard to see that it does not happen. "Remember this angle," an editor advised. "Too much brains around make revolutions—and we don't want that!" (510-6.) No case has come to my attention where an Internal Communications Specialist—either through raising membership expectations or playing union politics—promoted the rise of the boss' opposition without being removed. Moreover, where new leadership is nurtured and trained by a representative of the administration, it can usually be integrated into the incumbent machine.

Some dysfunctional consequences are unavoidable. In the role of agitator and propagandist, the Communications Specialist occasionally promotes membership militancy when militancy is inappropriate. An editor reports a large wage gain in one place; this promotes discontent in another. He writes belligerent editorials during negotiations, and is caught out on a limb when a highly amicable settlement is reached. An education director tells a group about what a fine program Local XYZ has going five hundred miles to the West; this raises questions about leadership performance in ABC. But the fact that the experts are aware of these consequences and have worked out ways to minimize or avoid them ("You have to be politic"), indicates this is no serious threat to stability.

It is true, too, that the Internal Communications Specialists at times become internal lobbyists whose goal is to divert leadership energies away from the core job of collective bargaining and union administration. They sometimes compete for a share of the boss' attention in an attempt to implement their private version of the proper role of labor in a free society. The education director may want to accent the urgent need for world government rather than the importance of knowing the contract. The editor may want to devote his attention to public affairs and legislative issues that are at best peripheral to the central interests of the union. But their programs and publications nevertheless lean toward the straight trade union side. ("My major job is time study, steward training—basic tool courses. My interest lies elsewhere. . . . But my job is defined.") The Internal Communications Specialist who is tempted to oversell either his version of the broad view, or his specialty as the answer to all the union's problems, like all the staff experts soon learns his place. If he fails to quiet down, if his orientation remains too "impractical," he is relegated to a peripheral position and ignored.[23]

On balance, the data point to the central function of internal communication and control and a net effect of enhancing the power and prestige of incumbent national leaders. Of the three types we have discussed, the Internal Communications Specialist seems least likely to have dysfunctional consequences for the union.

The Internal Communications Specialist buttresses top officer prestige and authority; but he may also promote new styles in the exercise of that authority—the substitution of persuasion for coercion, of manipulation for persuasion. Many of the top officer interview comments point to a new concern with the worker's mind, a new demand for total, not partial, loyalty and commitment. The worker should not only do as the union tells him; he should have the conviction that what he's doing is right and good. The Internal Communications Specialist makes the officer desire to conquer the worker's mind more feasible and thereby promotes it. He supplies the liberal rhetoric that accompanies trade union action; he supplies a kit of communication tools with which to oil the officer's political machine (audio-visual aids, role-playing, modern discussion group methods, "permissive" leadership techniques, streamlined journalism). A move from coercion to persuasion as the dominant mode of union administration may be succeeded by a move from persuasion to manipulation.[24] For the means of winning the minds

23. The conviction among some education directors that their work is misunderstood, viewed as a "frill," the expression of "fashion," and that their position is more tenuous than that of other staff experts, is in part explained by a conflict between their role orientation and the functions they fulfill. Officer lack of understanding is often merely a lack of appreciation of the large private purposes of the staff expert. See below, Chapter VIII, for analysis of this phenomenon.

24. Manipulation defined as a means of control whereby the person controlled is unaware of the goals toward which his activity is directed.

of men are becoming more efficient, and the Internal Communications Specialists more enlightened and enthusiastic in their use. Moreover, worker susceptibility to organizational and propagandistic manipulation is increasingly characteristic of our society.[25] Thus, while our data here are limited, it is possible to speculate that the Internal Communications Specialist not only enhances authority, but introduces a "manipulative bias" in its use. It is possible that the trade union leader of the future may talk like this atypical incumbent:

> Such sciences as anthropology, sociology and psychology trade union leaders have not taken near advantage of the way they could. When I have a problem like increasing dues—on any problem in the day-to-day administration of the union, if I had a better understanding of what makes people tick, what builds good and bad attitudes, we'd have a better union. I'd like to have more of these scientists in to train my staff. . . . Techniques—these are adjuncts to any intelligent operation. (3-5.)

Summary and Conclusions: Part II

In order to explore questions about the uses unions make of the staff experts, the sources of their indispensability, the consequences their presence in the union is likely to entail (i.e., the direction of their influence), I constructed a functional typology of staff experts. The typology was based on three criteria: distinctive job content; their functions; and the nature of the bias introduced by their presence. Application of these criteria to interview and questionnaire and participant observation data, as well as to documentary sources, yields three types: the Facts and Figures Man, the Contact Man, and the Internal Communications Specialist. The characteristics of each type are summarized and compared in Chart I.

My tentative conclusions with regard to the net effect of each type's presence in the union have direct bearing on the theories advanced by Schumpeter, Mannheim, De Man and others about the role of the intellectual in society, discussed in Chapter II. As

25. See Philip Selznick, "Institutional Vulnerability in Mass Society," *American Journal of Sociology,* LVI (Jan., 1951), 320-31. Cf. Mannheim, *Man and Society* . . . , *op. cit.*

Chart I—A Functional Typology

Functional Type	DISTINCTIVE JOB CONTENT (Focus of activities, talents, knowledge, background)	AREAS OF UNION DECISION	
		Directly and Primarily	Indirectly or Secondarily
Facts and Figures Man	Supplies technical-economic-legal intelligence, builds the "case." Primary concern and skill with facts, figures, records, arguments. Analysis of economic characteristics and conditions of industries and companies union deals with; jobs, contracts, wage structures; laws and administrative regulations. Skill in producing quick, simple answers to complex technical-economic-legal questions. Human relations skills less prominent. Background in the law, the social sciences (especially economics, industrial relations and statistics), and engineering. High education level.	Collective barg. and through this governmental relations	Public relations Internal control and organization Rival union relations (Relatively little field contact.)
Contact Man	Supplies political-ideological intelligence leader needs to find way around modern society. Mediates relations between union and outside world. Primary concern and skill with facts about and techniques of manipulating the thoughts, feelings, conduct of men. Valued for his (1) knowledge of political-social topography of American Society; (2) nontransferable contacts; (3) skills in "working" the contacts—his skills in private consultation, negotiation, mediation. Background heterogeneous: law, journalism, politics, teaching, religion—most have had jobs in bureaucracies with which the union deals.	Governmental relations Public relations Collective bargaining (Occasional concentration on internal union and rival union relations)	
Internal Communications Specialist	Supplies political-ideological intelligence for internal control. Mainly transmits union policies downward; sometimes reports on locals. Involved in factionalism as part of boss' machine. Work has contact and trouble-shooting aspects. Primary concern with and skill in manipulating union members—especially leadership-activist core. Has propaganda, group-work skills; ability to gauge group reactions; knowledge of labor politics. Background in radical and/or union politics.	Internal control and organization Rival union relations	

DISTINCTIVE FUNCTIONS *(Manifest and Latent)*	NET EFFECT *(Probable net balance of aggregate consequences)*
Builds pressure on employer via the state and the public—which gives bargaining a "public responsibility" flavor, encourages counter argument, fact for fact, helps employer size up union power and intent.	Introduces a "rational-responsible bias" into union decision-making—more conscious examination of alternatives, of relevant factors beyond power, even "long range" consequences.
Persuades and impresses arbitrators, quasi-judicial boards, promotes reorientation of the negotiators towards data.	(In a few cases this becomes a "conservative-take-less" or "play-it-safe" bias.)
Strengthens the conviction and morale of union committee and in turn the rank and file, thus boosting bargaining power with employers and rival unions, enhancing leaders' control over members.	
Smooths officer's contacts with nonunion world, helps him find his way around complex bureaucratic entanglements; this promotes a "beat-the-game" mentality, strengthens officer's conviction that wherever there's a clash of interests, some way can be found to "put in the fix," bail union out of trouble.	Moves union towards a "beat-the-game" "cut-red-tape" bias. Smoothing, fixing, expediting side of his work is paramount.
Interprets officer and union to important publics, interprets these publics to officer; this may act to build image of officer and union as "respectable" and "responsible"; officer's new self-image tends to make him "play it safe" to cultivate good-will of these (real or imagined) publics.	(The "play it safe and respectable" or "go slow" bias operates only in long run. Embryonic as yet.)
In role of "glorified business agent," he facilitates maintenance of internal unity and discipline—but this is a less prominent function.	
Builds top officer prestige, enhances his control over members in internal union affairs (and increasingly in American politics as well), and strengthens the leader's political machine.	Building power and prestige of incumbent national officers, increases efficiency of union administration.
Maintains union morale, builds membership loyalty in crisis situations—negotiations, strikes, rival union raids, local leadership disaffection or deviation, etc.	Promotes changes in the modes of exercising authority. Possibly promotes a "manipulative bias" in union decision-making—a move from coercion to persuasion, persuasion to manipulation.
Allays minority group pressures when they threaten stability.	

Schumpeter suggests, intellectuals invading the labor movement as staff men have probably ". . . worked it up into something that differs substantially from what it would be without them." But the data would seem to contradict Schumpeter's hypothesis that they have "radicalized" the labor movement, ". . . eventually imparting a revolutionary bias to the most bourgeois trade-union practices."[26] The "rational-responsible" bias introduced by the Facts and Figures Man, the "beat-the-game," "cut-red-tape" bias of the Contact Man, the "manipulative bias" of the Internal Communications Specialist, could hardly be said to have "radicalized" the American labor movement—whatever the degree of influence we attribute to them. The function fulfilled by all types—that of buttressing top leader power and prestige—must, indeed, work in the long run to suppress radical tendencies pushing up from below. The "civilized" bargaining style promoted by the Facts and Figures operation, the smoothing, fixing and expediting contributions of the Contact Man—these inevitably work toward the more rational accommodation of conflicting union and nonunion interests. They further the integration of American labor into the complex bureaucratic machinery of a private enterprise economy and a pressure group polity. Any worker disaffection that may result from this trend will result in increasing employment for Internal Communications Specialists, whose propaganda and group-work skills are indispensable in the transformation of discontent into loyalty, opposition into properly constructive participation.

On a deeper level of analysis—cross-cutting all functional types and focusing on the place of labor in the social order—one can argue that the staff expert as verbalizer, sloganizer, specialist in symbolic manipulation, may in the long run promote the "substantial irrationality" which Mannheim sees undermining modern "mass" society. In this view, the rise of propagandists in the private association, business enterprise, political party, in the machinery of military and civil government, tends to multiply contradictions, insecurities and crises, and intensify competing hatreds and passions. The propaganda of one interest group induces the counter-propaganda of another and discredits both sides in the eyes of their

---

26. *Op. cit.*, pp. 153-54.

followers. This leaves them more susceptible to the appeals of new fanatical faiths of nation or race, religion or state.[27] In the case of the free trade union, such an outcome would lessen its hold over its members and ultimately destroy it.

On the other hand, one can argue just as plausibly that it is not disillusionment and a hunger for faith that the propagandist in a pluralist society creates. The battle of words via the mass media, the public forum and the mass meeting may on the contrary be a catharsis, safely channeling energy and latent hostility that might otherwise be directed into militant political action, violence and revolution. Instead of a baseball bat, says the up-to-date union leader of his new style in negotiations, you bring in your editor, your lawyer, your economist. Indeed, the participants and followers on both sides in (let us say) a labor-management national emergency dispute may get emotional release and stability-inducing satisfaction from watching the progress of the propaganda war, and in the end nod their heads peacefully when the Internal Communications Specialists on both sides tell them they have won a great victory.[28]

The typology above provides an idea of the distinctive talents and knowledge that give various groups of experts entree to the union; it serves as a clue to the likely *direction* of influence of each functional type. It also gives us a hint of the probable impact on the union of the increasing use of specialists approximating each

27. This is essentially the argument of Mannheim in *Man and Society*. . . . An increase in the "functional rationality" characterizing bureaucracy has not brought an increase in "substantial rationality." "A few people can see things more and more clearly over an ever-widening field, while the average man's capacity for rational judgment steadily declines once he has turned over to the organizer the responsibility for making decisions." "Fundamental democratization" and the vehement competition for ascendancy between different interest groups makes for the debilitation of norm-supplying elites and a consequent breakdown in community control. *Op. cit.*, pp. 51 ff., 81-105, 350 ff. Compare Lasswell, *World Politics* . . . , *op. cit.*, pp. 114, 281-83, who similarly argues that propaganda at a time of rapid social change maximizes insecurity and helps lay the groundwork for totalitarian social movements.

28. The kinds of social psychological studies that can permit an informed assessment of such speculation—studies of the quality of mass apathy and participation, of the content and impact of the mass media coverage of conflict and crisis situations, etc.—are beyond the scope of the present effort.

type. But this leaves out half the picture: the orientations and identifications of the experts themselves and the impact the organization has on them. Part III deals with the "subjective" side of the story; it seeks to view things from the perspective of the staff man.

ORIENTATIONS AND IDENTIFICATIONS OF THE STAFF EXPERT

CHAPTER VII

A TYPOLOGY OF ROLE ORIENTATIONS

WHAT THE EXPERT DOES is one thing; the meaning he assigns to what he does is another. His job activity has consequences; but what he experiences may correspond only dimly to those consequences. We need to know both how the variety of motives, loyalties, understandings and interests that people bring with them affect the organization, and, conversely, how the organization molds and shapes the person and his motives, loyalties, understandings, and interests.[1]

The Theoretical Context

Much sociological discussion of the plight of the modern intellectual has centered around the consequences of his involvement

1. One of the major problems of sociology is that of relating "institutional" and "motivational" levels of analysis. See discussions of formal and informal organization, institution and person in Chester I. Barnard, *The Functions of the Executive* (Cambridge, Massachusetts: Harvard University Press, 1938), Chapt. 9; Philip Selznick, *TVA and the Grass Roots: A Study in the Sociology of Formal Organization* (Berkeley and Los Angeles: University of California Press, 1949); Robin M. Williams, Jr., *American Society* (New York: Alfred A. Knopf, 1951), pp. 455-61; Everett C. Hughes, "Institutional Office and the Person," *American Journal of Sociology*, 42 (1937), 404-13; and Merton, "Bureaucratic Structure and Personality," *op. cit.*, pp. 151-60. The best empirical studies that have come to the writer's attention which attempt to relate these levels of analysis in the study of bureaucracy are: Leonard Reissman, "A Study of Role Conceptions in Bureaucracy," *Social Forces*, 27 (1949), 305-10; and Kurt Lang, "Bureaucracy in Crisis: A Case Study of a Military Bureaucracy" (Unpublished Master's Thesis, University of Chicago, 1952).

as a functionary in large-scale organizations. Whether these organizations are expanding units in a successful social movement or relatively stable bureaucracies with long histories and fixed traditions, the man of knowledge who enters them is pictured as experiencing a drastic transformation in outlook (see Chapter II). Merton's formulation of this theme is typical: ". . . bureaucracies provoke gradual transformations of the alienated intellectual into the a-political technician, whose role is to serve whatever strata happen to be in power."[2] There are two problems here for this study: (1) To what extent do unions share the bureaucratic characteristics said to provoke such a transformation; (2) what is the outlook of the man of knowledge who enters the trade union and how does it change—is it a transformation from alienated policy-minded intellectual to apolitical, means-centered technician, or something else? Part V deals with the first problem. This Chapter and the next deal with the second problem.

The occupational role of each expert consists of the behavior the union expects of him by virtue of his holding the job (this is the job-content component of the functional types). But no actor merely plays a role, even if the role behavior is explicitly and clearly defined for every situation. Each man brings to the role his conceptions of what it is, what it should be, what it might become. These meanings he assigns his job activity might be called his "role orientation."

The staff expert orients himself in the job role in a direction determined in part by his past and present group identifications. These become important in explaining how he acts and how he feels in his job role. They may include identifications with groups outside as well as inside the union. The typology below describes both his stance in the role and the main job-relevant group identification which supports that stance.

To say that a man is identified with a group is to say he is willing to subject himself to the controls and standards of the group. This does not necessarily signify active participation.[3] A staff ex-

2. *Op. cit.*, p. 167.

3. On the nature of group identification and its relation to participation see Edward Sapir, "The Group," in *Selected Writings of Edward Sapir*, ed. D. G. Mandelbaum (Berkeley: University of California Press, 1949), p. 360. Cf.

pert may no longer participate in any concrete political, religious, or professional group and no longer feel himself to be in a significant personal relation to some or all of its members. Nevertheless, he may have so internalized the values, expectations, and demands of such groups that they become either (1) crucial guides for action in his job role; or (2) sources of role conflict where union values, expectations, and demands run counter. His primary job identification is indicated by his willing acceptance of these group controls or by the dilemmas experienced when deference to an outside group is incompatible with the job. In the latter case, though he may choose to conform to union expectations, the fact that he does it with misgiving marks him as having an outward orientation.

Getting at a man's job-relevant group identifications through interviews or any other method is not easy. We must often be satisfied with indirect clues. To type these experts by role orientation and main job identification, I analyzed interview content and questionnaire responses under eight major rubrics—the best clues I could devise. The eight criteria were: (1) job frustrations; (2) job satisfactions; (3) enemy targets of his work activity; (4) view of hypothetical or actual company job offers; (5) how he describes his work; (6) the presence or absence of research product pitched to a professional audience since he has been with the union; (7) his concept of the ideal expert; (8) the character of his colleague group in so far as this is indicated by frequency of contact with outside professionals, labor movement experts and own-union line and staff officials.

Methods for constructing the typology of past and present role orientations are described in Appendix D. In the following discussion, interview material is used only to illustrate the generalizations derived from an attribute analysis, or to point up the more subtle differences lost in the process of coding. The eight types which emerged from this analysis have these labels:

1. Missionaries
    (a) Party Missionary
    (b) Legislative-Liberal Missionary

R. K. Merton and A. S. Kitt, "Contributions to the Theory of Reference Group Behavior" in *Continuities in Social Research,* ed. Merton and Lazarsfeld (Glencoe, Ill.: The Free Press, 1950), pp. 40-105.

(c) Religious-Ethico Missionary
2. Professional Service Experts
    (a) Program Professionals
    (b) Technician Professionals
3. Careerists
    (a) Outside Careerists
    (b) Rank-and-File Careerists ("Porkchoppers")
4. Politicos

Missionary Types

. . . the terrible dilemma arises,—either support what is going on, in which case you count for nothing because you are swallowed in the mass and great incalculable forces bear you on; or remain aloof, passively resistant, in which case you count for nothing because you are outside the machinery of reality.

—Randolph Bourne, *Untimely Papers*

The Missionary is oriented in his job towards some abstract concept of the labor movement; he is highly identified with an outside political or religious-political group. Looking outward toward national politics and larger (though sometimes amorphous) social movements, he sees the union as a vehicle for social changes in accord with his private goals. These goals, which constitute his mission in the union, are derived in part from his past or present participation in radical or liberal movements and organizations. His main problems and frustrations stem from a conflict between his private mission (legitimized by these political groups), on the one hand, and the requirements of the job and the values of union officials, on the other.

The Missionary tends to structure the world as hostile to his values. His job satisfactions come from combat on behalf of the cause. For instance, he enjoys a sense of identity with the union rank and file in their defensive struggles, especially strikes. He gets a kick out of thwarting the designs of reactionary forces, which he identifies with the symbol, Big Business.[4] He invests the union's

---

4. It is interesting as an index of the Missionary's spirit of rebellion that eight of the nine cases in my sample whose fathers are big business execu-

day-to-day activities with large meanings centered around their long-run effect in this struggle against Reaction. This struggle, he is convinced, is going to be decided in the political arena, not at the bargaining table, though the union's economic and organizational strikes may serve as schools for political combat or, at minimum, fortify the generalized rank-and-file loyalties to the union which can later be redirected into political channels. "We all know," a typical comment goes, "that our economic gains can be wiped out by the political power of business. "(302b-3.) Where it is apparent that union officials do not see their activities in this same light, they, too, become target symbols. Thus, the Missionary can seldom describe his work without invoking both "Big Business'" and "immoral," "racketeer," "sell-out," or "reactionary" union leaders as enemy targets. He often adds "reactionary Catholic circles" in the labor movement to the list.

No Missionary, whatever the adaptation he has made to trade union reality, would seriously consider accepting a company job, even if the salary and the work were quite congenial. Prominent in his concept of the ideal staff expert is dedication to the "labor-liberal movement" (or something similar), measured by a willingness to sacrifice money, health, or time with family for Labor. He works hard and he works with a sense of mission. "I've put in seven days a week, 14 hours a day for . . . years. . . . I believe in it," explains one hard-driving Missionary.

There are some people around the union who think they can do a job in 40 hours a week. . . . They're not willing to put in the number of hours necessary. This isn't a job—it's a mission that requires dedication. Practically anything I do I exploit for the union. I go to an art exhibit. I come back with a design [for a union publication]. I go to a movie, read books, attend the theater—everything I do finds expression ultimately in my work. . . . I use my kids' experiences. . . . I happen to be interested and satisfied with my work. With some it's horses or women. With me it's my work. It's true of a lot of people

---

tives entered the labor movement as Missionaries and seven of these remain Missionaries. In general, however, the men who entered with a mission are more heterogeneous in social origins than any other type (considering all sixty-four cases who entered as Missionaries). This seems to contradict Lasswell's view of "social radicals" as "run-away adolescents from bourgeois families" who dash into exciting social movements. Lasswell, *World Politics . . . , op. cit.,* pp. 263-64.

around here. . . . You have to understand [this union] as more than a union, it's a social movement like the Christian Temperance Union or the Townsend Plan. . . . Our people have something to do and a reason for doing it. . . . (514.)

The Missionary is not too concerned with the intrinsic nature of the job. He can stand much grubby routine so long as he is convinced it has some meaning—and the case quoted above goes on to describe the rather undramatic, often clerical core of his work. Moreover, his time perspective is often long enough so that the tenuous link of his day-to-day union work with the ultimate emergence of his Utopia does not press too heavily upon him.

Union leaders are aware of the Missionary's enthusiasms, and if relative salaries are any indication, do not hesitate to exploit them. Median annual salary for 123 cases on which I have data is $7,500; for the twenty-nine Missionaries, however, the figure is $6,500. (Careerists top the list with $8,500; Politicos and Professional Service types both get $7,500.)[5] One staff expert, an ex-Missionary turned Careerist, observed of his Missionary colleagues, "Like professors in small colleges, they get paid in titles and non-monetary incomes. . . . In the past, unions attracted people who thought the trade union is a way of life. . . . Unions use their illusions and in fact pay them off in illusions." (338.)

This pattern of rewards is made possible by the narrow range of the Missionary's acceptable job alternatives. Jobs in the business world, though some offers are forthcoming, are out of the question. Other worlds are scrutinized carefully in terms of potential for social action in pursuit of the mission. Typically the choice narrows down to a few social action agencies, very few government labor agencies, and occasionally a university. Even labor-movement jobs are restricted in acceptability; the Missionary sometimes can envision working for no other union but the one he is in. Cut off from

5. Low median salary does not appear to be related to a high proportion of newcomers (men whose date of first service to the labor movement was in the period 1945-51) in each of the four main role orientation types. The newcomers are distributed as follows: Missionaries, 8/29; Professionals, 27/53; Careerists, 6/32; Politicos, 1/12. Low salaries cannot be explained by short service. In fact, the median salary of the Rank-and-File Careerist group, which includes no newcomers, is below the overall median, while that of the Program Professionals, two-thirds of whom are newcomers, is above the median.

so many possibilities, it is easy to understand why his sense of job insecurity is greater than most of his colleagues whose ideological commitments are less weighty.

How did the Missionaries get that way? Marx, Keynes and Christ take center stage in the story of the genesis of this type. After first-hand or second-hand exposure to the ideas these gods stood for, the Missionaries found themselves looking to the labor movement for a chance to put their political, economic or ethical philosophies to work. These symbols of idea systems can serve to introduce the three types of Missionary found in my sample. All share the general role orientation discussed above; but there are some crucial distinctions among them, stemming from their different approaches to politics.

The Party Missionary.—The Party Missionary entered the labor movement with eyes ablaze. He was an ideological fanatic, a member of some faction or fraction of the socialist movement, totally committed to the idea that the unions were the vanguard in a class war whose inevitable outcome was a new planned social order, and that the Marxist missionaries in the unions were in the forefront of the vanguard. Prior to his entry he had already embarked on a life of dedication and submission to discipline; he had begun to develop a sense of conspiracy and martyrdom. His conversion to the true political gospel may originally have been intellectual (accomplished in a library or classroom or college campus, with the assistance of books); it may have been more a matter of emotional affinity. In many cases a large element of chance was involved—chance exposure to a pamphlet, a riot or strike, a teacher, a party zealot. Here is a story which combines several of these elements (some minor details are changed or omitted):

I was working in a factory and going to high school at night. I was reading crime stories in the newspaper and I wrote a paper holding that crime was the result of poverty. So the way to limit it was to guarantee everyone a job. The teacher called my theme rank Bolshevism. I didn't know what that meant so I went to the library and started reading up on Bolshevism. . . . I came in contact with various youth organizations. . . . [When I got on the CCNY campus] I took a look at the Commie organizations—but somehow they were emotionally repulsive to me. I ended up in the YPSL's finally—not through any particular logic, just accident and emotional compatibility. I might have ended up in the YCL, but I liked the YPSL's as people more. Actually my first job was pretty much accident, too. A lot of YPSL's were going to Brookwood Labor College because of a general interest in the labor movement. I went along and this put me in contact. . . . [Describes subsequent teaching assignment in WPA workers' education project, research in other New Deal agencies, then various union jobs.] (302a-3,4.)

However casual the initial exposure, once he became fully involved the thing became immensely serious. The Party Missionary's political conversion may have been accompanied by a sharp break with family and friends. "I joined the SP in ——," said one, "and through that became interested in unionism. I practically got thrown out of school and my family practically disowned me." (513-3.)[6] The party commitment was not lightly undertaken. "It was plainly the answer for me," recalls another. "It wasn't a shallow or superficial thing. It was stern and grim." (910-4.)

His occupation just prior to his first full-time, paid union job reflects this early commitment: he was an outsider whose job duties were defined in terms of the promotion of some political program (i.e., a Communist Party plant in a New Deal agency, a Socialist Party journalist or administrator, a college campus radical, a "synthetic rank-and-filer" who went into the shop on party assignment, etc.); or he was a radical party activist from wage-worker ranks who became an inside organizer.

Typically, he got his first union staff expert job by demonstrating loyalty or skill in some union activity, usually at a local level. Often this meant volunteer work in strike situations, organizing

---

6. The Party Missionary's total commitment is often revealed in his marital history. Several cases, unable to bring their wives or girl friends along on their ideological journeys, got divorced or remained single. In one fascinating document a Party Missionary of the late thirties recalls his first wife: "She was a capable housekeeper and a devoted mother, but union activity just wasn't in her scheme of life!" C. Fountain, *op. cit.*, p. 59. Another adjusting socialist says, "I'm a bachelor and . . . I have no outside interests. It's easier for me to be a fanatic. Most of my life I've been an activist. I still consider it a crusade." (606-4.) We are reminded again that a variety of social reformers and leaders of radical social movements have seen marriage and the family as basically anti-social and corrupting because they prevent a man from doing his political duty.

drives and the like; or participation in a CP caucus in a white-collar union. The party sometimes got him the job via its contact with party members in official positions.

In keeping with his sense of martyrdom and sacrifice, the Party Missionary typically had the satisfaction of taking a cut in annual salary when he came to his first full-time union job.[7]

What of the Party Missionary today? About 30 per cent of the sample (thirty-six of 122 cases typed by past role orientation) entered the labor movement as Party Missionaries. Only eight cases have retained an approximation to this type of role orientation; they are members of a fading fraternity. The first and most poignant complaint of these men is the lack of opportunity to radicalize or politicalize the rank and file. Just as CP agents who infiltrate peace organizations, veterans' organizations, and powerless educational groups are on the fringe of CP action ("The basis of the Party organization, its fortresses, are the factory nuclei," said Lenin[8]), so the Party Missionary staff expert in the trade union is on the fringe of the fortress, feeding the militants ammunition as if by long distance telephone. Thus he exhibits a deep sense of isolation from the "real struggles" of the masses. Desk-bound, he'd like to be "out there pitching," "working closely with the problems of the locals and the men—that's the guts of the thing." (704-4.)

Now, some isolation from rank-and-file contact is characteristic of most of these experts; the sheer fact of their location in the international headquarters is enough (aside from their job functions). What makes the Party Missionary feel it most deeply is his firm belief in the Myth of the Sublimity of the Proletariat—the myth that the "masses" have a monopoly on the virtues of militancy, heroism and courage, tolerance and good-will; indeed, that the practical earthy wisdom of the proletariat is the only source of truth and goodness.[9] This idealization of the masses, common among Marxian

7. While about two-fifths (40/98) of all known cases took a cut, two-thirds (16/24) of the Party Missionaries made a clear-cut financial sacrifice to take a union job. Figures are based on Main Sample cases for which both Career Theme (Past Role Orientation) and Salary Transition are known.

8. Quoted in Philip Selznick, *op. cit.*, p. 22.

9. A typical phrasing on the truth point: "The answers the workers themselves develop are likely to be better than those of all the university experts put together." (D15.)

socialists everywhere,[10] prompts the Party Missionary to adopt a spurious identification with imagined proletarian styles of life and conduct. If he cannot boast of his wage-worker parentage, he will often invoke the briefest experience in a factory, e.g., his few weeks of a summer vacation from college, as a means of maintaining self-respect.

The Myth of the Sublimity of the Proletariat is more easily held if sustained and intimate contact with real-life proletarians is lacking. It is suggestive, for instance, that seven of the eight Party Missionary holdouts can be described as "bourgeois intellectuals" by occupational origin and training. In contrast, nine of the ten workers who entered as Party Missionaries have experienced a drastic transformation in role orientation.[11]

The Party Missionary is not only isolated from rank-and-file workers by his occupational history and the requirements of his job—an isolation he feels more deeply than other experts who structure the political world in different fashion—but he is typically isolated from the officialdom of labor as well. For example, in contrast to the Legislative-Liberal Missionary, he has little contact with other staff experts outside his own union. This isolation is especially acute in the case of the CP Missionary. With the demise of the Communists in the CIO, with the proliferation of public and private loyalty programs and pledges and Congressional investigations, the CP intellectual has long been effectively cut off from respectable labor and government contacts (and, of course, job opportunities):

Off the job some years ago I did have personal relationships with a lot of government and union people. Now that's no longer so. Guys

---

10. For a brilliant account of some bizarre aspects of the "cult of Proletarian chauvinism" in the American socialist movement, see Daniel Bell in Egbert, *et al.*, *op. cit.*, Vol. I, pp. 286, 294-99. For similar treatment of this phenomenon on the European scene, see Henry De Man, *op. cit.*, pp. 31 ff. S. M. Schwarz notes that during the period of the NEP in the Soviet Union (1921-28), it was ". . . a great advantage in the Communist Party to be or to have been a manual worker or of 'proletarian origin.'" F. Bienstock, S. M. Schwarz, and A. Yugow, *Management in Russian Industry and Agriculture* (London: Oxford University Press, 1944), p. 27.

11. Compare De Man's observation that "The manual worker who rises in the social scale, even if it be only in and through the socialist labour movement, can be embourgeoised far more readily than the socialist intellectual [of bourgeois origin] in like circumstances." *Op. cit.*, p. 235.

can actually lose their jobs by being friends with me. They don't take the risk and I don't try to impose it on them. It wouldn't be fair. I have friends in ———. I never call 'em up. . . . My social life is very much confined. In fact [recent events] have killed it. (704-8.)

Paradoxically, this further isolation from the movement may serve to reinforce his party commitment, even when doubts about the true gospel begin to plague his intellect. His sense of conspiracy and martyrdom is nourished by the concrete sacrifices his party affiliation involves (incidentally, the staff experts in CP-dominated unions are among the lowest paid). It is possible that his ideology is further sustained by intimate association with his colleagues in a CP cell (though, even here his labor assignment may afford little opportunity for off-the-job contacts).

The CP fellow-travelers and anti-Stalinist radicals in my sample in some ways find it more difficult than CP members to maintain a wholehearted, total commitment to a political ideology. Surrounded by ordinary trade union functionaries, often cut off from the psychological sustenance of face-to-face contacts with a well-organized political group, their conception of themselves as revolutionaries must find nourishment from within. Their sense of martyrdom is sometimes sorely attenuated by a medium-good salary. One Party Missionary, a case of extreme isolation, was described in these terms:

——— is an old-fashioned Marxist—a Karl Kautsky disciple who carries in his heart a poisoned virus. . . . He's a devoted man, has utter contempt for the time-servers and 'those who speak for labor and live like kings.' His conscience bothers him when he gets a raise! He'd just as soon be getting $25 a week. [He actually makes the highest salary in the Party Missionary group.] He's an old bachelor, spends all his time working. He has no outside associations. His room and his office is his whole life. . . . He's completely ineffective. He's wrapped up in Socialist writings—has fixations. He hates bosses, reds, fascism, monopolists, and corruption as expressed in the workings of the modern labor movement. He reads the foreign labor press. . . . He pays little attention to the problems concerning workers. . . . He's an anomaly here because the union doesn't recognize the class struggle the old man is engaged in. (522-1,2,11.)

In all cases, as in this one, what sustains the Party Missionary's dedication is his belief that with all its limitations, with all the "betrayals" of its leaders, the labor movement is still the decisive vehicle for promoting a new social order. "The union is a better instrument for achieving the things I want to see done than anything else I know. That doesn't mean I won't maybe change my views in years to come, if the organization aims no longer correspond to mine, but right now I think they do. . . . You work at any time within the possibilities of the existing situation." (302a-6,7.) Within those possibilities, his chief job satisfactions come from even an occasional chance to plant a socialist idea with the rank and file and/or leadership, and from infrequent opportunities for close contact with the idealized masses, with a view to advancing their class (political) consciousness. When the union officials he works for make it clear, even to him, that their interests lie elsewhere, he may fall back on the conviction that inexorable forces (another Great Depression, an aroused rank and file) will bring the leadership around or, better, sweep more receptive leaders into power. "It's my early training and struggles in the labor movement that keep me going," explained the Karl Kautsky disciple. "I have a certain conception of the labor movement; I wouldn't be happy if I weren't in it. . . . The next depression will force the leaders of labor to become socialists." (N529.)

It should be clear from my description of the Party Missionary today that few, if any, in my sample fit perfectly the image of the unreconstructed True Believer. A case or two (such as the one just quoted) come close. In their initial career theme probably all come close. But today their ideological commitments are not total, their hesitations and reservations, while only dimly and uncomfortably admitted, are clear. Several have scaled down their expectations and demands. Even the Missionaries in CP-dominated unions do not match the stereotype of the hard-core conspirator. Some data suggest that even these last-ditch holdouts are too intellectual to invest political doctrine with the certitude of holy writ, that they are unable to see party action in strategic and tactical "dialectical" perspective, unable to subscribe so firmly to an "ethic of ultimate ends" that none of the agonizing problems of ethics and politics bother them.[12] These quotations from a party-line intel-

---

12. See Weber's discussion of the relation between ethics and politics in Gerth and Mills (trans. and eds.), *op. cit.*, pp. 228-35. The Party Missionary type obscures differences that may be significant in other connections—e.g.,

lectual, for instance, could hardly be said to suggest a full-fledged political fanatic:

SE: . . . I wouldn't feel competent to go out in the field [to do organizational work and carry on the battle in the front lines]. You have to be too thick-skinned and have strong nerves; whereas I can do something in a research way satisfying to myself and useful to the union. . . . But there's no use kidding ourselves that the trade union movement is flourishing, because we're definitely on the defensive. And when you come from a business background, there's an inevitable problem; higher education costs money—and the technician is likely to come from a well-to-do family. Your former associates look at you as if you're nuts. . . . My family has frowned on it. They're disappointed that I'm not in business. I get a kind of perverse satisfaction in at least holding out! . . . I feel this is something that people are coming to accept, but there's still a ways to go. My [relative] is always telling me, "Why don't you stop wasting your life?" It's hard for him to realize the trade union is anything worth working for. I can remember when working for the New Deal was worse than working for the labor movement now. [Describes his gradual political awakening and the development of labor sympathies which led to casual exposure to CP unionists and eventual conversion] . . . I wasn't forced into it, I didn't learn the hard way. I read about it and had professors who influenced my thinking. . . .

HLW: Do you get much chance on your present job to come in contact with other [union staff experts in your specialty]?

SE: Unfortunately, I'm cut off. I used to meet with ———. The mutual exchange was good . . . I miss that. . . . They don't want to be seen with us. . . .

---

between the Trotskyite fundamentalist who believes, like the Christian evangelist, in an "ethic of ultimate ends" and the Socialist Party gradualist who subscribes to an "ethic of responsibility." Such distinctions help explain the former's intense preoccupation with doctrinal purity (as with the Socialist Workers Party member today), the latter's more measured concern with specific program, strategy and tactics. Cf. Selznick's distinction between the total commitment of the "well-integrated Marxist," and the partial, anxiety-laden commitment of the "petty-bourgeois Stalinoid." *Op. cit.,* pp. 297 ff. See also W. F. Ward's characterization of the "lost generation" (Hook, Burnham, Lewis Corey, Edmund Wilson, Dwight MacDonald, etc.) as intellectuals who never really accepted dialectical materialism. "From Revisionism to Social-Chauvinism; I. The Degradation of Sidney Hook," *Fourth International,* III (June, 1942), 174-78. The contrast between the cold professionalism of Communist agent Maxim and the hesitancies of party sympathizer Laskel depicted by novelist Lionel Trilling are similarly suggestive. *The Middle of the Journey* (New York: The Viking Press, 1947), p. 128.

HLW: How about [outside professionals]? Do you get a chance to keep in touch with current notions in the profession?

SE: Not as much as I'd like. That's one of the problems you run into on a union job. You don't have time to do the reading you'd like or attend the meetings. . . . The demands of the job are such that you have to make everything you do fit into it. . . . [Discusses research vs. advocacy. Previous jobs had been too constrained. "You'd report the facts but confuse their meaning. . . . Union jobs are better in that respect—you're doing research for a purpose." He also says, however, that he'd like to teach in a university ". . . next to the union job, that is. I guess it's because there's less pressure in the university; you don't have to be so thick-skinned."]

HLW: You keep using the phrase "thick-skinned" as a quality needed on a union job. What do you mean by that?

SE: Well, it's hard to find the right word. I don't mean cynicism, but I mean being able to . . . see what kind of stupid bastards [people he has to contact in the line of duty] are and yet deal with them as if they were fine people. You have to be able to deal with anybody. (337-5-7.)

Here is a Party Missionary long dominated by a Communist ideology, yet we see considerable ambivalence. He takes his main cues from the Party, but he is still sensitive to the expectations and values of family, his former non-Party friends, even the profession. Moreover, he finds it hard to accept any assignment—"deal with anybody" —in the interest of the cause.

In sum, whatever they were at their initial conversion, the present Party Missionaries embrace a wide range of political ideologies; they show varying degrees of commitment to party program. In some cases they have no personal participation in any political group. All, however, have a primarily outward orientation in their union job roles, toward either some concrete radical political party or an image of past experience in one.

The Legislative-Liberal Missionary.—This type of missionary takes his main cues from the "liberal-labor movement," symbolized by a set of interlocking political organizations such as Americans for Democratic Action, CIO's Political Action Committee, Labor's League for Political Education (AFL), American Veterans Committee, Liberal Party (N.Y.), American Civil Liberties Union, various minority-group defense agencies (e.g., NAACP), various units of the workers' education movement, in some places the Democratic

Party, etc. Highly identified with the people and/or programs of these groups, he is convinced that legislative and administrative action by the federal government along New Deal-Fair Deal lines would solve most of the nation's—and even the world's—problems. He sees labor as the core of the political coalition necessary for enactment and appropriate administration of "liberal" laws in such fields as taxes, trade, social welfare, civil liberties, union-management relations, atomic energy, etc. Hence, his main satisfactions in his job role come from the belief that he is encouraging union officials' interest in these reforms, pushing them beyond business unionism to a newer, more political unionism, "keeping them Left." This belief is buttressed by his opportunity for a liberalizing impact on nonbargaining policies (see Chapter IX). At the same time, his hope that labor will take the lead in social reform on a broad front constitutes the main source of his job frustrations. Line and staff officials at all levels resist the push forward. His influence on the nonbargaining issues is too often on paper only:

> Sweat goes into it. What an armful of work. Breathless stuff. But it's just a damn dumb show. There's no better way of keeping a secret than putting it in a [federation] or [union] convention resolution. (705.)

Typically he holds memberships in several liberal organizations and has frequent contacts with organizational liberals both in and out of the labor movement. When the ideas held most dear in these circles are not readily implemented in union action, he feels thwarted. Though he finds the resistance from within wearing, he tends to be a bit more tolerant of the internal enemy than the Party Missionary, a bit more appreciative of the consuming nature of the boss' administrative and bargaining tasks. The officers don't spend a reasonable amount of time in important social reforms, observes one case. "But I understand. They've got so much on their minds. Their range of attention is broad enough. This is just an added headache." (513-2.)

Preoccupied with short-run legislative issues (a little more security for the aged, a little more equality in the tax structure, more protection for minority groups, more opportunity for education and medical care for all, etc.), he shares little of the Party Missionary's sense of isolation from the masses. He seldom embraces the Myth of Proletarian Sublimity. In fact, a rather realistic view of where the rank and file are now often leads him to a class-uplift theme in his description of his work satisfactions. When his job puts him in touch with the members and lower leaders, he enjoys the feeling that he's developing leadership potential, strengthening democratic unionism, counteracting bureaucratic tendencies, promoting a "thinking loyalty," and helping labor achieve power and prestige positions in the community. The Legislative-Liberal Missionary, a strong believer in democratic processes, is invariably an enthusiast in the anti-apathy crusade, which, as Riesman and Glazer have suggested, is based on old middle-class assumptions that obvious self-interest and patriotic social duty are adequate motivations for political participation.[13] The belief that these motives, especially the one of self-interest, can be tapped to activate the membership on behalf of his legislative goals, sustains him in his mission.

To clarify self-interest for the working people, to overcome the feelings of impotency that block their proper political participation —these are the hard tasks he sets himself in his internal contacts. The ultimate goal is to bring about social reform on behalf of the less privileged through national legislation.

The Legislative-Liberal Missionary is far less doctrinaire than his militant Party colleagues. His hopes tend to be modest ones, phrased in moderate tones. An ex-Socialist says:

> I love the job. It never is work. I could live without working with the union; at one time I thought I couldn't. But life would sure lose a lot of its zest. . . . My whole philosophy makes me believe in it. . . . In 1936 I voted for Roosevelt. . . . I think the labor movement is the best hope towards moving toward a world we once believed we were moving toward rapidly. Another thing, I once thought I knew all the answers. Salvation was to be sought in a labor party, nationalization of industry, etc. Now I'm not so sure. I have my doubts about the Democrats—like many of us. Still—X [Party Missionary] wouldn't agree—but I think it's wise. But I'm not *sure*. It looks practical. World conditions have to be considered. I keep my belief in certain basic principles— like Civil Rights. [Describes political slogans of labor, is worried that "the specific ingredients are lacking."] . . . I believe that with strength comes responsibility. It's easy to be a soap-boxer. . . . (513-4,5.)

---

13. "Criteria for Political Apathy," in *Studies in Leadership,* ed. Alvin W. Gouldner (New York: Harper and Bros., 1950), pp. 520 ff.

Political feelings may still be strong, but the dominant tone is one of cautious, critical realism, tempered by an underlying principled sympathy with the underdog. Confronted with the statement that his own goals and the action program of the union seem to be somewhat different, this type typically falls back on the most "left" of labor's official policy pronouncements: "We're for TVA, MVA, government ownership of steel if recurring shortages make for unemployment. . . . As the years go by, everybody seems to get more practical. In and out of our union this seems to happen. Maybe we're getting older and we want to see some of our hopes put into action—even a little bit." (517.)

What about the origins and background of this type?

Of nineteen cases in the sample who are now Legislative-Liberal Missionaries, twelve entered the labor movement as Party Missionaries and the other seven entered with (approximately) their present orientation. Of 122 cases whose career themes are known, twenty-six entered as Legislative-Liberal Missionaries. These men typically got their jobs by working first as an agent of a third party serving or regulating unions (three-fifths of them made labor contacts while officials or experts in government labor agencies, newspapermen covering labor, or consultants to labor). Three out of five had "ideological" occupations just prior to entry, including many from college campuses and many from New Deal labor agencies; the rest have scattered occupational origins.

Many cases demonstrated in the circumstances of their entry considerable willingness to stick their necks out for their political beliefs, typically in some sacrifice of career because of labor sympathies. As with the Party Missionary, Depression experiences were often crucial in the genesis of this type, though a radical party may not have presided over the process, and the conversion experience is missing.

The Religious-Ethico Missionary.—A professional or lay preacher of the social gospel of Christianity or a social actionist of the Roman Catholic Church, this type sees the labor movement as a channel for promoting a new social or industrial order that will implement ethical standards in human relations and promote brotherly love. The mandate for this mission comes from a religious group whose precepts demand action in this world.

Though his political program goals may be similar to those of other Missionaries, his ultimate goal is to make all men behave in accord with Christian principles. Hence his response to such a symbol as Big Business is not so virulent; indeed, he may want to reduce class conflict and coercion, and promote more understanding and tolerance at the bargaining table ("All they that take the sword shall perish by the sword").[14]

In further contrast to other Missionary types, his approach to his job is religious, not secular, in the sense that it involves a belief in a supernatural God whose will he expresses by working in the labor movement. Before coming to labor, he had no significant non-church-connected political affiliation. In fact, God's official servants on earth may even have presided over, or at least prompted, his entry into the unions. One case describes this sequence of events: "I read Father Keller's book, *You Can Change the World.* That convinced me. I wrote to [union official] and said I want to work for a union. He gave the letter to X." After learning that his technical skills could be used by labor, he went to his boss, a management consultant, and told him that he'd seen the light, that he could better act out his religious convictions in the labor movement, and was therefore quitting. After long discussion and the offer of a sizeable salary increase, the boss called up Father Keller and persuaded the latter that the cut in salary necessitated by the shift to labor would threaten the integrity of the staff expert's large family. "I told the boss. 'Give me the phone and I'll convince him it'll be injurious to my conscience if I stay here.' We finally submitted it to [the Diocese] for decision on the moral issue. They decided in my favor." (406a-2.)

Preoccupied by moral problems, subscribing in large degree to an ethical absolutism, the Religious-Ethico Missionary is apt to view the political means used by union leaders as evil and corrupting. He is not a political infant—unaware of the universal dilemmas posed by the problem of ethics and politics—or he would not have been admitted to union headquarters in the first place; but he is

---

14. Several ex-experts who probably had a Religious-Ethico role orientation in their labor jobs were pacifists. Judgment of their role orientation, however, is based on scattered information and casual impression.

plagued far more by this problem (good ends vs. morally dubious means) than his colleagues.

There are only two cases of this type in my sample; both have since left. One became a church missionary abroad; the other went back to management consulting.

Professional Service Types

[He] . . . lives in a world which, by and large, is not asking, "Is Smith trying to get at the facts? Is he trying to be fair and constructive at the same time that he is unwilling to pull his punch?" but which asks, "Are you for us, or against us?"

—ROBERT S. LYND[15]

The Professional Service expert is oriented in his job role toward an outside colleague group; his primary job identification is with his profession. Whether he maintains a current participation in a concrete professional group or has merely internalized its values and subjected himself to its controls, the consequence in his work experience is the same. It is seen especially along these dimensions of analysis: job frustration and satisfactions, concept of ideal staff expert, view of company employment, colleague contacts, and research product.

His main job problems and frustrations can be interpreted in terms of a conflict between the requirements of the job (and/or the values of union officials), on the one hand; and a professional ethos—expressed in a desire to render competent, efficient, objective, technical service of which professional colleagues outside the union would approve—on the other. He complains about the uses to which data or professional skills are put: "I'm supposed to supply the data, but what the hell do I do if the data isn't there. . . . I spend half my time proving the X workers are being beat to death by the SOB corporations. The other half I spend proving that the X workers are the highest paid, best treated workers in the country." (301-1,5)[16] He complains about officer indifference to professional

---

15. *Knowledge for What: The Place of Social Science in American Culture* (Princeton: Princeton University Press, 1948), p. 10.

16. In his concept of the ideal expert, this type often points to the ability

standards or lack of respect for data or technique. An editor: "I
don't know if you know how newspapermen regard publicity press
agents. We regard them with tolerance, not respect. . . . It's a
helluva note that publicity should be valued more than putting out
a good newspaper, but it's a fact, unions don't know the value of a
good newspaperman. The publicity racket is what gets the pay-off."
(501-6.) An economist: "These . . . people don't want to discuss a
memorandum. They want yes and no. That's not our job but that's
what they want from us. . . . They don't know how to use technicians." (306a-3.) A lawyer: "We're not given the full facts; they
hold back. After you're in, they sometimes forget you're there. . . .
I've been used to government, where you'd have information from
both partisan parties . . . as well as your own investigation. I was
used to a well-rounded set of facts. Both the company and the
union attorney suffer." (915-2.) He thinks the officers cannot fairly
evaluate his work because they don't understand it: "There's a
lack of any real understanding . . . of the meaning of engineering
techniques. . . . Your supervisors don't know what the hell you're
up to. . . . So your reputation depends on chance events. Reports
from the field for instance. . . . There's little or no attention given
to the nature of the problem giving rise to the report." (454-1,2.)[17]
He is concerned about the loss of professional craft competence due
to job requirements: "I don't have time to keep up in the economics literature. It wouldn't help on the job, but I miss it, anyway. Intellectual stimulation and professional competence are
hard to keep on ice." (317-6.)

In contrast to all other types, the Professional Service expert
seldom complains about a lack of influence *per se.* He is in general
more disturbed when the officers do not fully utilize his professional skills and training: "The staff is not large enough to permit
original or creative work. . . ." (Questionnaire.) "There's a lack

to reconcile "professional integrity" or "objectivity" with the necessity of
advocating union policy. Some also say you have to be a person "interested
in the field [of professional specialization] rather than in making a lot of
money"—one clue to a professional ideology of altruistic service.

17. Along with this go occasional complaints of favoritism and strained
intra-staff relations: the officers don't give credit where due, other staff experts play politics and this violates his sense of staff-line propriety, etc. Of
eighteen cases who register such complaints, eleven are Professional Service
experts.

of facilities and of time to turn out the polished sort of job you'd like. . . . It often has to be superficial; it's hit and miss sometimes." (406-1.) "There's a constant conflict between the necessity of meeting the immediate situation vs. doing something constructive and long-range. . . ." (454-2.)

What the Professional Service expert seeks most is work that is "professionally gratifying." By this he means work that measures up to his own standards derived from past training and experience and the judgments of his professional colleagues. In contrast to Missionary types, the intrinsic nature of the work is very important to him. He is pleased when the union gives him freedom and leeway within his area of competence and makes good use of his professional advice. If he is a lawyer he gets special satisfaction "mapping out a line of litigation strategy," or, best of all, getting a decision from the Supreme Court. If he is an economist he takes pleasure doing a piece of more-than-routine research; or he is proud that management and neutral sources accept his facts as facts and accord his opinions respect. If he is an editor, it is quality journalism that counts: "Putting out the paper is most satisfying. . . . It's my own show. You know, you labor and labor and labor, baby comes out very small, but it's good. I think it's the best."

His central focus on the chance for full utilization of his professional skills and his desire to render efficient and competent service, tend to foster in him an instrumental view of his function.

Case 66: When I go to work for a union, I've got a job to do. I think it's too damn bad that there aren't more carpenters and fewer architects. And that's what my job is, I'm a carpenter. I'm supposed to be skilled at putting out a paper and writing a speech and getting out a radio broadcast. There are too damn many editors in the labor movement who don't know the first thing about editing, or newspaper work. If there's anything I respect, it's the good technician, the man who knows his job, does it well. We need more carpenters. . . . (501-13.)

Here again, his comments about his colleagues of different disposition are revealing.

Case 69: A lot of the problems he makes himself. The trouble is that the technician expects far more from his union than he expects from other employers. I believe you can't apply a double standard. These same people if they were personnel technicians for a company would recognize the facts of life. The company hires you only if they'd make more money with you around than they would without you. . . . The union has just as definite objectives as management. They're quite clear: to enlarge the membership, to collect dues, to expand the leadership's job security, to add to the prestige of leadership. . . . The technician who is perfectly willing to accept the profit motive for management in a system of private enterprise is unhappy, feels he's not doing his job if he can't be in the boss' office every Tuesday haranguing him with a lecture on race relations. . . . That does not mean I can't hold opinions. I have a right to my views on race relations or anything else. My views are well known to the officers. (610-1.)

The heavy accent on professional neutrality—the impartial performance of duty regardless of personal sentiment and opinion—is somewhat tempered by a concomitant dedication to professional objectivity and independence. (Be a pliant tool, yes; but don't let your desire to please the boss interfere with honest advice based on professional knowledge.) Discussing colleagues less oriented toward professional values, a Professional Service expert says:

SE: They're sloppy in their use of data. They don't give a damn. They're philosophical relativists with no real belief in truth or in scientific objectivity; or at least they think the search for truth is too difficult, so they abandon it and excuse themselves from it by saying, "Who's interested in the truth, anyway—management?" Basically, it's because they have a Marxist or a social reform attitude. Everything becomes a matter of partisan advantage. . . . All they want to do is build up the prejudices of the leader.
HLW: It sounds to me like you ought to be in a university, not a union.
SE: I sometimes wish I'd gone into university teaching. . . . [Getting back to "objectivity."] It's like honesty in general—there are degrees. We all break the law, but does that mean we have to be habitual criminals? A kid may break a window once in a while, but should he become a juvenile delinquent? (335-6; 335a-3.)

Consistent with his acceptance of the norms of professional neutrality and objectivity is a respect for specialized professional competence. Standards of job proficiency, for example, are prominent in his concept of the ideal expert—and the qualifications he names are sometimes stringent, indeed. One case named graduate degrees in three fields as a partial requirement for his job. Other cases show a general concern with raising the level of competence of their labor colleagues:

For all these years I have insisted on high-caliber technical competence among the "technicians" and a high regard for facts among all. (The latter has paid off, incidentally, since employers in our industry have publicly affirmed they will accept facts that I submit, however much they may disagree with my conclusions.) The lack of appreciation for quality performance in labor generally has also been reflected in the kind of work many have performed. I have strenuously insisted, argued, urged and implored all to make themselves most qualified. (D3-3.)

Consistent with this emphasis on competence is the fact that this type has more formal education than all others.[18]

The Professional Service expert, in contrast to Missionary types, is less concerned about labor movement loyalties (e.g., in his concept of the ideal expert), though he often shows some ambivalence on the question about taking a company job. (A qualified "yes" is the typical answer: "It would require some soul-searching, but would be very tempting. . . ." "Yes, if it were an established union employer. . . .") His reservations about company employment are sometimes rooted in the belief that it would be a violation of professional ethics if he moved directly from the union to the opposing party, in effect selling information to be used against the union. Thus, one case specified that he would be quite willing to take a company job "if I took another job in between the union job and the company job first"—much as the widow who tells the hasty suitor she'd be quite willing to remarry, but, in deference to her dead husband, a respectable time lapse must first smooth the way!

Beyond these minor reservations the Professional faces few self-imposed limits on his job opportunities. Just as the Missionary would tend to move to those places where his private political goals can best be accommodated, so the Professional Service expert would tend to move to those places where his professional skills can best be utilized. This may mean that the former is locked up in the labor movement. But it implies that the latter has considerable job space to move around in.[19] We see this not only in his view of

---

18. Median years of education around seventeen. More than two-thirds of the Professionals have done graduate work. The proportion for other types: Missionaries, fewer than one-half; Careerists, about one-third; Politicos, one-quarter. Of the eighteen cases who have a Ph.D. or more (out of a total of 126 cases), thirteen are Professional Service types.

19. That there is some relationship between self-imposed limits in job choice and the job offers received is suggested in these facts: the Missionaries report proportionately fewer job offers from industry-business and govern-

company employment and the way he talks about prospects in other fields, but also in scattered information on recent job shifts of specific cases. There are, for instance, the Industry Refugees: they came to the unions in part because they anticipated more freedom of operation and fuller use of skills. The move may have meant a large cut in salary. In some occupational groups with especially high transferability of skills (e.g., experts in engineering, pensions, insurance) there are instances where a man shuttles back and forth between company and union jobs in search for the right work situation. Similarly, some data on ex-experts and information about experts who quit since field work was done suggest that our Professional Service type includes the Professional Sojourner: a technician who comes to Labor briefly to broaden his professional experience and then moves back (or on) to teaching, research, or private consulting. It is noteworthy in this connection that one of the job satisfactions the incumbent Professional Service experts mention is the chance to enhance their professional skills.

I have said that the Professional Service expert has a primary job identification with his profession and is oriented towards an outside colleague group. What exactly is the character of this group? What are the ways in which his identification with it is sustained in a union setting?

The great professional association which ideally acts as guardian of a body of esoteric knowledge and technique, administers professional training, controls entry to the occupation, sets up standards of work performance, disciplines the members, fosters growth of technique and information-sharing, promotes a professional ideology of "service" and idealizes its social responsibilities—this, where it exists, is ultimately the reference group for our Professional Serv-

---

ment than any of the other three types. (*Government:* Missionary, 4/29; Professional, 18/53; Careerist, 14/32; Politico, 3/12. *Industry-Business:* Missionary, 6/29; Professional, 16/53; Careerist, 14/32; Politico, 5/12.) The Professional Service type, as one might expect, gets proportionately more job chances in the *Education* field than the other types: Missionary, 3/29; Professional, 8/53; Careerist, 1/32; Politico, none. He also comes out on top on offers from commercial publications. He gets many offers from government and from private consulting firms. About one-fourth of all cases report no job offers, but there are no marked concentrations of the "no offers" response by main role orientation types (though proportionately fewer of the Professionals, 12/53, and more of the Missionaries, 9/29, report no job offers).

ice expert. Of course the state or county bar association, the city press club and the American Economics Association exercise vastly different degrees of control over their members and fellow-travelers. Moreover, the controls the main professional associations *do* exercise are sometimes mediated by subgroupings within the occupation, made up of those who work on behalf of a set of special interests within the larger society. Thus we see the labor federations holding periodic press and public relations conferences, meetings and symposia of labor lawyers and the like. Meetings of advisory boards called by government labor agencies similarly act as information clearing-houses for union economists and researchers. The Inter-Union Institute, a co-operative association of labor staff intellectuals, which from 1945 to 1952 published *Labor and Nation,* has for more than a decade acted as a cross-occupational channel of communication.

"These people," observes a government official, "have developed a professional attitude among themselves. They value the esteem of their colleagues in the labor movement—you can see that at these meetings." (917.) This apparent separation of the labor professionals from the larger professional world is deceptive, for the men most active in the organization and control of these labor grouplets are also active in the mainstream of professional life. These men, attuned to the standards of the profession, act as norm-suppliers for the labor professionals with less first-hand contact. A union attorney lists several leading labor lawyers (both house counsel and fee counsel) whose main satisfactions, he thinks, come from recognition in the profession and yet whose contacts within the labor movement are broad and solid. He contrasts them with the "mouthpiece—a lawyer with no independence, who just does what he's told and doesn't even offer his opinion . . . like 'Y.' . . . Now 'X' [house counsel] won't do that. . . . When it comes to having a meeting of the American Arbitration Association . . . or the ––– Bar Association and they want a labor representative, who do they appoint? X, not Y." (233-2.)

Whatever the channels, the Professional Service expert typically has high exposure not only to labor professionals in his specialty outside his own union, but also to nonlabor professionals. Sometimes he gets his professional cues from academicians:

We take every periodical in the field. . . . I write and visit and see innumerable people in the field of —— particularly. . . . I get a call from [university professor] every week or two. I teach his class every once in a while. I taught at ten universities this year. I make it a point to maintain broad contacts with experts in this field. . . . (401-5.)

Sometimes his colleague group includes a management component:

We have as much stature in management circles as within the union. . . . There's some degree of fraternity among engineers—regardless of affiliation, union or management. The newer group of engineers coming in have a different view—they mean to get along with the union. . . . . This is also one of the sources of conflict. On the one hand, the professional point of view and an affinity for other engineers vs. the basic conflicts that may be there. I may have that conflict more than others. Having worked in his capacity I understand his problems. My sympathy may make me less effective for the union, maybe more; I don't know. (454-3.)

Few of the Professional Service experts have frequent off-the-job contacts with own-union staff and line officials. They often explicitly cite recognition from or a chance to contact outside professionals as a major job satisfaction. Asked about his off-the-job social life, one said:

I don't see any of them [people in his own union] except X, or the guys in the car pool, or an occasional poker game. [Describes friends in labor and government.] . . . I try not to make it so—that type of inbreeding is harmful to your intellectual development. One of the finest qualities in a person is curiosity. . . . I try to keep up professional contacts. . . . I'm active in the [learned society. Enthusiastically decribes participation.] . . . My biggest kick comes from my own self-esteem. Second: recognition from my peers—professionals in universities. . . . Third, and last of all: recognition from the officers. (335a-2.)

A final clue to his professional identification—and another way he sustains it—is in his willingness to subject his work and his opinions to academic criticism. At least two in five of our Professional Service experts can claim, since working for a union, some research product aimed at a serious professional audience. A few cases show a truly prodigious extra-curricular research effort, despite the obviously heavy demands of their union jobs. (One person, over a decade of union employment turned out several books, parts of books and monographs, and literally scores of articles, which have contributed to a wide reputation among academic specialists in his field.)

What of the origins and background of the Professional Service type and the patterns of change in his role orientation? Of twenty-two cases who entered as Professional Service experts, twenty-one remain so (one became a Politico). Thus, this type shows marked stability. Even more striking is the fact that the Professional Service orientation seems to be the main destination of other types. Of the sixty-four cases who entered as Missionaries, twenty-three have become Professionals; of the thirty-five who entered as Careerists, six have become Professionals.

In occupational origin, the Professional Service expert typically enters from a New Deal or World War II government labor agency (of twenty-two known "career theme" cases, eleven had this background just prior to entry; a few came from college campuses, a few from other outside professional occupations). Limited data suggest a concentration of social origin among Jewish business, professional and white-collar families.[20]

My sample of 126 has fifty-three cases whose present role orientation can best be called Professional Service. This main type may show some interest in social mobility via a union career, but this is not dominant as in the case of the Careerist. He may also show some satisfaction in the "excitement of a game of chance," but the political process is not his major preoccupation as in the case of the Union Politico. His professional identification, the content of which is specified above, is what distinguishes him from other types.

Nevertheless, this category obscures some important differences of degree and kind among the fifty-three cases grouped in it. A further breakdown shows that while all cases fit the general type delineated above, twenty-two of them can best be called "Program Professionals," thirty-one "Technician Professionals." A brief description of these subtypes will clarify the distinction.

---

20. While fewer than half of all known cases, 50/105, had business, professional, or white-collar fathers, eleven of the fifteen Professional Service entries whose fathers' occupations I know had this family background. As for religious background: while about one-third of all known career theme cases were of Jewish origin (42/121), almost two-thirds of those who entered as Professionals (13/21) had this background; while about two-fifths of all present cases (45/126) are of Jewish origin, today about half (25/53) of the present Professional Service experts are Jews.

The Program Professional.—The Program Professional combines his high professional identification and his desire for full utilization of his professional skills with an interest in heavy program impact within his area of specialization. Like the Missionary, he tends to see the union as the vehicle for the promotion of some strongly held ideas. Like the Missionary and in contrast to the Technician Professional, he is less preoccupied with the intrinsic nature of the work. Like the Missionary, he may even point to a liberalizing policy influence on nonbargaining issues as a source of job satisfaction. But the program development he has in mind does not involve any vision of a transformed unionism in a new social order. In fact, this type can best be distinguished by the neat coincidence of his private goals with current organizational goals. One Program Professional sorts himself out from the Missionaries in these terms:

> You can and must separate "policy-making" from the job of the adviser. . . . I'm not trying to infiltrate. My thinking is completely different from these intellectuals who come into the labor movement and use the union as a setting to push an ideology. They screw up the works for themselves *and* the union if they do this. If you want to fight the class struggle you've got this last problem [how hard to push]. If you've got something to contribute that the union needs, then it's no problem. [The top officers] have to have technicians who give them the content for a program [in collective bargaining] and that's my job. I found out exactly where they stood [on policy in my area of competence] before I took the job. There is no disagreement on program objectives. To implement that program—their program—is my job. (401, Questionnaire.)

On the frustration side, too, the meaning of "program" is quite narrow. He typically feels the job is too limited because the officers resist (1) program goals which are close to or the same as official union goals, or (2) new means of achieving old trade-union goals. These goals and methods, he feels, are within his sphere of professional competence; his knowledge of the field indicates they are feasible and desirable. "The job is more limited than I thought it would be," says one Professional. ". . . It's hard . . . to sell the policy of the International itself! . . . Basically the problem is selling what's sounder to the officers and negotiators [in my field]." (224-1,2.)

Phrases like "selling what's sounder," "getting them to recognize a solid approach to their problems instead of a quick, immediate political gain" (327), etc., are typical and indicate the modesty of his aspirations for program impact. If he is an insurance expert, he wants the union negotiators to understand the soundness of a service approach to medical care rather than a cash indemnity approach. If he's a publicity specialist, he wants the union to exploit its public relations opportunities more fully; he may feel he is "helping to even up the propaganda battle." (502-8.) If he is a legal advisor, he wants the union to avoid "blundering cases" that weaken its position in the long-run effort to reshape the framework of labor law through legislation, precedent, and public opinion; or he wants the union to participate more fully in the defense of our threatened civil liberties.

His job satisfactions are much the same as other professionals', plus the element of policy impact within his area: "furnishing content for a program." This is often put in the context of a comparison with previous jobs:

My main satisfaction is working in [the field of specialization] and the feeling that this is the one place in the country where most is being done. Once it was Washington, now it's the union. . . . From the time I went to school I thought of work in [professional field] and labor. Here I can combine both. (224-3,1.)

The occupational origins, job-getting methods and salary transition of these Program Professionals throw further light on their motivations. Of the twelve cases who entered with this role orientation, seven (in eleven whose occupational histories I know) came directly from New Deal agencies in the federal government. Nine in twelve made their labor contacts through (or as) government or company functionaries dealing with (usually serving) labor. While only one of the Technician Professionals took a cut in salary to come, several of the Program Professionals did so.

Two cases will illustrate the nature of the Program Professional's career theme. Both took a salary cut to come to the unions, one from a government job, the other from a company. Both are highly trained technicians with high professional identification. Both operate within relatively narrow fields of specialization.

Case 55: It was a cold, calculating move. I made the decision to spend some time in the labor movement—years ago. I wanted to see what kind of a program could be promoted. So my last two years in government, I spent much time exploring the labor-management situation. My major interest is in [one aspect of the field of specialization]. . . . When we first talked about the job . . . I explored [my program ideas] with the officers. I wanted to be sure I knew what I was getting into. (401-5.)

Case 51: There's usually a resentment on the part of the workers to whatever piece rates ₁you set. The initial reaction is always bad. . . . These are the same problems of the management engineer everywhere: there's a psychological conflict between possible and historical outcome of engineering techniques and the social attitude of the practitioner. That's one reason I left industry: because I couldn't express myself as an engineer. If you worry about ten people you're putting out of work, you can't do your job. You wonder about the social effect of your work. Can get philosophical about it and say in the long run these workers get absorbed, but it's hard when you see the ten people out on the street. At least in the union I can think about that problem and try to cope with it. [Note the merging of Professional and Program interests: in context and throughout the interview "express myself as an engineer" has both connotations.] (454-2,3.)

The job moves of these Program Professionals are perhaps part of a larger drama acted out by strategy-oriented professionals in many corners of the bureaucratic machinery of modern society. Government technicians, who in New Deal days moved from agency to agency to follow the program to which both their skills and social philosophies were bound, may more recently (during the period 1948-53) be following these programs into social agencies, educational institutions, civic organizations, foundations, etc., as well as the labor movement.[21]

---

21. That the Program Professional in unions has his counterpart in government is suggested by Dimock and Hyde, who observe of government bureaucrats: "The elements of prestige, of appeal to service and patriotism, and of belonging to an agency that is 'doing things' (or, at least, has been for the past decade), serve in large part to counteract the handicaps of lower salaries and shorter tenure for the top men." Marshall E. Dimock and H. K. Hyde, *Bureaucracy and Trusteeship in Large Corporations* (Washington, D. C.: U.S. Government Printing Office, 1940), p. 64. See also Stephen Bailey's account of the work of Congressional staff experts involved in the passage of the Employment Act of 1946: ". . . the staff became the central mechanism for mobilizing widely dispersed intellectual resources and a coalition of pressures, public and private, behind the legislation." Bailey adds, however, that "the imaginative, strategy-oriented, staff expert is rare at all levels of government." *Congress Makes a Law* (New York: Columbia

The Program Professional's concern with the direction of policy within his area does not violate the norms of professional neutrality and objectivity (which all the Professional Service experts embrace in some degree). When the congruence of his program ideas and the union's policies becomes significantly less, he will leave— just as he left government or the company in the past. Meanwhile, he shares the Technician Professional's desire to render competent, efficient professional services, which occasions some difficulty. The role orientation of this type involves a constant balancing off of commitment to program vs. commitment to quality work, with first one coming out on top and then the other.

Case 43: This job turned out much better than I expected. . . . I have a lot more freedom and discretion than I'd get anywhere else. . . . It's a job where you could get ulcers. But in [government agency] I worked for a guy—a good lawyer, a real technician. He felt it's a lousy business being a lawyer—you're a mechanism. You can have the satisfaction only of being a good craftsman. There we labored over litigation —everything that had to go out had to be a fine jewel. A year before I even got a letter out I had to submit everything to the boss and go over it in fine detail. It was exacting training. Here it's exactly the reverse. There's not time to do a craftsman-like job at all. You go into a hearing with ten minutes preparation. But if you're smart you can do it and come out about as well as the craftsman. . . . The amount of stuff we're expected to turn out is fabulous. I still take longer than most labor lawyers to work up a brief—my government experience slows me down. (226-3.)

Case 50: If you want to do studies this is not the place to come. In government—you're working in a Research Department. You have more time; but in an *operating* department of government when you spot a research problem it has to be solved that afternoon. That's the way it is here only worse. It's similar to an operating department in wartime. Like any operating agency it's not too adequately staffed. As far as having a chance to do studies it wouldn't be a problem for a person who wants to be part of an action movement. It *would* be a problem for a person who wanted to do more careful research. I put myself in that category. I do not intend to stay here forever, but it is extremely interesting and helpful. My longer-term research later will be helped in having watched

University Press, 1950), p. 78. There is much that is tragic in the exodus from government of thousands of intellectuals, trained in the social sciences and humanities, after the Eisenhower victory of 1952—both in the disruption of individual life plans and career expectations and in the loss to our society of valuable social skills. On this point, see Daniel Bell, "Hard Times for the Intellectuals," *New Republic,* 129 (August 17, 1953), 8-10.

practical operating decisions. . . . In other words, if you're careful and
thorough and occasionally like to stop and get a sabbatical to evaluate
—then stay away from this job. . . . It's very hectic—phenomenal hours
of work and exhausting; but extremely interesting. You see a side of
the . . . problem you can't see from a Research person's point of van-
tage. You feel you're useful also. The program itself is [benefiting]
people in and out of the union. It can improve services the country
over. It's a tremendous impact that the whole program has—a remarkable opportunity for service. I know this sounds YMCA'ish. . . . [He
adds, when asked about company jobs, "It would depend. I can't imagine
a company doing this kind of work. Now a foundation job, that might
be different. . . . I could do better work, evaluate both sides, analyze
where the program is headed. I have no objection to working for industry if the program is sincerely geared for useful service. . . . But
industry is not interested in these problems."] (410.)

While all types of staff experts complain of the pressure of
time and work, it is significant that almost every one of the Program Professionals (19/22) cites this as a source of job frustration.
Why this type should feel the pressure most constantly and acutely
may be explained by his dual loyalty to program and profession:
he feels the urge to move ahead on his particular program and
lacks staff and time to do so, and yet he also feels the necessity of
doing careful, professionally respectable work. In contrast, the
Technician Professional lacks the urgency of a program (only half,
16/31, complain of this work pressure). In the absence of any
serious commitment to professional norms, the Missionary can slop
through to achieve his larger political mission (10/29); the Careerist (9/32) or Politico (3/12) can do the same to achieve organizational goals and work out their personal strivings.

One final difference of degree between Program Professional
and Technician Professional—again reflecting the former's commitment to a program and the happy coincidence between that program and union action—is the difference in the degree of hostility
to management. A few (six) of the Program Professionals name
Big Business as a target of their work; none of the Technician Professionals invoke that symbol. The typical response of the Professional Service expert to the prospect of taking a company job
is a qualified yes. But contrast the two subtypes: not one of the
Program Professionals gave an unhesitating, "Yes, I'd take a
company job," while five of the Technician Professionals gave an

unqualified yes.[22] Moreover, the qualifications the ambivalent TP's name tend to be less severe, their hesitations less marked than those of the Program Professionals.

The Technician Professional.—Like the Outsider Careerist and in some contrast to the Program Professional, he is solidly means-centered when he describes his work. He exhibits a preoccupation with technical detail, technique, "pitch"; he does not speak in terms of values or goals. He never cites a liberalizing impact on nonbargaining issues as a source of job satisfaction. He often makes an unelicited denial of any mission or private programs.

An exaggerated humility cross-cuts all our role-orientation types and probably reflects typical patterns of union administration and a basic officer-expert relationship. The Technician Professional, however, tends to accent this more than other types. Prominent in his concept of the ideal expert, for instance, is the notion of a man who knows his place, stays in it, has humility, and has no power strivings or at least gives the impression that he has none.[23]

No Technician Professional rejects without qualification the idea of using his skills and knowledge in a company setting. None has a preoccupation with any enemy targets inside or outside the union.

The Technician Professional at the time of entry had a central focus on the chance for full use of his skills within his area of competence, though he typically also received a salary increase when he made the move.[24] In his initial discussion of the job with

---

22. There are only ten cases in the whole sample who say without qualification that they would take a company job. Five are TP's, four are Outsider Careerists, one is a Rank-and-File Careerist.

23. Distribution of such responses: Party Missionary, 2/8; Leg.-Lib. Miss., 5/19; Tech. Prof., 16/31; Pgm. Prof., 6/22; Outsider Careerist, 2/18; Rank-and-File Careerist, 1/14; Politico, 4/12. In succeeding footnotes the distribution of responses mentioned in the text among the seven role-orientation types is indicated by fractions (denominator, the number of cases classified in the type; numerator, the number of cases of that type giving the coded response). The types will be abbreviated.

24. While about two-fifths (37/98) of all career theme cases whose salary transition is known got an increase, five in seven of the Technician Professionals and about half (15/31) of the Careerists report an increase. Income and status mobility via the union, however, was not the TP's primary motivation; it was overshadowed by a professional orientation. In time, however, as his union career develops and his salary rises, he may find it increasingly difficult to leave for a greater fulfillment of professional aspirations, however strongly these may be held. Consider this statement by a

his prospective boss he may have made explicit his desire to preserve a professional-client relationship. The self-changing nature of the expert's role may in time pull him into a wider range of decisions (see Chapter XI), but this type tends to resist the process or, at minimum, rationalize it by an especially strong adherence to the staff-line myth.

Ten cases entered as Technician Professionals; all ten have maintained this type of role orientation. Thus, this is the most stable type. (Of the twelve who entered as Program Professionals, eight remained so, three became TP's, one a Politico.)

Aside from these differences from the Program Professional, the Technician Professional shares all the marks of professional identification delineated in the general treatment of the Professional Service expert above—which distinguish him clearly from the Careerist. In general, what sorts him out from the Program Professional are his stronger adherence to a means-centered professional neutrality and the absence of major interest in program impact.

Careerist Types

It was a promotion for me, so I went into it full-time. I was a great success in ———. I got a build-up in my own career there. I traveled around the State. The new issues brought on by the surge of the war— the conferences and all—that meant my contacts were broader. I made a lot of contacts with people—CIO and AFL—who seemed to be on their way up. (524-5.)

—Interview with Case 107.

The Careerist is highly identified with the hierarchy of his

Technician Professional: "I wanted to get into this job to see what it was like. If you want to see how labor worked there's no substitute for it. . . . Historically in Germany you could go into teaching, leave, get mature experience and then come back to teach. . . . I wanted to see what makes labor tick. I wanted to get in there and see first-hand. I would have liked to go back to teaching, but they offered me a little less than my secretary is paid [in his union], $4200. People who have important places in the large universities are well off; but those are few; most of the people in the field of college teaching are plodders. . . . I love teaching but I got to eat. I like to think that in my lifetime that universities looking for people in the labor relations field, they'll look for (a) academic training plus (b) applied training. I hope the relative standing of labor relations will go up in the academic curriculum. Then I'll go back." (338-3.)

union and is oriented towards a career within it. He has no ideological motivation, no dilemma-producing nonorganizational goals, and very little if any professional identification. His job satisfactions center around the chance for social mobility via the union career; his job frustrations, if he has any, stem from anything that stands in the way of that career. He is a man with few conflicts in loyalty, and tends to feel that the union has treated him well.

The dominance of middle-class mobility strivings in his role orientation is reflected both in his present appraisal of his job and the circumstances surrounding his entry. He expresses his chief job satisfactions in terms of any or all of the following: (1) Money —the job pays well and thus permits a good life, time with the family, etc. (2) Opportunity for promotion—the job has brought increasing responsibilities, broader experience; it may even be a means for a better job outside the union. (3) Security—in the form of retirement benefits, a steady salary, etc. When he reports these job satisfactions, it is often in the context of a description of thwarted mobility strivings on previous jobs.

SE: Myself—I came from [a business firm]. . . . I was fed up with the company. I felt the Labor Movement was something worthwhile, has real promise. . . . I'd been with [business firm] for —— years.
HLW: How do the two jobs compare—the company and the union?
SE: Oh, there's no comparison between them. Working conditions are much better here—and salaries are *extremely* better. There's greater personal understanding. . . . Working for a large corporation you're just another hand; in a labor union most of the people you meet have a personal interest in you and your work. As time goes on I've got the feeling it's done a lot for me. Here you have opportunities you wouldn't have in a company. A man can come out of the shop and up through the union. How often would a man out of the shop be picked up to an executive position—unless he has a pull? In a union if you have ambition and knowledge you can get ahead. . . . In a company, junior executives are given titles of assistant to the assistant to the assistant—but only a few cents in salary increase. Here ability and ambition are recognized. . . . Not only that, you'd be surprised how many companies won't hire a man if he's of the wrong religion. [The union, in contrast, he adds, does not discriminate.] (N342.)

Much of the Careerist's job satisfaction stems from the process of prestige-borrowing or -lending. His union job means a chance to bask in the reflected glory of great men. Or he enjoys making the union respectable in the public eye—looking after status for the union and hence for himself as an employee of the union. The first satisfaction is especially apparent in this case:

Case 107: It is a pleasure to travel with [top officer]. When he steps into a room you know you're with an important guy. When he rides on a train, you'd think you were with the President of the Company or something. He's always treated with great deference. . . . I'm not one of these business-hating crusaders. I like to fraternize with businessmen. I'm really fond of some of them. There's nothing wrong with a man because he's with business. They just work for something big and I work for something big, too. (524-1,5.)

As this suggests, "career" for this type (in contrast to the Professional Service expert) typically has a broad, community-at-large focus. The coercive comparisons of income and prestige are made with reference to the dominant respectable groups in the community—of which a professional colleague group, if included, is only one, a relatively minor one. If he has any professional identification—and this is rare—its main significance is in terms of the central focus on income-prestige mobility. Case 107, for instance, adds that he gets along very well with certain industry people— but not just his counterparts among company staff experts. His social life does include participation in a profession-connected social club:

A certain number [of the people who run this club] look down their noses at you because you work for a union. With some I am a sort of minor celebrity, though. I've had a break on national publicity a few times. . . . That helps you in the profession. (524-6.)

But he goes on to explain that it's the same with other high status groups in the community: "When I go to a doctor, he's interested in what the organization is and my job. Labor is getting pretty respectable and it's only right it should." He adds that it's a source of satisfaction to him that when he has come in contact with the rank and file in his union, he's found little difference between his "economic level" and theirs. "These workers are home-owners who send their kids to college." (524-6.)

The broad, respectable community reference comes out again

in the job frustrations this type cites. Many complain of a loss of community prestige because of the labor tie. Case 110, for instance, who moved to a new upper-middle-class suburb as his union career developed, is eager to make the union acceptable: "I don't want my kids growing up in an atmosphere that can label a man a radical or a racketeer just because he works for a union." (500-2.) Other complaints, where they do not cross-cut all our role-orientation types, center again on the income-prestige issue: the salary is insufficient, promotion chances are limited, etc.

Confirming this interview picture of mobility striving are three correlates of the Careerist orientation: the "objective" indices of social origin, religion, and associational memberships. The men who entered as Careerists have the largest proportion of wage-worker fathers; they are typically upwardly mobile in terms of inter-generational comparison.[25] Answers to a question on religion can also be taken as a clue to aspirations for community status. Not one of those who entered as Careerists answers "None" on religion; all but one (who says he's an inactive Protestant) mark some religion.[26] Perhaps more significant is the great number of "respectable" nonprofessional affiliations the Careerist group lists: churches, fraternal orders, alumni associations, the American Legion, the YMCA, the Boy Scouts, even businessmen's clubs, country clubs, the Republican Party, etc.[27]

---

25. While almost 46 per cent (48/105) of all known career theme cases came from wage worker (skilled, semi-skilled and unskilled labor) families, more than 63 per cent of the Careerists whose fathers' occupations are known had this background (19/30).

26. Of twenty-five "None's," twenty-two are past Missionaries. Eight are present Missionaries, sixteen are present Professional Service types, one is a Politico. The "no religion" answers are thus concentrated among past and present Missionaries and present Professionals who entered as Missionaries —confirmation, perhaps, of the thoroughgoing secularism of Party and Legislative-Liberal types. The twenty Catholics are concentrated in the Careerist group, both past and present. Present distribution: Missionary, 2/29; Professional, 6/52; Careerist, 10/31; Politico, 2/10. Past distribution (religion by career theme): Missionary, 3/62; Professional, 3/21; Careerist, 14/34; Politico, none. This Catholic concentration is probably a reflection of the lower social origins of the Careerists.

27. As suggested in Chapter III, these affiliations are often line-of-duty public relations functions of the union staff expert. Thus many experts of all types score in the "respectable nonprofessional" affiliation column. However, there is a noteworthy concentration of Careerists in this category: Eighteen

Though he may see his job in terms of its effect on his income and his income in terms of its uses in raising his community prestige, the Careerist, in contrast to the Missionary or Professional, is oriented inward in his work role—he tends to have a strong identification with the incumbent leadership of his particular union. When he describes his work, he shows no interest in policy impact in the nonbargaining, nonadministrative areas. When asked about his job problems, he reports few difficulties. Several Careerists—even after considerable probing—articulate no job frustrations at all, either because they have none or because they do not want the boss pictured in a bad light (this in itself may reflect their identification with the union hierarchy).[28]

Consistent with this inward orientation is his pattern of colleague contact. Like the Party Missionary, but for different reasons, he is typically isolated from other staff experts in the labor movement, and has little contact with outside professionals. As might be expected, he has no research product. He attaches little importance to such contacts and activities. How could they help in his career within the Gadgetworkers Union? On the other hand, he typically cultivates the off-the-job own-union staff and line contacts necessary to boost his promotion chances and security within his union.[29]

The Careerist's union identification may not imply hostility to the values of the business community (e.g., enemy targets in his work are very minor or nonexistent, and many cases describe

---

of the twenty-seven whose affiliations are known as compared with: Missionary, 11/28; Politico, 3/11; or Professional, 10/50. Moreover, the specific associations of the Careerists within this category seem to be more middle-class community-oriented—e.g., the Lions, the Masons, the Podunk Sportsmen's Association or Businessmen's Club rather than Phi Beta Kappa, or a national public affairs committee.

28. Distribution of cases who cite no job frustrations: Missionary, 2/27; Professional, 1/53; Careerist, 7/32; Politico, none. The problems the other Careerists cite either cross-cut all types or are focused on the question of getting ahead. The job frustrations of the Careerists also seem to be phrased in a less pointed, this-really-gets-in-my-hair style.

29. For the Missionary such own-union off-the-job contact has its meaning in the promotion of the mission; for the Politico in the preoccupation with the political process. Distribution of High own-union contact: Missionary 12/27; Professional, 13/53; Careerist, 15/32; Politico, 10/12 (other two unknown). Of the fifteen cases who score Low own-union contact, all but two Outside Careerists are Professionals or Missionaries.

fraternization with management). If he has a positive view of straight trade-union goals it is coupled with a feeling that what helps the union helps his career, and helps the community, including the business segment of the community. It is suggestive that proportionately more Careerists report job offers from business-industry (14/32), as well as government (14/32), than any other main type. On the assumption that job offers are in part a product of cultivation—are themselves a consequence of a man's role orientation—this suggests a willingness to contemplate eventual company employment with some favor, given superior career possibilities. Analysis of other dimensions of his role orientation—the respectable community-at-large focus of his mobility strivings, his associational memberships, etc.—would also point to this conclusion.

Of the thirty-five cases who entered as Careerists, twenty-eight remain so; six became Technician Professionals, one a Politico. Of the 126 cases typed by present role orientation, thirty-two are Careerists. All thirty-two fit the above delineation of Careerist, but important differences in the routes by which they have moved up suggest a subdivision which puts the label "Outsider Careerist" on eighteen of them, Rank-and-File Careerist (or "Porkchopper") on fourteen of them. A brief account of the consequences and correlates of their different occupational origins follows.

The Rank-and-File Careerist.—This type got his start as a rank-and-file worker and union activist. Like the Party Missionary, he typically came to the attention of union officials through (1) general activity as a functionary in a local union; (2) demonstrating loyalty to such officials in the early struggles of the union; (3) demonstrating special "technical" skills in union work (e.g., editor of local paper, member of job evaluation committee or compensation committee, etc.).[30] His transition to the staff expert job was typically accompanied by a (sometimes large) increase in annual salary and by an effort at self-improvement through reading, night school, correspondence school, or apprenticeship to incumbent experts.[31] By 1951 the Rank-and-File Careerist group was making a

---

30. Staff expert appointments in two cases, however, were awarded as sinecures for length of service in union staff or line.

31. Nine of the thirteen cases who entered as Rank-and-File Careerists and whose salary transition is known got a salary increase out of the move;

median salary of $7,000—just under the overall median of $7,500, much under the $9,500 of the Outsider Careerist, but much more as a rule than they had made as wage workers. The Rank-and-File Careerist, while he feels he got a good break in moving up to the staff job, may find the current disparity between his salary and the outsiders' annoying: "When a professional [a staff expert hired from outside] goes in to the President and asks for a raise," one complains, "he doesn't give him any song and dance about loyalty to the organization, but when I go in I get, 'After all, it's your organization as well as mine.' He can't tell the outsider that. It's either yes or no." (339.)

Another consequence of his occupational origin—and confirmation of his union identification—is the high valuation he puts on "practical experience." In his concept of the Ideal Expert the Porkchopper stresses (1) knowledge of the craft, trade or industry gained through actual working experience and/or (2) practical experience as a rank-and-file member or leader in a local union.[32] One Professional Service expert comments, "These 'experts' who've worked their way up from the rank and file are very proud of their knowledge and will not hesitate to tell you about it." (G 309a-2.) Such comments as well as first-hand observation suggest that this type is most likely to exaggerate what is an occupational characteristic of all experts—the anxious effort to preserve the mysteries of the trade.

Having come from the ranks, the Rank-and-File Careerist may still retain in his vocabulary the phrases of dedication to service for the common man: "I like the feeling I'm helping someone else who hasn't had the chance I've had." (612.) "I have a warm feeling towards the working class of people." (301-9.) The reference, however, is to an entity he is glad to move away from. Scratch the surface a bit and you get an upward salary transition, a steady

---

only two took a cut. The Rank-and-File Careerist is like the Technician Professional in this respect.

32. This is in part a reflection of the "Practical Experience" Myth discussed below, and cross-cuts all types. But it is especially prominent among Porkchoppers. The distribution of such responses: Missionary, 5/27; Prof., 10/53; Outside Careerist, 3/18; Rank-and-File Careerist, 12/14; Politico, 6/12.

career climb, plus comments like the following (from the man with the "warm feeling"):

You couldn't get a better job as far as liking the work goes. As far as union beliefs, I believe unions are cold, hard, business propositions. Still, underlying it, I believe that they do good. I got no religious tendencies but . . . I want to contribute my part toward evening the struggle up. . . . Also, I'll be frank. I don't know where I could get a salary like this. I'm making a lot more than I'd be making in the plant. I'm for sale in that respect. If someone offers me twice as much as what I'm getting I'll tell you I'd take it. . . . [Describes the previous company offer. They didn't meet his figure, and also he felt ambivalent about it, insisted on a free hand in labor relations, etc. Asked how he'd feel about it now, he said:] The decision would be rather difficult. My attitude would depend on the way I'm being treated by the Gadget-workers Union. As it is right now, no. I'm getting good treatment. The President never asks you to play politics . . . I don't have to be a ward-heeler within the union. If there were a shake-up, then I might have an attitude of the heck with them. . . . (301-9,10.)

Occasionally this type shows a budding professional orientation, though this rarely blossoms forth full-blown. The effort at self-improvement may lead him to an exposure to academe. His "technical" job exerts pressure for the development of specialized skills, and his association with more highly trained experts in his union may nurture professional aspirations or pretentions. At the same time, the Rank-and-File Careerist wants to enjoy the fruits of a union career—money, good suburban residence, etc.; he may sharply separate work and nonwork spheres ("I'd like to study at X University. . . . But when I get through here at night . . . I want to spend some time with the family").

His occupational history, his relatively uncomplicated outlook and career aspirations, probably put the Rank-and-File Careerist closer than any of my role-orientation types to the thousands of full-time functionaries in the labor movement who carry such titles as Organizer, or International Rep. The label these men often apply to one another, "Porkchopper"—Porkchops symbolizing food on the table—captures one important motivational pattern among them.

The Outsider Careerist.—This type contrasts sharply with the

Porkchopper in occupational origin, salary transition, and present salary level.

The men who entered as Outsider Careerists typically came from nonlabor, nonideological occupations usually relevant (but sometimes irrelevant) to their first union jobs—such occupations as commercial advertising or newspaper work (no Guild activity), industrial engineer in a company, management consultant, private law practice, civil service unconnected with the New Deal, etc.[33] Though most of them took a salary cut or stayed on the same level when they made the transition to Labor, this was often a necessary or calculated risk in the interest of long-run earning power.[34] Thus, the median figure of $9,500 puts the present Outsider Careerist group at the very peak of the staff expert salary scale. As one of the transitional salary-cut cases said, "Now I'm getting a good salary, but at the time I came I could have got more outside. I won't kid you, though. It was not much of a sacrifice to come." (527-4.) Several cases felt that they had climbed to the top in their previous occupation and the union, whatever the starting salary, offered a situation with high growth potential. Several others were either unemployed or facing a job loss when the chance for a union career opened up.

Aside from occupational history, salary transition, and present income, there is some contrast with the Rank-and-File Careerist in the way the basic own-union identification is expressed. Like the Technician Professional, the Outsider Careerist tends to be means-centered in describing his work—indifferent to any goals, straight trade union or otherwise. The Rank-and-File Careerist, however, speaks in terms of policy impact on bargaining or administrative issues. This appears again to some extent in the concept of the Ideal Expert: several Outsider Careerists feel the compulsion of specifying as a needed qualification belief in or loyalty to the union worked for, its policies in general, or its policies in the area of the expert's specialty.[35] The Rank-and-File Careerist

33. Thirteen of the twenty with an OC career theme score here on occupational origin. The rest are scattered—three from New Deal or World War II agencies, four from college campuses.

34. Of the eighteen whose salary transition is known, six got more, four stayed the same, six got less, two had no previous job.

35. Distribution: Missionary, none; Prof., 5/53; OC, 5/18; RF Career., 1/14; Politico, 5/12.

seems to take this for granted—perhaps on the assumption that the possession of the practical wisdom that comes from rank-and-file shop and union experience automatically produces the proper own-union loyalty. With his previous professional experiences, the Outsider Careerist may be more conscious of the possible range of loyalty conflicts, though such conflicts seldom plague him except in very minor degree.

The Union Politico

. . . . Work [in the modern "Age of Sport"] gives a man the joy of victorious force, bestows on him the harsh pleasure of feeling his personality triumphant. . . . Since the joy which he seeks is to be found only in the possession of a powerful personality, the actual result of his work becomes a matter of indifference. The important thing is the joy of having been shrewd enough to accomplish that result. . . . Thus work tends little by little to change itself into a game in which the important thing is not the goal, but the skill of the player.

—ADRIANO TILGHER, *Work: What It Has Meant to Men Through the Ages*, trans. D. C. Fisher (New York, Harcourt, Brace and Co., 1930).

My biggest kick is planning something big that pans out. Anticipating certain results. . . . It was a big, costly battle. . . . My prediction came true. . . . It's like shooting craps when you bet on the right number. There's no greater satisfaction than victory in a game of chance. (222-6.)

—Interview with Case 102

The Politico, like the Careerist, is highly identified with the union hierarchy. What is unique in his role orientation is a basic preoccupation with the political process. While the Missionary craves influence and power as a means of promoting his private political goals, and the Careerist as a means of enhancing his income and prestige, the Politico strives for influence and power as ends in themselves. His outstanding job satisfaction is in the "excitement of the game"—meaning the political game within and between unions and between unions and other groups. He is a man who enjoys the "big play," the planning and execution of a slick maneuver.

True, almost half the Careerists cite this sort of satisfaction in their work,[36] and a few Professionals and Legislative Liberals come close to it. But for the Careerist it is eclipsed by the overriding preoccupation with social mobility; for the others it takes on a value connotation.[37] The Politico's interest in broad policy impact and his enjoyment of the "big play" are focused on the intrinsic *process* of policy formulation itself, not on the *direction* of policy.

If the Politico shows any interest in program, it is likely to be of low intensity. One Politico says he'd like to push the thinking of the officers and staff a little beyond where they are now and mentions a specific program idea. Then he adds,

> But nothing much gets in my hair. You see, I don't feel any fire the way some of these guys do. The union isn't going to solve the world's problems tomorrow—or even the next day. So I don't get excited when the problems are still with us. I'm satisfied with small gains. Missionaries are good to have. But I am not one. . . . I'm accepted. In the field I make a leaflet distribution, walk on picket lines, drink beer with the boys—not because I feel the necessity—it's my normal way of doing things. (405-3.)

Another case gave this interesting definition of "idealism."

> There's another sort of satisfaction [in addition to excitement of the game]. You understand the problems of your clients and you are one step ahead of them and you can supply that needed step. (222-6.)

Being "one step ahead," being "accepted"—in general, being in the know and on the inside is his chief job preoccupation. The man who says he is "not on fire" speaks of a previous point of choice in his career:

> Several years ago I set myself to take this job. [Describes preparation, says he could have gone into the plant and run for office instead.]

---

36. Distribution: Careerist, 14/32; Politico, 12/12.

37. This Program Professional, for example, describes one job satisfaction in these terms: "I've enjoyed tearing apart the smug attorney who has a Victorian approach to [collective bargaining issues]—the kind who'll tell you 'We don't believe in *principle* in [contract clause].' I've enjoyed . . . a personal kind of satisfaction in destroying these 'principled' arguments —and we have much opportunity for that." (411a-3.) While this might be interpreted as satisfaction in the excitement of the game, in the context of an overriding concern with program promotion it can more appropriately be set apart from satisfaction in the negotiation process itself, which characterizes the Politico.

. . . My area of influence in this spot is greater than what a [middle leader] has. [Note, though, that the latter functionary makes more money.] I'd have been a second-rate [middle leader] in the same number of years if I'd have gone into a plant. You can tell your chances to get into an elective spot. . . . (405-3.)

When the choice is between a chance to operate on a high level in union politics, on the one hand, and money and lower-level official responsibility, on the other, the Politico would rather play the operator. His ideal is the celebrated "man behind the throne," a fellow who not only is in the know, but is known to important people as part of the inner circle (whatever the homage paid to the imperative of staff anonymity).

Similarly, if the Politico shows any of the marks of professional identification, they take on a special meaning in the context of his central preoccupation with the political process. For instance, if he turns out any research product aimed at an academic audience (one case), or participates in meetings of professional associations (four cases), he does these things in the spirit of a task force commander on "D" Day. He conceives of his role as invader, his research presentation as a political maneuver (like leaflet-drop assurances to the civilian population that his bombs are aimed only at military targets). Such meetings give him a chance to "wise up the ivory tower boys," tell them off in their own language—so they will know, for instance, how things *really* are in labor relations. The Politico is a man who loves a good fight.

The problems that bother the Professional Service expert—maintaining a reasonable balance between objectivity and advocacy, upholding professional standards of work, preserving craft competence, etc.—these are matters of no moment to the Politico. The contempt he sometimes feels for the Professional is suggested in this composite quotation in which two Politicos contrast a third, departed Politico with his Professional successors:

X was no technician like Y. But he understood the use of facts and figures: to advance trade union aims. He massacred statistical method with wonderful abandon! Some of our more academic economists shuddered. . . . Y makes it into a counting agency, complete with line graphs, correlation coefficients, etc. . . . This is ridiculous. . . . X had boldness and imagination. He knew how to dramatize issues. He used to toss a hatful of statistics in the air and catch them the way they fell.

. . . [The study] may have been nonsense, but it [served the union's purpose]. (G220a-2, 308-2.)

Like the Missionary and the Program Professional and in contrast to the Careerist, the Politico never complains, even incidentally, about thwarted mobility strivings (though two cases do mention income as a source of job satisfaction). Asking the question, "under what conditions would this man sever the labor tie, assuming he maintains his role orientation intact and has alternative possibilities?" is a helpful way of thinking about these cases. The data seem to suggest these answers: the Missionary would leave when he is convinced the union is no longer the best vehicle for carrying out his mission; the Professional Service expert when his technical skills are not sufficiently utilized; the Careerist when his income-prestige strivings are seriously checked. Finally, the Politico would depart when (1) things get dull ("The job no longer offers a challenge. . . . Even hysteria gets routine!" 451-3); or (2) he is deprived of the feeling of being on the inside, part of the inner circle. On this point, one ex-expert, a Politico when he left, was described in these terms:

He became a little psychotic towards the end. If X and Y went in to see the boss and there was a policy matter under discussion, he'd be finished for the day—he'd stew over it, he'd say, "I'm not being utilized." He'd get livid. (NG 519b.)

The Politico in question adds the postscript, "I had a grand time for . . . years. It was time to get out. You either reconcile yourself to a lesser role, or get in the hair of some [line officer] and get your throat cut." (903-5.)

What of the character of the Politico's union identification? Clues to it are found mainly in his concept of the Ideal Expert, his job satisfactions and his pattern of colleague contact. The data are sketchy, the number of cases (twelve) is small, but an attribute analysis is suggestive and confirms the overall interview impression.

In his concept of the Ideal Expert he tends, like the Outsider Careerist, to emphasize loyalty to the particular union and its policies. Like the Porkchopper, he also makes much of "practical experience" in shop and union—even though he himself may be an outsider.[38]

Consistent with this inward orientation is the frequently expressed feeling that he is rendering service to the rank and file in terms of straight trade-union gains—contracts improved, plant grievances won, safety enhanced, bad working conditions exposed, etc. The Politico tends to be immersed in the core function of the union. As with the Professionals (especially the Technician Professionals), the intrinsic nature of the work—with trade-union aims assumed as given—is quite important to him. But the focus is not on technical performance within an area of special competence; it is on general political maneuver. The Politico sees the straight trade-union job as interesting, varied and exciting, especially where work initiative in pursuit of important union goals is allowed.[39]

This inward orientation is both reflected and reinforced by his colleague contacts. Of all types, he has the most contact with own-union line and staff officials. He tends even more than the Careerist to share political and social contacts off the job with such functionaries.

There is much similarity between the Technician Professional's instrumental definition of his function and that of the Politico.[40] The main difference is that the Politico's willingness to accept trade-union goals as given is untempered by any commitment to professional objectivity and independence. More than other types he bends easily to the requirements of the moment and the situation; indeed, sometimes the necessity of facile adaptation to changes in the union line is elevated to an austere virtue:

There is no place for an outsider who doesn't believe that the union is generally doing the right thing. . . . The intellectual in the labor

38. Occupational origins of present Politicos: six outsiders, six rank-and-filers.

39. Distribution of "satisfaction in straight TU gains": Missionary, 4/27; Prof., 9/53; Careerist, 5/32; Politico, 7/12. Also, from combinations of other job satisfactions one can infer the above formulation.

40. Aside from the data above there is one other clue to this instrumental view. Proportionately, more Politicos and Professionals score one or more of Ideal Expert codes 9 (know and understand personalities, politics or policies of own union), 2a (loyalty to own union and its policies), or 10 (know your place, etc.): Missionary, 12/29; Professional, 34/53; Careerist, 16/32; Politico, 9/12.

movement has to sincerely feel he's willing to attach his life to the job of
the union and that the straight union job has some historical meaning.
. . . Take these people who've never been schooled in loyalty or never
walked a picket line. [Describes two departed Missionaries.] . . . There
is no place for missionaries or hypocrites in the labor movement.
(318-5,6.)

The Politico's preoccupation with the political process, his identification with the union hierarchy, his instrumental view of his
role as well as the militant coloration in his manner of speech (as
exemplified in the case quoted above)—these are in large part a
product of his past political experience and present job functions.
The Politico is typically an old-timer who entered the labor movement before 1941 as a Party Missionary; through the years he has
acquired a position of Medium to High Influence as a Contact
Man or Internal Communications Specialist.[41]

This background helps explain the railing cynicism the Politico
exhibits in political discussion. Having been burned in his political
past, he never wants to be taken in again by anything or anybody.
He has drastically scaled down his past aspirations, tends now to
sneer at them. He still retains strong political affect and would
rate fairly high on any scale of political competence, but both
emotion and skill have become reoriented around the means of
political conflict, not new ends.

The Politico's cynicism is a reflection of the absence of a stabilizing set of values. The Missionary's political energies, while put
out in less "realistic" style, are goal-directed, attached to principle,
typically guided by some image of Utopia. The Professional types
have some commitment to a professional ideology of dispassionate
service; they prize the values of objectivity and independence,
respect technical competence. Finally, the Careerist is typically
oriented toward middle-class values sustained by church, family
and community. The Politico, in contrast, lacking the stabilizing
influence of a firm set of values, reacts to politics with a hard-

41. Nine of the twelve entered as Missionaries (seven PM's, two LLM's);
one as a Professional, one as a Careerist, one as a Politico. Ten of the twelve
entered before 1941 (one is a wartimer, the other a newcomer). Eight of the
twelve are Contact Men or ICS (and two of the four Facts and Figures Men
have many characteristics of the Contact Man in their work). Only three
cases—all ex-Missionaries with Facts and Figures functions—rate low on
Influence (and this because of a high degree of specialization).

boiled manipulative outlook.[42] This cynicism, however, is often a kind of wounded idealism overlaid with a shell of overcompensating "realism." Hence the Missionary hangover in the talk of some cases.

As this discussion of the Politico suggests, the variables of past role orientation (career theme) and functional type can be used as guides to analysis of the impact of organization on person. What transformations of the staff expert's role orientation take place in the union setting? What are the typical patterns of adjustment and how can they be explained? How is a man's role orientation related to his functions?

---

42. Many writers have noted this sort of mentality among a variety of intellectuals and professionals. Leo Rosten describes the cynicism of the Washington Press corps in *The Washington Correspondents* (New York: Harcourt, Brace and Co., 1937), pp. 250 ff. L. Sussman notes "an all-inclusive cynicism" as "the most striking trait of many, if not most, public relations men. For them the world divides itself into two kinds of people: those who can be led by the nose and those who can be bought." "The Public Relations Movement in America" (Unpublished M.A. Thesis, University of Chicago, 1947), p. 97. Cf. Riesman's "inside dopester." *Op. cit.*, pp. 199 ff.

CHAPTER VIII

SHAPING, SELECTING AND
ELIMINATING THE EXPERTS

ALL OF THESE eight role-orientation types can be seen as directions toward which the mentality of the intellectuals and staff experts who enter a social movement develop. Some orientations are appropriate to the demands of the movement at a given stage of growth; others are not. Conflicts between the meanings the experts assign to their activity and the functions they fulfill exert a strain toward change in both person and organization. The person faced with long-range, conflicting expectations of two groups to whom he is responsive (job vs. profession, job vs. mission) can (1) try to reshape the role in which he acts to make the demands compatible; (2) change his role orientation to exclude the demands of one, i.e., leave the job role or adapt to the job role.[1] The absence of such conflict, reflecting a congruence between function and role orientation, could be expected to result in stability in both organization and person.

1. Some of the adaptations a person caught in the crossfire of competing claims can make are likely to be temporary and are not considered here. For instance: (1) The double life—a person can play the approved role in each group and ignore its expectations when in contact with the other; (2) illness—failure to conform to conflicting role expectations may result in mental or physical illness, resolution by socially approved escape. For an analysis of several such adaptations, see Jackson Toby, "Some Variables in Role Conflict Analysis" (Unpublished paper, hectographed, undated).

Patterns of Change and Stability
in Role Orientation

Table 1 presents a picture of the transformations that have taken place in the role orientations of the incumbent staff experts since they first entered the labor movement. The most stable of the types are the Technician Professional and Careerist (both Outsider and Rank-and-File). The least stable is the Missionary type. While all of the ten who entered as Technician Professionals and twenty-eight of the thirty-five who entered as Careerists have remained so, more than half of the Missionaries have been shaped in the image of some other main type. Only about one in four of the men who entered as Party Missionaries and the same small proportion of Legislative Liberals have maintained their special outlook. The Program Professional is a type with middling stability.

Confirmation of this picture comes from data on the staff experts who have been eliminated. They are generally the same types who, when they stay with the unions, become most drastically reoriented. The CP Missionaries who were thrown out in factional struggles—and whose role orientation at the time of departure can be inferred from their affiliation—constitute the largest group. Aside from the departed Communists, there are twenty-six ex-experts whose role orientations can be reasonably guessed from interviews and/or reputation (eighteen were interviewed; these include four of the incumbents who left since field work was completed). Of the twenty-six, seventeen were Missionaries of one kind or another (including five Religious-Ethico Missionaries), five were Program Professionals. Only two Technician Professionals, one Politico, and one Outsider Careerist were among the departed. Not one was a Rank-and-File Careerist.[2]

Explaining Stability

It may be that the Technician Professional and Careerist are types whose years of service are few, and that they simply have

---

2. Only one case in the sample, an old-timer, was a Politico at the time of entry; only one of those who have left was a Politico at the time of his departure.

Table 1—Distribution of 122 Cases by Past and Present Role Orientation*

PAST ROLE ORIENTATION (Career Theme)		PRESENT ROLE ORIENTATION								TOTAL PAST
		MISSIONARIES			PROF. SERVICE		CAREERIST		POLITICO	
		Party 1	Liberal 2	Religious 3	Program 4	Technician 5	Outsider 6	Rank and File 7	8	
Mission-aries	Total	8	19	2	14	9	1	2	9	64
	Party	8	12	0	3	5	0	1	7	36
	Lib.	0	7	0	11	4	1	1	2	26
	Rel.	0	0	2	0	0	0	0	0	2
Prof. Service	Total				8	13			1	22
	Pgm.				8	3			1	12
	Tech.				0	10			0	10
Career-ist	Total					6	17	11	1	35
	Outs.					3	17	0	0	20
	R and F.					3	0	11	1	15
Politico	Total								1	1
Total Present		8	19	2	22	28	18	13	12	122

* Insufficient data on Past Role Orient. for three present Technician Professionals and one present Rank-and-File Careerist. The 122 cases include representation from all 15 first priority unions, eight second priority unions, and two "extras" (included because full data available on scarce types). Five administrative assistants who were once staff experts are included.

not had the time to become reoriented. Or, if my hypothesis is correct, these are the types who experience least tension between the work they do and the meanings they assign to it.

The first thing to note is that the Technician Professionals are indeed very recent arrivals; seven of the nine known cases are postwar entries (1945-51). (See Table 2.) But short service cannot explain the stability of those who entered as Careerist types: none of the Rank-and-File Careerists are newcomers; only about one in three of the Outsider Careerists is a newcomer. Moreover, the seniority pattern cannot account for the contrast in personal stability between Party Missionary and Porkchopper, both early entries, or Technician Professional and Program Professional, both late entries. Finally, when we control the time factor by looking only at the thirty-eight newcomers of all types, we find that 50 per cent of the Missionaries, but only 20 per cent of the Careerists and only 6 per cent of the Professionals have changed to another main type.

The explanation of stability in role orientation, while in part a matter of length of service, is thus more a matter of the degree of

Table 2—Distribution of 126 Cases by Past Orientation (Career Theme) and Time of First Service to Labor Movement

PAST ROLE ORIENTATION	Before 1941 (Old-timers)		1941-44 (War-timers)		1945-51 (Newcomers)		No Information		TOTALS	
	N	%	N	%	N	%	N	%	N	%
Missionary	33	51.6	13	20.3	16	25.0	2	3.1	64	100.0
1 PM	25		7		3		1			
2 LLM	8		6		12		1			
3 REM					1					
Professional	1	4.5	3	13.6	17	77.3	1	4.5	22	99.9
4 PP			2		10					
5 TP	1		1		7		1			
Careerist	21	60.0	4	11.4	5	14.3	5	14.3	35	100.0
6 OC	7		4		5		4			
7 R & F	14		0		0		1			
Politico 8	1								1	
Unknown	2				2				4	
Totals	58	46.0	20	15.9	40	31.8	8	6.3	126	100

TIME OF ENTRY

* Date of first service in any capacity—staff or line, paid or unpaid, elected or appointed, volunteer or regular and in any unit of the labor movement. Newspaper Guild activism, or the lawyer's first act of taking on an important union client, are counted. Newer unions are included on the assumption that their leaders count long service in an older unit as demonstrated loyalty.

role conflict. The three most stable types share a thoroughly instrumental view of their job. There is little conflict between organizational and personal goals in the case of the Careerist (Rank-and-File *or* Outsider); his inward orientation and his identification with the incumbent leadership make him nicely adaptable to union ends. Moreover, on the things that count for him—salary, prestige— he is making out very well, as has been shown. The desire of the TP to render competent, efficient service, coupled with his strong commitment to the norm of professional neutrality, makes him similarly adaptable.

I have traced the many conflicts between professional and union identifications, but these rarely occasion real crises among the Professional Service experts. A Technician Professional departure is likely to be provoked more by insufficient acceptance of the professional injunction of impartial service than by his acceptance of professional controls in his standards of work performance. One top officer described an extreme case, a Technician Professional whose role conflicts were resolved by a parting of the ways:

> He had an outstanding background and was a good economist. But he did not see eye to eye with us or organized labor in a general way. . . . We knew before we employed him, but we didn't think there was enough of a difference. . . . While he carried out assignments, his heart wasn't in it. Since there was a fundamental difference of opinion, it was too difficult to work with him. . . . He'd try to write a brief setting forth our position but never strong enough or slanted enough if it involved a question he had his personal ideas on. There was a number of things he was hot on. . . . (23-4.)

More typically, the Technician Professional is able to rationalize these conflicts without much strain. Even if his heart is not in it, he can act as if it were. A man whose professional identification is very high, for instance, observes:

> There are certain circumstances under which any kind of partisan discourse is distasteful. You're asked to make a case; o.k., you make a case and the employer's economist makes a case. In collective bargaining it's a game—a debating trick. But when it comes to broader economic analysis it's different. (335-5.)

Since his boss is not as vitally concerned with broad economic analysis as with collective bargaining (see, e.g., Chapter IX), and since the bulk of his work is of a bread-and-butter character, these dilemmas of job vs. profession do not occasion too much difficulty. In fact, it is an important reason for the marked stability of the Technician Professional (and the medium stability of the Program Professional, despite his additional conflicts) that there is a basic congruence between his role orientation and the functions he fulfills. Table 3 shows a heavy concentration of Professional Service experts among the Facts and Figures Men. While only one in six of the Missionaries (one in nineteen of the LLM's), one in three of the Politicos, and fewer than half of the Careerists fulfill Facts and Figures functions, about seven in ten of the Professionals are of that functional type. Only five of the fifty-three Professionals are Contact Men. An orientation which stresses utilization of professional skills acquired typically through long training is likely to be more at home handling the facts and figures than working the contacts. As one expert put it:

A lobbyist has to sell his product without knowing how the darn thing is put together—a different type from me. He has to be a negotiator and a bargainer. Imagine a salesman who really *knew* his vacuum cleaner! (705.)

The low degree of role strain among Technician Professionals thus reflects (1) the congruence of the Professional role orientation and the Facts and Figures function; (2) an increased demand for competent, better-trained technicians to serve the movement in its administrative and bargaining maturity. Few of these men leave the labor movement; fewer still experience much change in their role orientation. Despite their relatively short service, this analysis would point toward continued stability in men of this type.

Explaining Change

What about the fifty-eight experts of less stability who stayed on the job and were transformed? What are the typical patterns of change in their role orientation?

The central movement of our staff experts has been toward the Professional Service types. Note in Table 1 that twenty-three

Table 3—Distribution of 126 Cases by Role Orientation and Functional Type

FUNCTIONAL TYPE

ROLE ORIENT.	Facts & Fig. Man	Contact Man	Int. Com. Spec.	Adm. Ass't.	Totals
Missionaries					
Party	3	2	3	0	8
Leg. Lib.	1	6	12	0	19
Rel.-Eth.	1	0	0	1	2
Total Mission	5	8	15	1	29
Prof. Serv.					
Prog. Prof.	15	1	6	0	22
Techn. Prof.	20	4	5	2	31
Total PS	35	5	11	2	53
Careerist					
Outs. Car.	6	7	4	1	18
RF Car.	8	2	3	1	14
Total Car.	14	9	7	2	32
Politico	4	6	2	0	12
Totals	58	28	35	5	126

of the sixty-four who entered as Missionaries became Professionals. So did six of the Careerists. Nine of the Missionaries became Politicos. Equally important are the patterns of change within these main types. In order of importance, the points of arrival in these role orientation journeys are: (1) Technician Professional; (2) Program Professional; (3) Legislative-Liberal Missionary; (4) Politico; (5) Careerist types.

The overall pattern can be seen as a movement away from ideas and toward jobs: the Missionary abandons ideology and moves to professional service, an immersion in the political process, or careerism; the Program Professional loses interest in program promotion and shifts to a preoccupation with technical and administrative detail. Quitting aside, the final resting places for all types beset with severe role conflicts are (1) Technician Professional; (2) Politico. Cases of every type end up in the Technician Professional slot. The Politicos are likewise an outgrowth of all main types, though the principal source is the Party Missionary. An analysis of the most frequent shift of each type will provide some insight into these patterns of change.

Party Missionary to Legislative-Liberal Missionary.—The transformations of the thirty-six party ideologues can be seen as different modes of resolution of the conflicts experienced between missionary dreams and trade union reality. As the union becomes established, with sanctions in contracts and in law, the doctrines of class struggle become less relevant. The interests of organizational survival and growth, of leadership tenure and prestige, become paramount. As Weber's work suggests, there may be no pre-established correspondence between the content of an idea (or the role orientation of a missionary) and the interests of the leaders and members who rise to power in a social movement. But in time, ideas are discredited in the face of history, unless they are compatible with the conduct that various interests promote.[3] Ideas, selected and reinterpreted from the initial doctrines, gain an affinity with the interests of the men in charge; if not, the ideas are abandoned. Like ideas and their publics, experts and their bosses in successful (i.e., institutionalized) social movements, by a selective process, find their affinities.

The forms this takes in the labor movement vary with the specific opportunities and experiences of the staff expert involved. In general, when the Party Missionary's opportunity for planting ideas declines, the intrinsic nature of the work, his isolation from the masses, his relatively low salary and his job insecurities begin to weigh on his mind. If opportunity for political activity aimed at the masses appears elsewhere, he leaves; if not, he adapts. We have seen some adaptation even within the Party Missionary category; the ideological commitments are no longer total, the hesitations and reservations are clear. In time, many move to the Legislative-Liberal orientation; they abandon doctrinaire views and adopt a cautious, critical realism, tempered by an underlying sympathy with the underdog. Even here, however, the pressure for change is strong; an inner weariness develops as the Legislative Liberal is again and again confronted with the unwieldy machinery

---

3. For Weber, in contrast to Marx, ideas do not simply "express" class interests or the social origin of the idea-holder; ideas may have little correspondence with these interests in the initial stages. Ideas and interests gain an "elective affinity" only in the course of the routinization of the social movement. Gerth and Mills, ed., *op. cit.*, pp. 62-63, 284 ff.

of the world-as-it-is-constituted. This case, who entered as a Party Missionary, shows this weariness, mentioning new family responsibilities as a cause:

> . . . The labor movement was the only place a young idealist who wanted to get personal satisfaction out of his work—to relate his day-to-day activity to his social philosophy—could go. The satisfactions are so few. And when you come down to it the satisfaction that's really important in life is those kids and that family. All the service to humanity, all the struggle and work and planning turns to ashes in your mouth, to mix a metaphor. For the impact the technician will make, it's not worth the tremendous personal sacrifice involved. (N 315b.)

New family responsibilities, of course, are not the only pressure for change. With age comes a declining fund of physical energy. The years of union experience may also bring increased professional competence, a rising salary, and broadened responsibilities. The Missionary's enthusiasm for the cause(s) diminishes or is redirected; he assigns new meanings to his work.

The tensions between job functions and role orientation among the Legislative Liberals are especially acute and act to intensify these pressures for change. Twelve of our nineteen LLM's are Internal Communications Specialists, six are Contact Men (see Table 3). Now these job functions are about as close as a Legislative Liberal can get to compatibility with his orientation. As an Internal Communications Specialist, he has some chance to broaden leadership-activist horizons (via political content in newspaper or education program); as a Contact Man, he can devote some attention to national legislative issues (via lobbying and public relations activity). Some people find enough satisfaction in these opportunities, whatever the resistances, to maintain their outlook intact. But the incongruence of the Legislative-Liberal orientation and the ICS and CM functions is still very great. One Internal Communications Specialist sums up this incongruence as he sees it:

> My major job is time study, steward training—basic tool courses. My interest lies elsewhere—in the long run—before ten years are up. Time's running out. [Describes world problems on which he thinks labor should be working and educating.] . . . I think it's a function of the unions to do it. . . . But my job is defined. I agree I must do the basic job of "training." (606-2.)

In his job role the Legislative Liberal functions to build top officer prestige, neutralize or suppress disaffection, maintain morale in crisis situations, etc.—small potatoes for a man with the long view. Or, as Contact Man he smoothes the boss' contacts with the non-union world, moves the union towards a "cut-red-tape" bias at the same time that he builds an officer self-image of respectability and responsibility. All of this tends to make the union less of a threat to the status quo than an integral part of it—hardly a joyous prospect for a man who wants to reshape the universe.

Under pressure, the easiest move for the Legislative Liberal (or Party Missionary) who retains a large fund of physical energy and high political affect is in the Politico direction. Here, while the ends of politics become subordinated to the means, the illusion of big doings can be maintained. An immersion in a kind of apolitical politics (for no political battle is without its "principled," goal-directed aspect), accompanied by compensatory sneers at his past aspirations, can serve as a new adaptation more in line with his job functions.

A more direct flight from politics is seen in the cases who move to careerism or technical professionalism. A lifelong functionary in the socialist movement describes this adaptation of several one-time party radicals who have "emerged absorbed in the experience of their particular calling":

They rationalize their role in the union. They say, 'We're building democracy for the economy. Sooner or later unions will be political.' Meanwhile they're so concerned with the details of their particular job they have no energy for anything else. X, for instance, works late at night—and there's only 24 hours in the day. Y, an executive, in —— corporation, is an ex-Socialist—an example on the management side. He's very much absorbed in the company vision—a very narrow life view. This is inevitable. Their jobs consume them. (958-3.)

As the mission is shed and the image of the labor movement re-cast, the day-to-day job—with the intrinsic satisfaction and the salary it affords—becomes more important. Whether this absorption in the job takes the form of a Technician Professional or a Career-ist orientation depends on a great number of factors: the man's previous training; the opportunities his work affords for profes-sional contacts and the character of the specialized competence it

demands; how much pressure for social mobility comes from family
and friends; the ease of his relationships with staff and line officials,
etc. The transformation from Legislative Liberal to Careerist or
Technician Professional occurs too seldom to permit any judgment
of the relative importance of these factors from my data.

Legislative Liberal to Program Professional.—The most frequent
adaptation of the Legislative Liberal takes this form: he acquires
professional identification and he narrows his focus of political
attention without becoming completely means-centered. Trade-
union reality occasionally provides a demand for specialized competence coupled with an opportunity for development of newer
programs for collective bargaining, internal administration or governmental relations (see Chapter IX). If satisfaction from small-
scale planning for mundane trade-union goals can be reinforced
by a full utilization of relevant skills, which in turn leads to
recognition from other professionals, we have the makings of a
Program Professional. This represents the beginning of an absorption in the job and a flight from ideas.

Program Professional to Technician Professional.—This shift
occurs when one of two things happens: (a) the demands of the
Facts and Figures role do not allow opportunity for thinking,
planning or promoting program ideas within his specialty—either
because the union loses interest in the area, or because the expert
moves up and out of his narrow sphere and himself loses interest
in program; (b) the conflict of commitment to program vs. commitment to professionally respectable work is resolved in favor of
the latter. With decline in program interest comes the development
of a stronger adherence to a means-centered, professional neutrality
and an increased absorption in the technical and administrative
detail of the job. The data here, it should be noted, are limited to
only three cases.

Careerist to Technician Professional.—A similar pattern is suggested by the six cases (three outsiders, three rank-and-filers) who
made this shift. They present a striking instance of the shaping of
role orientation by function. These cases also point to the locus of
what instability exists among Careerists. All of these transformed
Careerists are Facts and Figures Men. All have experienced a disparity between the demands of the job role and the technical equip-

ment possessed. None have had graduate school training; three were forced to quit college before obtaining a degree.

The seeds of professional aspiration may have been planted early in their occupational histories. All six, for example, had a taste of white-collar or professional work sometime prior to their present jobs as staff experts. Latching on to a Facts and Figures job as a means of social mobility, they begin to come up against men of higher education and perhaps superior technical knowledge on the company side. They feel the pressure to cultivate professional prowess. Three of the six go to night school to make up the deficiency. A fourth says he would like to get training in another, highly specialized discipline; he admires the consulting experts he has seen in that field. A fifth says he intends to become a consultant—not just for the money, but mainly because of the independence he'll get in the conduct of his work. All six become exposed to professional norms—through participation in professional societies or through contact with professionally oriented colleagues in the labor movement.

None of these men, as they acquire more training and experience, drop their mobility aspirations completely, but all have developed considerable professional identification. This identification is sometimes more exaggerated than in those professionals who lack the marks of middle-class mobility striving. It appears, for instance, in a proud announcement of dedication to "sound principles" and the facts.

Several of the Careerists—especially among the Porkchoppers—show a budding professional identification, though the dominance of income-prestige preoccupation in their role orientation precludes classification as Technician Professionals as yet. This analysis would suggest the hypothesis that those Careerists who fulfill Facts and Figures functions will in time develop a professional orientation.

Summary and Conclusion

In order to grasp the interaction of person and organization in various units of a successful social movement, I have analyzed the transformations of the staff expert's role orientation—his typical pat-

terns of adjustment—and related these to his job functions. Data
on the past and present role orientations of 122 incumbents and on
the role orientation at time of departure of many ex-experts (including 25 non-Communists) point to these conclusions:

1. The most stable types are Technician Professional, Outsider
Careerist, and Porkchopper. Program Professionals, considering
both incumbents and ex-experts, have medium stability.

2. The most unstable types are Party Missionary and Legislative-
Liberal Missionary. Considering departures, the Religious-Ethico
Missionary is the most unstable of all.

3. The labor movement, as it has become established, has shaped
its men of knowledge in the Professional Service mold.

4. The most frequent shift of each type shows these specific
patterns: from Missionary to Legislative-Liberal Missionary to Program Professional to Technician Professional; from Careerist (Outsider or Rank-and-Filer) to Technician Professional. Any main type
can move in the Politico direction, though the typical source is the
Party Missionary. Quitting aside, the final resting place for all
change-prone types are Technician Professional and Politico.

5. The overall movement is thus away from ideas and towards
jobs, from a goal-centered outlook to a means-centered outlook.

The import of these findings is once again to confirm that people
fulfilling similar functions in an organization, exposed to similar
working climates and institutional pressures, can display an extraordinary diversity in the meanings they assign their activity. The
consequent role conflicts constitute important levers for both personal and organizational change. The degree of role conflict helps
explain the patterns of stability and change established above. The
stable types are those who experience least role conflict and exert
least pressure for organizational change, e.g., the Careerist and the
Technician Professional. The unstable types are those who experience most role conflict and exert most pressure for organizational
change, e.g., the Missionaries.

The distribution of role-orientation types by functional types
suggests these conclusions and affords illustration of the tendency
for the man and the job to find their affinities:

1. The relative stability of the Professional Service experts is in
part explained by the basic congruence of role orientation and

function: seven in ten are Facts and Figures Men, a good "fit" of man and job. This is also confirmation of the analysis in Chapter IV of the "rational-responsible bias" of the Facts and Figures operation: men with professional orientation could be expected to have this sort of impact on union decision-making, an impact appropriate to a labor movement in its "maturity."

2. Men with political experience and preoccupation tend to show up in political jobs—witness the concentration of Politicos and Missionaries in Internal Communications and Contact Man specialties (Missionary, 23/28; Politico, 8/12; Careerist, 16/30; Professional, 16/51).

3. Where the "fit" of man and job is uneasy, the two-way process of change begins.

(a) The transformation of Careerist into Technician Professional is explained by pressures in the job role: the six cases who made this shift were all Facts and Figures Men. Their acquisition of professional identification in turn strengthens the "rational-responsible" bias inherent in their functions.

(b) While the pressures in the job role tend to move the Missionary away from ideas, the definition he gives his job while the process goes on helps shape the organization. It is likely, for instance, that the Legislative Liberal has his best chance to promote his larger mission in the internal and external propagandist roles he is selected to fill (18 in 19 are ICS or CM). His impact in the nonbargaining areas of union decision-making may be heavy (see Chapter IX). In the long run, however, the role conflicts he experiences even in these relatively compatible jobs are likely to result in a transformation in his outlook, as the patterns of change in my sample suggest.

The diversity of adjustment patterns available to the man with a mission suggests some modification of the hypothesis that "bureaucracies provoke gradual transformations of the alienated intellectual into the apolitical technician." The movement of all types toward Technician Professional is strong support for this hypothesis. But the deviations in the direction of Program Professional and Politico do not constitute a simple flight from politics. Moreover, many people find it possible to maintain a Missionary orientation over a very long period of union service—which at least suggests the necessity of relating the changes in person to the degree of bureaucratization of the organization under study. In fact, the use of the term "bureaucracy" in this generalization when applied to the trade union may obscure more than it reveals of the consequences of institutional involvement of intellectual life.

The final parts of this study, therefore, describe (1) the expert and the boss in the decision-making process; (2) the skills, functions, and outlook of the men selected for high influence positions; (3) the institutional pressures that impinge upon all types of union experts, whatever their functions, whatever their role orientations, whatever their influence. How much influence does the staff expert have? Where in the decision-making process is it most felt? On what kinds of decisions? What are the conditions (of union structure, of the national political economy) under which experts are used most and acquire maximum influence? Which of the functional types, which of the role-orientation types is likely to reach a position of high influence, and how?

A rough attempt at systematic analysis of these questions can help us see how well bureaucratic types of people make out and provide a picture of the bureaucratic and nonbureaucratic elements in union administration. It may also help clarify the speculation about the staff expert as powerless tool vs. prime mover, and yield some necessary refinements of the "managerial revolution" hypothesis.

PART IV

THE INFLUENCE OF
THE STAFF EXPERT

CHAPTER IX

THE LEADER AND THE EXPERT
IN THE DECISION-MAKING PROCESS

THE LITERATURE on large-scale organization is full of references to the "decision-making process," the "decision-making continuum," "power," "authority," "policy decisions," and "decision-making patterns." Analysis of the question, "Who makes what kinds of decisions with reference to what values," is widely seen as a crucial guide for the understanding of any given organization. And in recent years, the terminological confusion that has accompanied discussions of "decision-making" has been lessened somewhat.[1]

Concepts

The following concepts are used in this analysis of decision-making in the trade union:

1. *Influence.* A person may be said to have influence to the extent that he alters by persuasion the covert or overt behavior of

---

1. See, e.g., the efforts of C. I. Barnard, *The Functions of the Executive* (Cambridge: Harvard University Press, 1938); H. Goldhamer and E. A. Shils, "Types of Power and Status," *American Journal of Sociology,* 45 (Sept., 1939), 171-82; Herbert A. Simon, *Administrative Behavior* (New York: The Macmillan Co., 1947); Robert Bierstedt, "An Analysis of Social Power," *American Sociological Review,* XV (Dec., 1950), 730-38; and R. Tannenbaum and F. Massarik, "Participation by Subordinates in the Managerial Decision-Making Process," *Canadian Journal of Economics and Political Science,* 16 (August, 1950), 408-18.

others in accordance with his own intentions (the test is whether the behavior of others would have been different without the intervention of the man with influence).

2. *Power* is the ability to employ force, i.e., to apply effective, coercive sanctions.

3. *Authority* (or "legitimate power," or "institutionalized power") is the right to exercise power, a right acknowledged by subordinates. When authority is exercised, the subordinate makes no independent choice of behavior alternatives, but instead uses the command as his basis for choice.

4. *Uses.* The expert may have no power, no authority, no influence, and yet be *used* to execute a policy decision allowing no discretion or to provide services not related to policy.

5. *Decision-making process.* "Decision-making" (consciously choosing from among behavior alternatives) permeates every organization from top to bottom. No organization perfectly prescribes the total behavior expected of the functionaries who fill its offices; and even if this were possible, no functionary would or could perfectly comply with the rules. Moreover, making "policy" decisions is only part of a sequence of decisions that must be made with respect to each problem that arises. For analytical convenience, I chose four key points in the decision-making process:

(a) EMERGENCE OF PROBLEM. This is the point at which any responsible official becomes aware of a problem that gives rise to a policy decision. The staff expert may define the problem, bring it to the attention of the officer, or act upon it himself. (E.g., the expert decides that the union has a legitimate stake in a Congressional hearing, and suggests that a union representative testify.)

(b) POLICY DECISION. Here is where the value element in the decision-making process is most obvious, though it is by no means the only kind of decision affecting organizational purposes. Here the question is, "What action, if any, is desirable with repect to the problem?" (E.g., the expert persuades the boss that the union should testify against the bill.)

(c) DECISIONS ON THE MEANS OF IMPLEMENTATION. This includes questions of feasibility, timing, and methods. (E.g., can the union get before the Committee; if so, when is best, what general line should it take, who shall testify, etc.) These decisions may be important, especially where subsequent decision-makers view the policy decision as impossible to execute, harmful to the organization, or even morally wrong.

(d) DECISIONS INVOLVED IN EXECUTION. Once the problem has been accepted as a union problem, the policy set and the means of implementation chosen, there may still remain many decisions of consequence. (E.g., the expert prepares and gives the testimony, making on-the-spot decisions on what answers to give the Senators' inquiries. The publicity man prepares a press release on the basis of the testimony.)

There may be much or little discretion for the staff expert at any or all of these points in the decision-making process.

It is clear that the union staff expert is used, has influence, and in very rare cases may exercise power. By definition, he exercises no authority over the top officer, though he may, by delegation, exercise authority in dealings with officials at lower levels of the hierarchy. An engineer may carry the full sanction of the International when he trouble-shoots on a work-load problem in the field (authority); on his boss' views of incentive systems he must persuade (influence). Unless otherwise specified, the following analysis deals with the expert's influence with respect to his boss—the top officer(s).

Decisions in the large-scale organization are always to some extent guided by knowledge. And the man of knowledge in such an organization inevitably has some influence. As Lasswell puts it, "the mere fact of persisting in a network of relations means that one . . . partly modifies the shape and composition of the current value pyramid, whether one keeps this in mind or not."[2] The question is rather, as I have said, how much influence, in what areas of union decision, and where in the decision-making process.

Points of Highest Influence
in the Decision-Making Process

With varying degrees of specificity, the problems a union leader

---

2. *World Politics* . . . , *op. cit.*, p. 20.

faces press in on him from many sources: employers, members, government officials, other union leaders, outside friends and advisors, etc., and, of course, his staff experts.

To get some idea of where the expert's weight is typically felt, I gathered information on specific problems each union visited had dealt with in recent years. The data elicited in interviews with line officers, staff experts and their assistants were supplemented wherever possible by intra-union memoranda, official union reports, administrative letters, correspondence, etc., as well as labor press coverage of the issues involved. In one case, published descriptions of union administration helped. In all, I have what I judge to be full and reliable data on decision-making with respect to 167 problems in 26 unions (including five unions outside the Questionnaire Sample, three of them with membership somewhat under 50,000). The time locus is 1944-1951.

There is no claim that these problems are representative of the universe of problems these unions acted upon in that period. An effort was made in each union, however, to get decision-making material (1) from all major areas of union decision; (2) involving all kinds of staff experts (in their roles as experts, not administrators or executives); (3) on problems where experts had both high and low influence; (4) where experts did and did not originate the problems; (5) on problems of some importance either to the top officers or the experts. The aim was merely to get some idea of the range of decisions on which the expert has very high and very low influence, and to suggest the points in the decision-making process where he carries least and most weight. In addition it was hoped to elicit instances where technical-economic-legal considerations and knowledge became overriding, and instances where such knowledge was relevant but political-ideological considerations became overriding. See Appendix C for details on the working hypothesis and the system of influence analysis and scoring.

The data suggest that the influence of the trade union staff expert typically increases as one proceeds from emergence of problem to policy, to selection of means, through execution. The experts originated fewer than one-third of the 167 problems, had "High Influence" on about 57 per cent of the "Policy" decisions,

and about three-quarters of the "Means" and "Execution" decisions. The most striking contrast is between the low proportion in
which experts originated, and the high proportion with high influence on means and execution.[3] Probably more significant than the
general picture, however, are the data on the kinds of problems
and the areas of union decision in which the expert's influence is
most and least. (See Appendix C for system of analysis.)

The Nature of the Problem as a Factor Affecting Influence of Expert

In the 167 problems considered, the experts had highest influence in the areas of public relations and relations with government,
lowest in dealings with rival unions, next lowest in dealings with
members and lower leaders (present or potential)—with influence
in the area of employer relations somewhere in the middle. A
breakdown by subject matter within each area suggests that the
expert has his best chance to originate problems and achieve high
influence in the entire decision-making process on the following
matters (typical examples are listed and an asterisk marks each
instance in which an expert originated the problem):

1. *Public Relations* (Expert influence high on seventeen of twenty-two
   problems).
   (a) Editorials on world conditions; speeches and press releases on
       broad social-economic issues; etc.
       *Shall we issue press comment on Truman's State of the Union
       Message?
       *Shall we take an editorial stand against Franco?
       What big name shall we get as keynote speaker for our Conven-
       tion this year?
   (b) Co-operation with friendly groups, civic organizations; aid to
       worthy causes.
       *Should we support the NAACP (encourage local resolutions,
       contributions, etc.)?

---

3. My method of analysis is likely to be biased against the hypothesis
suggested here—both because of the attempt to elicit decisions where the
expert originated (examples where he did not originate came more readily
to the respondents' minds), and because of the system of rating influence (See
Appendix C).

*Shall we launch a college scholarship program?

Should we take a stand on the drive for grain for India?

2. *Relations with Government* (Expert influence high on thirty-four of fifty-two problems).

    (a) Bargain with government on wage or fringe wage issues.

*What to do about changes in the Bureau of Internal Revenue ruling making employer contributions for insurance nontaxable for the employee?

*Shall we petition for an increase in the Walsh-Healy minimum wage so substandard companies will be pressured into line?

What to do about nonunion standards on government work?

    (b) Defend employer interests *vis-à-vis* government.

*Should we take a stand on a government agency basing point ruling?

Should we join companies in petition for tariff relief in hearing before tariff commission?

Should we protest government agency stockpiling ruling at request of companies?

    (c) Policies on broad legislative issues (no cases of overall low influence).

Should we take a stand on the McCarran Communist Control bill?

Should we take a stand on the relation of speculation on the commodity exchanges to inflation?

*Should we support federal aid to local public health units?

3. *Relations with Employers* (Expert influence high on twenty-nine of fifty-nine problems).

    (a) Efficient organization of technical-economic-legal intelligence.

*Should we set up a system for contract analysis and record-keeping?

*Shall we appoint and use an advisory committee of outside consultants and experts on this bargaining issue?

*Should we work up and distribute a digest of arbitrators decisions to aid preparation of cases in X Company?

    (b) Formulate and apply policies on job evaluation, time study, workload, wage inequities, etc.

*What shall we do about the area wage differential problem in X industry and X companies?

What shall our policies be on the general problem of wage rate inequities?

How shall we apply wage increases to the basic wage structure?

    (c) Formulate and apply policies on benefit programs.

*Is permanent and total disability protection a desirable and feasible collective bargaining goal?

Shall we move for a pension and insurance program in coming negotiations?

How shall we apply the benefit program formula arrived at in a key bargain to other companies, industries, local situations?

4. *Internal Control and Organization* (Expert influence high on twelve of twenty-five, but the most important problems—internal opposition, discipline, changes in administrative structure, etc.—show little or no expert influence).

(a) Train and recruit lower leaders; build membership loyalty.
  *Shall we make educational films on union history, political action, etc.?
  *Shall we encourage local unions to set up local union newspapers?
  Should we print pictures of Negro members in our paper?

What emerges from this is support for the view that the staff expert typically has consistent, sustained, high influence on problems that the top officers see as far from the core function of their union. High influence, yes. Leeway and discretion in initiating policy proposals, yes. But on matters that don't count in the eyes of the boss.

An editor: I can write what I want on political issues or anything like that. It's sort of *papier-mâché,* though. If they [officers] don't understand what you're doing—and generally they don't—then what's it mean that you write a liberal editorial? Or that some paper picks it up? So you have an hour or two of glory and then fall back into depression. [Here he mentions the Negro question, and says what effect could he have on that—nothing. Whatever he'd print, it wouldn't mean anything] . . . (524-3.)

A lobbyist: In the old days [in Washington] you worked on a labor bill; now you work on genocide, atomic energy, everything. [A friendly government bureaucrat] calls me on the phone, says the FCC is going back on its stand for educational channels on television. [Describes decision-making here.] . . . We [specifies key experts] can get them [officers] to adopt a stand on rent control and housing. . . . It's different on other things. (700a-2.)[4]

The experts frequently complain about the officers' lack of interest in these "extracurricular" activities; at the same time it gives them a chance to have some sustained impact.

---

4. Compare Sussman's observations about company public relations consultants: "Sometimes public relations men do make policies, but only very minor ones; they decide that the employees need cleaner lavatories and more recreation, but they have nothing to say on union recognition or wages; they announce that a more attractive slogan is needed to sell the product but their advice is not asked on price policy. . . ." *Op. cit.,* p. 127.

The officers' indifference often reflects more than traditional
routine, ignorance, or a Perlmanesque "theory" of the labor movement; it may reflect a realistic appraisal of the limits of union
power. The price of steel, famine in India, oligopoly in industry,
the problems of genocide, DP's, etc—these are matters substantially
beyond the control of the union. Some of these nonbargaining issues
on which the expert has consistent high influence, however, may
objectively be closer to the central needs of the membership than
wage negotiations:

> *An economist:* Take taxes. There's no doubt in my mind that the
> real income of our members will be affected by taxes more than through
> collective bargaining this year. Yet any statement I'll make on taxes,
> they'll listen to. But any opinion I hold on collective bargaining will be
> duly ignored. (610-3.)

The expert's high influence in these areas—in so far as it has consequences in the political process—cannot be dismissed as unimportant. What actually reflects a thoroughgoing leadership indifference
or, at best, a lukewarm academic interest in the broad social problems of the day may be interpreted on the outside as a serious,
calculated expression of high policy. The outside liberal, the government official, or the labor reporter who hears the union staff
expert speak on these matters may project his own hopes, professional experience, or job routines into his perception of union
reality—he may see a "new unionism" arising on the scene. From
the union staff perspective, this is sometimes a bitter joke. One non-
UAW expert comments about Mr. Reuther's interest in world
politics:

> Walter goes out and makes a speech on foreign policy. Every liberal
> in the country has an orgasm! Walter goes out and makes a speech on
> pensions. The liberals are not excited about that one. But the speech
> on pensions gets the full backing of the union and the Executive Board;
> you know what the Executive Board thinks of the speech on foreign
> policy. (451-5.)

Another expert comments about government and employer reception
of his pronouncements on issues of national economic policy:

> The government technicians and the employer technicians haven't
> caught on that unions don't know about it and care less when their
> technicians take stands on these issues. . . . The jerks mending the leg-

islation don't realize the union's membership and the officers don't have
any opinions on these things. . . . These government bureaucrats are so
bound by their routines that they generalize them to the union. . . .
When the Fifth Secretary of the Interior speaks for the Secretary unless
he's disowned specifically it's assumed he's represented the Secretary's
policy. . . . So they think I'm representing [the union officer]. It occurs
on a whole host of things. . . . (610-3).

It is significant that in much of the court litigation involving John
L. Lewis' United Mineworkers Union, articles in the union's official
publication were alleged by opposition lawyers to represent union
policy, and in each case, the union successfully argued that it was
not the union speaking, but editor K. C. Adams.

My working hypothesis that amount of influence is positively
correlated with distance from the core function of the union as the
top officers see it finds further support in interview comments on the
expert's influence in relations with membership and with rival unions.
That important problems of internal union control and organizational strategy are areas where the expert treads with caution is not
only suggested by a limited statistical breakdown of degree of influence by type of problem, but is emphatically underscored in
self-appraisals by the experts.

An Internal Communications Specialist: On [legislative issues the
officer] is a damn sight more interested in his new house out in _____,
or in the baseball scores. This is not true when it comes to internal political affairs. . . . There we wouldn't dream of taking a stand. We know
it's a taboo subject. (522-10.)

A Contact Man [who has a top rating on influence]: I get into internal union operations. . . . I get into all areas. . . . I actually voice
sharp opinions on such matters as appointments [to union jobs]. Of
course, the ultimate judgment rests with them. My comments there are
not taken with the weight they have on other issues.[5]

Similar comments are made with respect to rival union relations
(where expert influence was high on only one in nine problems).
For example, several editors who do not normally clear copy or proof
with their officers mentioned coverage of other unions' activities
and settlements as the rare instances when they cleared carefully.

It follows from the above analysis that when a union becomes

---

5. The Bar Association study of labor lawyers confirms this picture of
relatively low expert influence on internal union affairs. R. M. Segal, *op. cit.*,
p. 359. Some limitations of this study are listed above, p. 63.

involved in all-out war with internal factions or external rivals, the influence of the staff expert—even within his sphere of competence —can be expected to decline. For at those times every decision— whatever the nature of the problem—is likely to be evaluated in terms of its effect on the outcome of the struggle. At the same time, all-out war may provide an opportunity for an expert with appropriate political skills and acceptable role orientation to move out of the role of expert and into a quasi-executive position (see Chapter XI).

These generalizations about the nature of the problem as a factor affecting the expert's influence need two qualifications:

1. Officer disinterest when carried to a logical extreme can mean that he will steer his union entirely away from nonbargaining problems. A pure-and-simple union leader with no interest in any of the problems I have labeled "extracurricular" will very likely never even hire staff experts (see Chapters IV-VI), let alone permit them to achieve high influence.

2. The expert in a Communist-dominated union presents a special case. There the top officers may include in their definition of the core function the promotion of Soviet foreign policy. Though the data are limited, it is probable that sustained high influence will be felt on problems that will shift with shifting party strategy and tactics *vis-à-vis* unionism. Moreover, the CP expert's standing in the Party, not the nature of the problem, may be the crucial determinant of influence. However, even here, there are hints of the applicability of the above analysis. The CP-line union officials (in the unions studied) face the same imperatives of survival as other union leaders, and their competences are similar. The nonbargaining issues even in a CP union are likely to require understandings and knowledge the officer grasps less easily than his hired staff man (party plant or not). These nonbargaining issues, despite party directives, may appear to him to be secondary to the time-consuming tasks of keeping on top of the bargaining situation and in control of the union.

There are a number of exceptions to the general picture presented above: (1) occasional instances of problems in collective bargaining or internal union control where the experts carried great weight; (2) occasional instances of problems of public relations and governmental relations pressing less close to the vital concerns of the union hierarchy where the expert had little or no influence. A closer look at some of these specific instances will (1) give us a feeling for the intricate interplay between technical-economic-legal considerations and political-ideological considerations in union decision-making; and (2) serve as an introduction to the analysis in Chapter XII of the channels of expert-boss communication, and in Chapter XI of the "managerial revolution" hypothesis applied to the competences, influence and power of both expert and officer.

The Interplay between Technical-Economic-Legal Intelligence and Political-Ideological Intelligence

What problems at the core of union functioning are so "technical" that the specialized knowledge and skill of experts (especially Facts and Figures Men) become overriding, despite the presence of substantial political considerations? They may be grouped as follows:

1. A series of problems which might be described as "secondary wage issues"—fringe wage benefits such as pensions and insurance; problems of wage structure and wage "inequities"; and problems of job content in relation to wage rates.

2. Wage bargaining where negative employment effects are clearly involved (or where the company persuades the union bargaining committee that such effects are certain if the union demand is granted); and problems of government action which employers allege have adverse effect on employment or ability to pay.

3. Problems of wage and strike policy or of internal control and rival union relations where government intervention is of crucial importance or potential large-scale litigation is involved.

Secondary Wage Issues.—Most of these issues—pension and insurance plans, time study, job evaluation, merit rating, incentive systems, etc.—are unique in their technical complexity; the staff experts employed to deal with them are among the most highly trained in the labor movement. Welfare bargaining has its actuarial tables, problems of funding, vesting, interest rates, eligibility, etc.

The various devices of "scientific" management carry their own vocabularies and conceptual apparatus. In both cases the union leader tends to feel lost. A typical comment from an officer:

> *On welfare bargaining:* The company had their actuaries in and we had ours in. They might as well have been talking Polish. Let's not kid ourselves—we put our contract in their [experts'] hands. (13-2.)

And from the bottom side up—a typical comment from an expert:

> *On welfare bargaining:* We've been in a tough spot in the past few months. We've got them [union hierarchy] in our clutches—they didn't know what to do in this area. . . . (401a-4.)

The full-time experts have carried the main burden for negotiation of settlements in the pension and insurance area in all the unions which used them.[6] Many officers, conceding that the issues raised by negotiated plans were beyond them, thought that once the plans were settled the need for expertise would disappear. They have discovered that the need continues after the contract is signed.[7]

When unions become enmeshed in the negotiation and administration of job evaluation programs (rationalization of wage rates in terms of job content), with the negotiation and policing of incentive systems, etc., the engineer plays a similarly important role: he carries the burden of negotiations within this sphere, and becomes even more indispensable in the handling of day-to-day workload grievances.

---

6. After the 1950 Steel Fact-Finding Board report, negotiation of welfare plans in key companies received much public attention—often obscuring the fact that the alleged "pattern" involved hundreds of separate agreements each distinguished more by its unique features than its similarity to the key settlement. The pension and insurance experts in auto and steel, for example, spent most of their time in the field during 1950-51 with local bargaining committees, district officials, and staff representatives applying and adapting very broad principles recommended by the International Union to local situations.

7. Among the problems: (1) inform members on rights under plans, interpret agreements to secure maximum services and benefits (e.g., what constitutes "disability," etc.); (2) review services used under an insurance plan and press to improve them; (3) review actuarial assumptions on pension plans and redetermine benefits on basis of cost experience; (4) put pressure on insurance plans on the basis of cost experience under them; and, where a jointly administered plan exists, (5) handle a series of form letters, application cards, and other procedural detail; and (6) train local leaders to serve on joint boards. "The administration of these pension plans," as one officer says, "is an involved business." (9-3.)

These two groups of experts have been fully used within their areas of competence, at times they have exercised considerable delegated authority in their relations with local unions, and have had high influence in many key bargaining situations.

Similarly, on problems of inter-plant, inter-area, and other "wage inequities," the Facts and Figures Men have often achieved high influence, despite complicated political implications. Here are typical examples of problems in which "technical" considerations and knowledge carried great weight (expert had high influence):

1. Shall we be serious in our demand for X cents per hour to adjust inter-plant, area and intra-plant inequities—inequities which may have unfavorable employment effects in the long run, but whose adjustment will immediately discriminate against a large and politically important segment of our membership? (Experts successfully pushed the long-run viewpoint.)

2. Should we hold out for X cents (much more than previous custom) in negotiations with a substandard, multiple-plant company? (Expert's research and argument buttressed weak local.)

The data suggest, too, that the expert's influence—especially the technical-economic-legal intelligence of Facts and Figures Men—will be greater in collective bargaining situations after a key bargain in a key company or industry is made. Bargaining for a breakthrough is more like a naked power struggle; but an employer—or a union leader—who knows the broad outlines of a settlement and accepts it as inevitable will be more receptive to rational arguments on the merits designed to fill in the details.

Union Expert or Company Assessments of Employment and Ability-to-Pay Effects.—In Congress, the public forum and academic debate, we frequently hear the view that union leaders should not, cannot, or do not take account of economic consequences. The trade union, we are told, is thoroughly and irrevocably a "political institution," little inclined to pay heed to the effects of union action on prices, production, or profits in particular firms and industries or in the economy as a whole.

My data, in a limited way, suggest that this picture of pure and unadulterated political unionism is overdrawn. In many of the decisions involving political considerations, the technical-economic-legal intelligence supplied by Facts and Figures men had high influence on union policies.

When it comes to employment effects of union wage policies, the expert's influence may be in the direction of taking less to preserve employment and the employer's competitive position; it may be in the direction of holding out for more (on the basis of the analysis that the company can stand it). In five unions in the Questionnaire Sample there are examples in which experts' findings of probable negative employment effects influenced union policies.[8] There are other instances where experts' analysis of the company's profit position led to tougher union wage policies.

When it comes to government action alleged by union employers to have adverse effects on their ability to pay or ability to give employment, the experts—in an antimonopoly, antiprotectionist spirit befitting an Adam Smith—typically strike their high influence blows for the free market. In at least nine problems of this sort, arising in six unions and requiring technical judgment, I found high expert influence in the face of political pressure from employers or members. They involved such issues as tariffs, price wars, stockpiling, and basing-point rulings. Typically, the story goes like this: the employer requests the union officer to join with him to prevent or protest adverse government rulings; the expert advises that the employers' allegations are groundless or exaggerated; the union refrains from participation or lets the government agency know (formally or informally) that the union is in sympathy with the ruling, not the employer.

Heavy Government Intervention and Potential Litigation.—Just as it is government intervention in economic life that constitutes the main source of the expert's entree to union payrolls (Chapters III-VI), so the impact of government (including court) decisions on union interests clears the way for his high influence—even in the face of important political pressures from members and other union

---

8. Compare the examples adduced for four other unions in Albert Rees, "Union Wage Policies," in *Interpreting the Labor Movement* (Industrial Relations Research Association, Dec., 1952), pp. 130-48. Times when market conditions (whether interpreted by experts or not) became overriding in the formulation of union wage policies are indicated from the history of collective bargaining in the bituminous coal, full-fashioned hosiery, cotton and rayon textile, and shoe industries. My examples—from other industries—confirm Rees' analysis: they were all in industries with a nonunion sector, or in firms with relatively poor competitive position.

leaders, even on decisions at the core of union functioning. Examples:

*1. Shall we change the timing of new contract demands to anticipate emerging Wage Stabilization Board policy (get demands on record in advance of contract date)?

2. What to do about union security and no-strike clauses under Taft-Hartley? What should our operating policies be with respect to the new labor law, June, 1947?

3. What should we do about litigation arising out of a long strike?

In the same category would be problems of approach to government fact-finding or mediation boards, or to arbitrators (government or private). "In major negotiations," says an expert, "the hunch and feel of the top officer is what it all boils down to. . . . Now when we get to arbitration where we don't have the strength —there the statistics and the preparations are important."

Political considerations may, of course, become all-important on any one of the issues discussed above. There are some striking examples in which the political-ideological aspects of a problem overrode important technical-economic-legal aspects in four decision-making areas:

1. *Relations with Employers:* How should we distribute money negotiated for temporary sickness benefits? The technical expert in insurance says to wait longer before initial weekly payment and pay more, so that the program provides for the most needy and discourages chiseling; but political pressures from the membership dictate a policy of paying less sooner.

Similarly, a pension expert says we should not attempt to go after pensions in weak companies unable to grant sound commitments; but the officers, under attack for flagging militancy, and pressured by members who don't see why they shouldn't get what everyone else is getting, ignore the expert advice.

2. *Relations with Government:* Should we risk a government fine for violation of injunction? Facts and Figures lawyers advise against the risk; officers weigh the net gains in terms of the possible bargain, the gain in reputation for militancy, the embarrassment to a disliked administration, etc.

Should we support the companies in their fight against a government regulation alleged to have a negative effect on their ability to pay? The expert here, on basis of a study of employers' cost position relative to other industries, advised no. The officers, however, decided to do the employers a favor.

3. *Internal Union Control and Organization:* Shall we suspend allegedly Communist leaders in area X? There were many legal complications. The experts were not consulted until after the suspensions were made. Experts then cleaned up the consequent NLRB cases and court litigation.

Shall we hold an educational institute in X area? The Internal Communications Specialist ordinarily would have high or medium influence here—if not on policy, at least on selection of the appropriate site, the form of the institute (camp, university, etc.), and the like. In this case the expert advised against holding the institute because in his view proper labor education facilities were lacking. The officer overruled the expert: it was needed to show headquarters interest in the area, take the play away from rival union, etc. The expert influenced only decisions of execution.

4. *Public Relations:* Should we give financial aid to X outside project? The public relations expert advised no because the project would not accord with intent of the donation. The expert's recommendation was ignored; the recipient was a friend of a middle-level union official acquired in his rise to power.

Thus far I have focused on the nature of the problem as a variable affecting the influence of the staff expert. The picture that emerges is this: the expert has highest sustained influence on problems that his boss sees as far from the core function of the union (these problems may nevertheless be objectively important to the members). The expert has least influence in the areas of internal union control and organization and rival union relations—problems lying at the heart of the officer's personal and organizational survival. Here the boss tends to be his own expert (though he may utilize to some extent the political-ideological intelligence of his Internal Communications Specialists and his Contact Men). Technical-economic-legal knowledge, as we have seen, does occasionally override political considerations and expediencies—especially on "secondary wage issues" of a complex character, on problems calling for assessment of possible employment effects of union and government action, and on problems in any area of union decision when large-scale government intervention is clearly involved.

"Crystallizing" Policy: The Importance of Means and Execution Decisions

To capture more fully the dynamics of the decision-making process and appreciate more fully the expert's chances for discretion and leeway throughout it, we will concentrate for a moment on decisions concerned with the selection of means and the execution of policy. The staff expert in a union—like the functionary in any private association—has many opportunities to influence "policy" at times and in ways far removed from formal or informal policy deliberations.

The union operates in a fast-moving, constantly changing situation. The executive in a democratic association must constantly adjust convention mandates, broad policy resolutions of official boards and committees, to cover new and unforeseen cases. To carry out organizational purposes, he must in fact change the purposes, adapting them to the needs of the moment. So, too, the functionaries who assist the executive, as they interpret and apply policy (even the executive's policy), can modify organizational purposes.

The staff expert gets his chance especially where official policy is loose, or the specificity of the problem as defined by the boss is low. In the role of "crystallizing agent," the expert affects the selection of means and makes decisions involved in execution. He articulates policy and gives it sharper definition; in doing so, he inevitably affects its direction. This occurs mainly when the expert is assigned to put something into words. He writes editorials, speeches, convention resolutions and reports—all within the framework of New Deal-Fair Deal "policies," perhaps, but "there's always room to move around" in a framework so broad. In fact, he may have "a helluva time getting them [line officials] to participate in the shaping of the report." (700a-1.) Or he writes up a wage pro-

gram, a contract clause, a statement on government mobilization.
Here he can expect closer scrutiny of the emphasis and tone (see
pp. 183 ff.), but, again, there is some leeway. There may be many
hours of policy discussion, and he may be assigned to draft a statement, "boil it down." And in boiling it down he selects some
things, eliminates others, gives this part a militant play, tones down
another. Sometimes, instead of boiling it down, he may have to
expand it. "He's the legalistic expert," said one informant, "and in
interpretation of a clause, he'll set up a new policy. That's the only
way I know how to put it. A three-word policy a lawyer will put
into seven pages, and you get three or four different policies out of
one. Read some of [expert's] releases and you'll know what I mean."
(453-4.)

The ambiguous character of "policy" and the gulf that divides
"policy" from "execution" are seen most vividly when the necessity
of speedy decision is combined with a heavy press of work. "There
is a surprising amount of freedom," muses one expert. "Part of it,
of course, isn't any great liberality; it's just that they're so damned
busy they *can't* supervise." (505a-3.) And decisions—policy or not
—sometimes can't wait.[9]

It is true that the expert's influence on the content of official
or semi-official convention resolutions, press releases, editorials, and
other "policy" statements is likely to exceed his influence on their
implementation. The expert may sell the union officer on the "right"
tariff policy for an after-dinner speech or federation resolution, but
when free trade appears to threaten employment in an industry
under jurisdiction the speech or resolution may be ignored. Nevertheless, these policy pronouncements, however loose, do upon occasion constitute a lever for expert influence. "As editor," says one
expert, "I hewed close to CIO policy. Sometimes closer than they
wanted me to! But they couldn't say anything—because they were
supposed to be following CIO policy themselves." (906-6.)[10] An

9. The experts working in small unions may have more frequent opportunity for exercising this sort of discretion. Such a union has a small headquarters staff; there is no raft of administrative assistants to keep things under
control while the line officials are gone.

10. Literal application of formal policy is a device frequently cited by
experts who want to influence union race relations decisions.

invocation of the union creed can sometimes be effective even where the issue is one vital to the union's interests:

Even where it hurts, you can appeal to the total framework within which they [officers] have been operating for years. Our policy statements over the years have been antimonopoly. So when X was pressured by the industry into taking a stand upholding price collusion, I could point to their tradition and he would have to say, as he did, "Oh, I didn't realize its implications." (G309a-1.)

Conclusion

Whatever the channels of influence, and whatever the area of decision, the ways of influence in all unions are strikingly similar: "crystallize" the policy when the policy is loose, sharpen the definition of the problem when its specificity is low, fill the vacuum when the boss is busy or time is short, use official policy pronouncements as a lever.

In the final analysis, however, what counts is the cumulative effect of thousands of statements of opinion and fact flowing through all the channels of influence, formal and informal, direct and indirect. "Most of it is creating a climate," says one expert, "and the boss may not even know he's been influenced." (305-5.) Day by day the expert articulates trade union aims and aspirations; day by day he invokes the documents (whose content and tone he helped shape) as justification for union action along a broad front. It is plain that the expert supplies the leader with a set of comfortable justifications for union policies and rationalizes the leader's prior beliefs; but he also gives some coherence to these policies, and—through a steady influence in the nonbargaining areas—he helps broaden leadership understandings and interests, helps create and sustain leadership views of the role of unionism in a free society.

CHAPTER X

TYPE OF UNION AND TYPE OF EXPERT AS THEY AFFECT CHANCES OF EXPERT INFLUENCE

IN ALL OF THIS TALK of influence and the factors maximizing it, a time perspective is essential. How much weight the skills and knowledge of the expert will swing depends upon the past history and present position and resources of the union and its leaders in the society as a whole, and on the career lines and resources of the individual experts involved. The relations of labor to society and of experts to union are in constant flux. Furthermore, not all experts acquire equal influence as their careers and skills develop through time.

In what kinds of unions, under what conditions do experts get used? Which of the Functional Types and which of the Role Orientation Types have the most influence? Who moves into the inner circle of key decision-makers by what routes?

Type of Union as a Variable in the Use and Influence of Experts

Again we come back to the changing role of the leader. The expert would never get the call to serve the union if the top officers did not feel some deficiency in their own skills and resources (or those of their political lieutenants). The union leader has typically climbed his way to national power from modest beginnings, and the climb has been fast. Starting as a wage worker in a single craft, trade, plant, or company, and elected or appointed line official at a local or regional level, he rises to the top of a vast and complicated administrative apparatus. Four trends in the labor movement predispose him to hire experts to assist in his new job (or keep on the ones his predecessor used): (1) the emergence of industrial, multi-industrial and amalgamated craft units as the dominant structural models in the labor movement; (2) the development of company-wide, industry-wide, or multi-employer bargaining on a national or regional scale; (3) an increasing involvement with and dependence on the federal government; (4) a tendency toward centralization of union government.

The centralization of union government (described in Chapter I) puts a heavier burden of responsibility for bargaining and administration on the shoulders of the national officers and complicates their job of internal control. The union membership interests and aspirations they must gauge are far more varied and contradictory than those of a lesser, smaller unit. With acquisition of these heavy responsibilities of the national union office goes a dramatic change in the leader's style of life and work. To many writers this has suggested the role of the union as an avenue of social mobility denied its leaders elsewhere in the industrial order. These writers have seen the union as an alternative way for wage workers to get ahead in a society in which entrepreneurial and managerial positions are (it is alleged) increasingly filled from other strata. [1]

Not only is the union a source of jobs within its own structure, but it is increasingly a stepping-stone to better occupations in other

---

1. *Industry and Society,* ed. W. F. Whyte (New York: McGraw-Hill Book Co., Inc., 1946), pp. 43-45, 187-88; W. L. Warner and J. L. Low, *The Social System of the Modern Factory* (New Haven: Yale University Press, 1947), pp. 159, 160, 177. N.B., C. W. M. Hart, "Industrial Relations Research and Social Theory" (Reprint), *Canadian Journal of Economics and Political Science,* XV, No. 1 (Feb., 1949), 7. Cf. Michels, *op. cit.,* pp. 273-74. The writer, in a study of a UAW Local in South Chicago, noted that all the top officers of the local either had been in business for themselves in the past, or currently have spare-time businesses or play leadership roles in other community organizations. Several other office-holders either have spare-time businesses or said they want to or once wanted to go into business. Harold L. Wilensky, "Local 166: A Study of a Union's Influence on the Political Orientation of Its Membership." (Unpublished Master's Thesis, Department of Sociology, University of Chicago, 1949), p. 24.

areas. As Labor becomes more powerful politically, state and federal appointments and offices become available to union functionaries. Even in industry the union is becoming a (sometimes reluctant) source of supervisory recruits. (Many companies now pick off local union leaders as they develop for supervisory jobs, both to drain off union talent and to get supervisors who can get along with the men.)

While the union may very well be a source of great mobility chances, the few who arrive at the International Headquarters seldom have anywhere else to go. Career lines run pretty much within the particular union—which, of course, makes the tenure problem loom large. The security of the top officer more and more depends on keeping his fences mended with the mass of office aspirants down below.

Centralization of union government—and the intensification of the tenure problem due to the nature of the leadership career line —generates one set of demands on top officer competence. Another set of demands stems from certain changes in union structure and the structure of the collective bargaining unit, which are in turn related to the public interest impact of union decisions and the increasing intervention of government.

Few modern unions fall in the pure craft category. Amalgamations of many crafts, trades, parts of industries, and industries defy simple classification, but students of Labor are agreed that the tendency is toward more inclusive union structures. So, too, with bargaining units. The company-wide and locality-wide bargaining areas have grown in importance.[2] Though it is not yet widespread, many unions press for industry-wide bargaining arrangements.

Now the officer of a multi-industrial, industrial, or multicraft union typically gets his experience and training in his own local or industry council, or his own craft. He finds it hazardous to generalize what may have been his narrow experience. He encounters strange terms, strange practices, new problems—especially when bargaining for those sections of the membership in industries not encompassed by his practical wisdom. So he hires staff experts to

---

2. David A. McCabe, "Union Policies as to the Area of Collective Bargaining," in Brooks *et al.* (eds.), *op. cit.*, pp. 110-29.

help him.[3] By the time he has acquired broader sophistication, he has also acquired new habits of administration and a large staff whose members are of demonstrated loyalty. Even if his own competence has increased enormously, he is not likely to get rid of them.

Even in the absence of centralization, inclusive structure, and heterogeneous bargaining units, a top officer who finds himself heavily involved with the federal government may be moved to bend an ear to the expert. In all the above discussion of the functions and influence of staff experts, the importance of government intervention has appeared again and again. Mobilization and world tension have given new urgency to the union leader's concern with government and have helped him capture a vision of himself as a statesman moving on a world stage. One top officer waxed enthusiastic as he described the great pressures (largely governmental and political) he had to cope with on his job:

It's great work—it's exciting work—there's a lot of variety—I don't have any two days alike. Why just in the course of the past few days, I've had occasion to talk with government officials at the highest level, of course with leaders of the labor movement [he'd just come from a United Labor Policy Committee meeting], with the university professors [names professors serving on government boards]; I've had [foreign labor leaders] over here as my guests. . . . I go to these international conferences. [Describes trip abroad.] . . . Hell, it's the most interesting work you can imagine. You're constantly meeting people, you cover a broad horizon. (22-6.)

This "broad horizon" means a set of experiences beyond the plant, beyond traditional collective bargaining, often in areas relatively new to the union leader. Here, again, we would expect to find large numbers of staff experts: Facts and Figures Men to advise on the meaning and import of government decisions, to prepare or render testimony before government boards; Contact Men to maintain steady relations with legislators and government officials; all types to herald the new responsibilities.

---

3. Even bargaining with one multiplant company may present a picture of tremendous diversity. For example, the Ford Department of the UAW-CIO, which makes extensive use of experts on and off the staff, has to deal with operations beyond those connected with auto manufacture. For Ford has its own steel division, its own glass plant, its own sand mine; it operates railroads, a plastics division, paint and leather processing units and more.

If the above analysis (derived largely from qualitative data) is correct, then the type of union making most use of national head-quarters staff experts would fit this picture: its structure would be industrial or multi-industrial, its government highly centralized; a large proportion of its membership would be covered by national or regional, multi-plant, company-wide, or industry-wide contracts; it would be highly involved with or dependent upon the federal government.

Data offer striking confirmation of the picture. Each of the 28 unions in the Questionnaire Sample was rated High, Medium, or Low on each of the four factors. A membership/experts ratio was used as a measure of relative use of experts (thousands of members per expert). The figure of fifty thousand was chosen arbitrarily to divide a high from a low ratio. (See Appendix B for ratings and a full explanation.) Negative cases were then sought in relation to two hypotheses: (1) the presence of a rating of High or High minus, on at least one factor, will appear in unions with an M/E ratio of under 50; (2) absence of H or H— on at least one factor will mean an M/E ratio of 50 or over. There was only one negative case for hypothesis one (union number 15); four borderline nega-tive cases for hypothesis two (unions 17, 20, 26, 27). Closer exam-ination of all cases showed them to be consistent with my analysis thus far.

Union 15, which rates high on all counts, has relatively few experts (M/E ratio of 86). It is large, militant, and strike-prone.[4] While industrial in structure, its membership is relatively homo-geneous. Its top officer is widely recognized as a versatile and talented leader, organizer, bargainer, orator, administrator. Finally, the union, while having a high M/E ratio, makes extensive use of outside experts, private and governmental. Moreover, some of the functions fulfilled by staff experts in comparable unions are spread among various line officials and administrative assistants.

Four unions without high ratings make more use of experts than expected, but they are not clear-cut negative cases: (1) they are small in size, which, because of the indivisibility of experts,

---

4. See above, pp. 53, 66-67, where the point is made that the closer bargaining is to a naked power struggle, the less relevant are the functions of staff experts.

distorts the M/E ratio as a measure (e.g., the presence of only three experts in a union of fifty-nine thousand gives it the very low M/E ratio of 20); (2) three of the four unions have Medium ratings on three of the four factors, and three of them have at least one M+ rating—close to the expected High; (3) the one without an M+ rating is close to the expected M/E ratio (it has an M/E ratio of 40).[5]

Officer Competence: Objective and Subjective.—The type of union affects the expert's entree in so far as it puts demands on the top officer's competence. But competence (or the lack of it) expresses itself in many ways. And men are not always aware either of their limitations, or of their capabilities. Whatever the objective situation demands in the way of expert knowledge and skill, the top officers' perception of that situation is what prompts his use or non-use of experts, as well as his receptivity to their advice once he hires them.

Union people, when asked how the boss' competence affects the expert's influence, run the gamut of the logical possibilities: (1) the officer has general low competence in bargaining and administration so the expert moves into the vacuum, takes over; (2) the officer is incompetent but does not know it, so he never calls on anyone for advice, or, if he has an expert or two around, he "won't listen because he thinks there's nothing new under the sun"; or (3) the officer "is statesmanlike," "alert," is "quick, sees things in perspective," is "generally competent," and therefore listens to the expert, accepting his ideas without resentment; (4) the officer is "capable of sifting and weighing expert opinion," is "a sharp guy," "brilliant," therefore he "won't take anything without proof" and "the expert can't do anything the boss doesn't understand and approve."

Thus, while general leadership competence is a factor in staff

---

5. Characteristics of negative cases:

Union No.	Size (thousands)	M/E ratio	Ratings
17	59	20	M M L+ M+
20	130	33	M+ M L ?
26	120	40	M M— L M—
27	175	44	M M M— M+

See Appendix B, Table 8.

expert influence, its effect must be seen in the context of the officer's administrative style. The leaders at the top of the unions I contacted could be classified roughly in these categories: (1) highly competent and also willing to delegate authority and responsibility (experts allowed maximum leeway, but kept under intelligent control); (2) highly competent but unwilling to delegate (experts closely supervised or advice is typically ignored); (3) highly competent now, but either unaware of it or relies on experts because of habits developed in the past when he was less capable; (4) not-so-competent and aware of it (problems left to the experts to work out with little supervision, or officer does not understand experts' advice and refuses to act on it, or union stays away from the complicated problems completely and does not use experts); (5) not-so-competent, and unaware of it ("they bull their way through, ignoring the advice of technicians or anyone else").

In dealing with this question of officer competence as it affects the position of the expert, it is important to realize that there are many things the expert does that his boss can do, too, sometimes better. Moreover, competence—either in general or in a specific problem area—is something that develops with the demands of the leadership role, whatever the humble beginnings of the incumbent. True, the officer may be lost when it comes to the funding of a pension plan; but he may become quite expert in handling the complicated grievances that arise concerning eligibility, worker rights and benefits under the plan.[6] Complexities of incentive systems and job evaluation plans are hard to grasp, but a few officers have acquired detailed knowledge of them. To formulate contract language for the rules of work sometimes demands the services of lawyers. But a few operating officials from the ranks in the Railroad Brotherhoods have acquired considerable specialized skill in writing such rules; they also prepare briefs for presentation to the Railroad Adjustment Board. Several unions—including the Oilworkers and Machinists—have long trained operating officials to handle NLRB cases. Other unions encompass in their jurisdiction a large

---

6. In several unions a line official is assigned to learn about these plans. Some of the officers in the Railroad Brotherhoods and the Letter Carriers helped write the laws covering their members' retirement; the meaning of these laws holds little mystery for them.

number of white-collar workers to whom the processing of words, numbers and memoranda may be old stuff.

The change in union leadership expertise is underscored by the frequent references in several unions to "sea lawyers" among the line officials. One lawyer says,

> You know, nearly every labor leader as I'm introduced to him and he hears I'm a lawyer—he immediately brightens up. So many times I get the reaction, "Say, I was going to go to law school myself." Especially among [middle leaders]. Some of them would still like to have a law degree. Whether they think it would give them distinction, I don't know. But an amazing number of them are frustrated lawyers. Take X. He just loves to go into a courthouse. You can see his eagerness when he goes in. He makes a wonderful witness. He understands how I handle these cases. He has a burning desire to lead one—he'd love to be up there himself. . . . The law is a real topic of conversation among our leadership. (203-7.)

Aside from the slowly increasing technical-legal-economic prowess of the line official, there has always been his political expertise. Here his talents—albeit a little less developed, a bit less polished—border on those of his political experts (see Chapters V and VI), and presumably will some day make him less dependent upon them.

To be sure, it is easy to exaggerate the expertise, political or technical, of the top official. His own self-estimate is frequently overdrawn. The estimate may be a reflection of his ignorance or a defensive reaction to demands in his new roles that tax him beyond his capacity.[7] The point is merely that some general skills of the leader and some specialized knowledge in some areas of union operation apparently increase with his rise to power. The deficiencies in competence of which the union leader is aware may be less sharply felt as his experience in the new era of managerial unionism broadens.

---

7. Staff experts in every type of organization sooner or later run into the "single case disease" ("You can't tell me how they feel about this settlement —I just got a letter from local X," etc.); the "many case disease" ("The cost-of-living can't be going down—I talked to thirty or forty people and they all said it was going up"); or the "I knew it all along" disease ("what you found by careful survey—it's no news to me"); or the "practical experience disease" ("I never heard that before and I don't believe it anyway. Besides, were you there?")

Functional Type and Time in the Labor Movement as Variables in Influence

The demands on leadership competence—reflecting the factors of structure, type of bargaining, degree of central control and involvement with government—coupled with the leader's own acquisition of expertise affect the expert's initial chance to move in. Which experts are able to make the most of that chance?

Table 4—Relation of Functional Type to Influence Rating[a] (Main Sample)

			FUNCTIONAL TYPE					
Influence Rating	Facts & Figures Man		Intern. Com Specialist		Contact Man		TOTALS	
	N	%	N	%	N	%	N	%
High (6-10)	4	6.2	3	8.3	14	50.0	21	16.4
Medium (4-5)	12	18.8	7	19.4	6	21.4	25	19.5
Low (0-3)	48	75.0	26	72.2	8	28.6	82	64.1
Totals	64	100.0	36	99.9	29[b]	100.0	128	100.0

a. See Appendix C for method of rating influence.

b. Two of these cases—19 and 107—are borderline between Contact Man and Internal Communications Specialist. One rates Medium on influence, the other Low. To eliminate them would strengthen my conclusion.

Table 4 shows that it is the Contact Men who make good: half of them rate High on influence, compared to about 6 per cent of the Facts and Figures Men and about 8 per cent of the Internal Communications Specialists. No Facts and Figures Man scored more than 6 (the lowest score for a High rating); the three ICS cases rated High were also on the border between Medium and High. The twenty-one cases with a High rating represent sixteen different unions.[8]

The relatively high influence of the Contact Man underscores

8. It is interesting that their occupational and professional backgrounds are quite varied: six are lawyers, seven are economists (broadly defined), and five are journalists.

the vital importance of human relations skills and contacts in the officer-expert relationship. Influence is won by gaining personal access to the boss, and the Contact Man has the resources to make maximum use of the informal channels (see Part V). The lesser influence of the Internal Communications Specialist despite his similar political talents is probably due to the narrow focus of his work. He gets into fewer areas of union decision. Moreover, his preoccupation with problems so close to the survival of the top officer stacks the cards against high influence. (As we have seen in Chapter IX, the closer the expert comes to a problem at the core of the union's function as defined by the boss, the less influence he has.)

A second factor which sorts out the experts according to influence is the sheer time they have served the labor movement. About 22 per cent of the old-timers (entered labor movement before 1941) have High scores, while only 4.8 per cent of the newcomers (served only after 1944) rate High. The old-timers, roughly, are the people who got in on the ground floor; they made themselves available to Labor in the Depression era or before—when a union was less respectable and had to make its way against odds. They are the fellows who "grew up with the organization," have a better claim to a voice in its affairs and easier personal access to the boss.

The importance of an early entry is also indicated by an examination of the cases which negate the notion that the Contact Man has the best chance to make good. All four of the Facts and Figures Men and two of the three Internal Communications Specialists with High influence scores are old-timers.[9]

Role Orientation as a Variable in Influence

Skills and functions, time of service—these affect the expert's influence. But what about his outlook? What are the role orientations of the men selected for high influence? Do they come closest to a bureaucratic mentality?

By all measures (median influence score, proportion High, pro-

---

9. Of the eight Contact Men who rate Low, three entered 1941 or after; one is unknown.

portion Medium or High, proportion scoring 5-10—i.e., upper medium and high—or proportion Low), the Politico, the Party Missionary, and the Legislative-Liberal Missionary make out best on influence.[10] The more bureaucratic types rate Medium or Low. The Technician Professional—closest to the Weberian model of professionalized bureaucrat—has middling influence. The Politico, who is likely to be a Contact Man in function and have high political affect and well-developed political skills, is the man of knowledge who has achieved highest influence as a staff expert. On the assumption that the character of a movement or of any social group is reflected in the orientations, skills and work of its successful men, these findings—especially the position of the Missionaries and Politicos—can be interpreted as an index of the low degree of bureaucratization of the labor movement.[11]

Table 5—Distribution of 120 Cases by Present Role Orientation and Influence Rating*

ROLE ORIENTATION	INFLUENCE RATING		TOTALS
	High-Medium (4-10)	Low (0-3)	
Politico	8	4	12
Missionary	14	14	28
Pgm. Prof.	7	15	22
Tech. Prof.	9	20	29
Careerist	5	24	29
Totals	43	77	120

* The focus is on relative influence of staff experts with different role orientations, so five Administrative Assistants who once were but are not now staff experts are excluded: One High and one Medium TP, one High Rank-and-File Car., one Med. OC; and one Low REM. One outs.- Careerist could not be rated by influence. A three-way spit on influence (columns) and a combination of role orientation categories (Politico and Missionary vs. Professional and Careerist in the rows) yields the same results with the same significance.

$$X^2 = 12.5$$
$$P < .02$$

The unexpected High rating of the Missionaries must be seen in the context of a protest movement hangover. The seven Missionaries

10. Contrary in some respects to the working hypothesis with which I started: those with the mission lack the influence and leave a successful movement; those with the influence lack or abandon the mission.

11. Note, however, that the more recent arrivals—the Professionals—are not the lowest in relative influence. Moreover, no Contact Man with a Professional orientation is relegated to a Low Influence position.

who rate High on influence work in seven different unions. In six of these unions the top executive is either CP-oriented or was once a participant in the socialist movement. The other union (as well as four of the six) has a very large proportion of its jurisdiction as yet unorganized. All face relatively strong management opposition. The position of the Missionaries in these unions can thus be interpreted as a reflection of: (1) receptivity to ideological penetration due to Communist domination; (2) the nostalgia of the one-time Socialist for his youthful ideological enthusiasms (the top officer salves conscience and achieves a sense of moral rectitude by keeping around a relic or two from his militant past);[12] and/or (3) the early stage of development in the cycle from sect to church, protest group to stable administrative organ (the unions which still face large unorganized territories and strong management opposition retain more of the character of the protest movement than unions of greater "maturity" and are therefore more receptive to the influence of ideologues).

If this analysis is correct, succession of new leadership types in unions now Communist-dominated or headed by nostalgic ex-Socialists will mean the departure of the Missionary staff experts, or a decline in their influence. Similar results would flow from successful organization of the workers now outside the fold and a decrease in management opposition.

Develop the skills and fulfill the functions of the Contact Man; get in on the ground floor; and acquire a role orientation appropriate to the stage of union development—this is a rough formula for achieving a position of high steady influence as a trade union staff expert.

But look at the negative cases. On function, seven Facts and Figures Men and Internal Communications Specialists have High influence, eight Contact Men rate Low. On time, almost half the old-timers are relegated to Low influence posts, and an impressive number of newcomers and wartimers have achieved Medium influence. A stricter interpretation of "time of first service to the labor movement" (e.g., substituting "first full-time paid job")

---

12. Many of these ideologues were hired *after* the union leader himself abandoned the cause.

would put several more High influence cases in the recent arrival category. On role orientation, there is no type all of whose representatives are relegated to Low (or to High) influence posts.[13] Finally, and most important, this picture of functional type, time of entry and role orientation as related to influence misses the many men of knowledge who have moved out of the sample into executive positions, the many who never get into a sample of "staff experts" because they make their way as private consultants, and the like.

For a more dynamic explanation of expert influence it is necessary to consider types of career lines among those who achieve high influence, to examine the process by which a specialist moves into a broad range of union decisions.

---

13. It is an impressive demonstration of the utility of all three variables considered together, however, that there is *not one case* of the following description: (1) *High* influence Missionary (serving in a union receptive to Missionary influence) of the *"wrong"* functional type and length of service (not Contact Man, not old-timer); (2) *Low* influence Missionary (serving in a union receptive to Missionary influence) of the *"right"* functional type and length of service (Contact Man, old-timer).

CHAPTER XI

THE MOVING-IN PROCESS:
MANAGERIAL REVOLUTION?

MANY WRITERS, on the basis of observation in a great variety of organizations, public and private, have noted in a general way the presence of an inner circle, a "kitchen cabinet" of key advisers who transcend the formal roles assigned to them. Many of these functionaries are technical specialists who have moved into the entire range of organizational decisions. Comptrollers in large corporations, Congressional Committee staff experts, scientists in government and business, lawyers and economists in government agencies —all are seen to face the choice between a life of technical service and job advancement.[1] The role of the expert, all these studies suggest, is self-changing: if he is successful within his sphere of technical competence, if his advice is taken on matters where his specialized knowledge is relevant, he is likely to be chosen for tasks outside that sphere of competence, where his specialized knowledge may be irrelevant.[2]

---

1. See Dimock and Hyde, *op. cit.*, p. 64; Stephen K. Bailey, *Congress Makes a Law: The Story Behind the Employment Act of 1946* (New York: Columbia University Press, 1950), p. 64; A. W. Macmahon and John D. Millett, *Federal Administrators: A Biographical Approach to the Problem of Departmental Management* (New York: Columbia University Press, 1939), p. 464; B. Barber, *Science and the Social Order* (Glencoe, Ill.: The Free Press, 1952), p. 176; V. Thompson, *The Regulatory Process in OPA Gas Rationing* (New York: Columbia University, King's Crown Press, 1950).

2. Note David Riesman's formulation of this theme: "The pressure towards social competence, with its concurrent disregard for technical competence

The difficulty with these formulations is that they seldom make clear (1) from what these men of knowledge move—the precise nature of their initial competence; (2) to what they move—the functions fulfilled and skills developed in their new roles; and (3) the process by which their roles change. In the union case, an examination of some types of career lines will help clarify and explain this moving-in process. I shall focus on the careers of High Influence experts in my sample as well as men of knowledge who have acquired much influence, authority, or power, but whose present position puts them outside my group of staff experts.

It is useful, first, to distinguish four terminal points in this moving-in process. The man of knowledge, wherever he begins his career, can become (at a local, state, regional, or national level) (1) a staff expert with High Influence and the beginnings of executive authority; (2) a "Braintruster-Confidante" or (3) a "Housekeeping Administrative Assistant"—both of whom have some executive authority; or (4) an elected or appointed line official who has power and wields formal executive authority.

1. *The High Influence Staff Expert.* This may be a Facts and Figures Man, an Internal Communications Specialist or a Contact Man, though the Contact Man is the one most likely to rate high. A few of the High Influence Experts acquire some executive authority;[3] Their skills and functions shade off into those of:

2. *The Braintruster-Confidante.* This is the general adviser to the top officer. He may be called "Executive Vice President," "Ad-

---

... is typical for the emergence of a new pattern in American business and professional life: if one is successful in one's craft, one is forced to leave it." As the engineer, newspaperman, doctor, professor move up their occupational ladders, they ". . . must bury their craft routines and desert their craft companions. They must work less with things and more with people." *Op. cit.,* pp. 133-34. Dael Wolfle offers some evidence consistent with this observation in his analysis of the occupational distribution in 1953 of living male college graduates (and also Master's degree holders) in the United States, classified by fields in which Bachelor's or first professional degree was earned. He shows much shift out of specialized fields into administrative and executive ranks. *America's Resources of Specialized Talent* (New York: Harper and Bros., 1954), pp. 48-61.

3. For instance, the Contact Man with the highest influence rating is viewed by his colleagues as an executive, not a staff expert. Faced with the allegation that the experts are moving in, several functionaries in one union denied it, citing in evidence the fact that the experts have to clear important matters with the General Counsel!

ministrative Assistant," or "General Counsel"; he may not even be on the official union staff. In all cases he has very high influence and operates in all areas of union decision. His authority and power rest upon his close personal, confidential relationship to the boss.

"Your power," says a retired Braintruster-Confidante, "stems from who you're representing. It's the kind of power Hopkins had with Roosevelt. Whether it's in a union or the government or a corporation, the chief executive officer has to have a couple people he can rely on. People who have no divided loyalties, who will do his bidding exactly and preferably who'll do his thinking for him, too. People who can be counted on to act exactly the way he would if he were around." (903-4.)

Sometimes, besides acting as general adviser and deputy to the boss, he does considerable trouble-shooting in the field:

X [braintruster] is Y's [officer's] alter ego in dealing with intra-union business. He represents him when he can't be there. He's Y's shadow, his right-hand man. He represents the maximum policy influence of any technician. . . . He's a diplomat and a trouble-shooter, a buffer and a fireman. He runs around for Y, he takes the heat off Y. . . . He's so good that he's developed an area of influence that is subdefinitive. He knows when to say yes and when to say no, when to press Y, when to keep quiet. . . . Strictly as a person he has important influence. He has a close personal relation—that's a large part of it. X is close enough to Y and is experienced enough so people tend to trust his judgment. . . . He's worth ten years on Y's life. (505a-1.)

The talents of the Braintruster-Confidante and the Contact Man are often described in identical terms. The distinction is one of degree; the former has more influence, has a closer personal relationship to the boss—a sustained, easy access the staff expert rarely achieves. Moreover, he is usually more visible and less anonymous in his operations; as deputy to the boss, he exercises some executive authority.[4]

3. *The Housekeeping Administrative Assistant.* Some of these are "pressure screeners" and in this their duties resemble those of

---

4. For a detailed description in similar vein of the Braintruster-Confidante role in government, see the references to Harry Hopkins in Robert E. Sherwood, *Roosevelt and Hopkins* (New York: revised, enlarged edition; Bantam Books, Inc., 1950), esp. Vol. I., pp. 2-3, 6, 134, 220, 247-49, 260-66, 456-57; Vol. II, pp. 23, 44-47, 94-96, 232, 280, 368-70, 380-86, 442-50, 468-73, 520, 553.

the Braintruster-Confidante. Moreover, their relationship to the boss is close, their contacts with him frequent. But their work is far more routine, their influence typically less, their authority more circumscribed, and their operations generally more anonymous. The Housekeeping Administrative Assistant may be "sort of a personal secretary to the President"; like the private secretary in other unions he may channel the important mail, answer some of it, arrange appointments, protect the boss from unnecessary visitors and problems. He may combine the handling of administrative detail with financial functions; he may supervise the expenditures of the departments, act as watchdog over union properties.[5]

In some unions there is a three-way split: one man (or set of men) handles the financial side, another the routine, nonfinancial administrative detail; a third acts in the Braintruster-Confidante role. In others one man or office combines aspects of all three.

4. *An elected or appointed line official.* Some men of knowledge acquire formal executive authority. In some unit at some level of the labor movement, they become President, Vice President, Secretary-Treasurer, etc.; director of an operating department; "International Rep." or business agent. The extent of this is unknown. But I have the names in thirty-nine cases where it has occurred; and several respondents allege that it is on the increase in specific unions.

Thus, there are four terminal points in the moving-in process: elected or appointed line official, housekeeping administrative assistant, braintruster-confidante, or staff expert with very high influence. All have acquired some executive authority; all possess managerial talent. From what beginnings do they move in?

The positions in which these men get their start (at any level of the labor movement) include: (1) staff expert recruited from the outside; (2) staff expert recruited from the ranks of union membership; (3) staff expert recruited from the outside who put in a brief ritual period in the rank and file; (4) professional or college man who enters as an organizer, paid or unpaid; (5) male

---

5. E.g., see description of the "Office of the Executive Secretary" in ILGWU-AFL, *Report of the General Executive Board to the 1950 Convention,* Part VIII, pp. 244 ff.

private secretary; (6) private paid consultant; and (7) outside adviser with no paid connection with the union administration.[6]

How men with these beginnings move into top positions of authority and power can best be seen in the career patterns of groups of specific cases.[7]

Emerging in a Crisis Situation

Most of the men of knowledge I know of who acquired executive or quasi-executive posts in the labor movement emerged in some period of crisis in either the larger society or the movement. Some examples are the upheaval of the Great Depression, the period of World War II, a factional battle leading to schism within an established union, or the creation of a new union to exploit virgin territory.

The Depression Era.—Many of these cases who moved into one of the four terminal executive positions entered the labor movement during a period of rapid, militant expansion, especially during the thirties (which ties in with the previous finding that High Influence experts are typically old-timers). A few made contact during earlier organizing campaigns in the sweated industries, e.g., the needle trades, 1910-30. Many were ideologues who moved in with a political mission.[8] "In the throes of an organizing drive," says one of them, "anyone could move in and become a leader of a union . . . anyone who happened to be on the spot and participated in the activities had a chance. This didn't exclude an intellectual. . . . Accountant, lawyer, preacher, anything—what did it matter then?" (961-2,3.) Whether these ideologues maintain their radical political orientations or become transformed into Professional Service, Politico, or Careerist types, their well-timed arrival on the

---

6. It is important to note that some cases are *hired* as administrative assistants from the start. Furthermore, in rare cases, the man of knowledge begins in a top executive post and moves *down* to staff specialist.

7. The subjective side of the career pattern—changes in the role orientation of the staff expert—is treated in more detail in Chapters VII and VIII.

8. See Chapter VII for details on the Party Missionaries among the staff experts.

scene of turmoil gives them an initial hold that in some cases lasts for many years.

Another group who moved in during the Depression (some, but not all, of these cases were also ideologues) were people who acquired some specialized knowledge of an unorganized industry into which the unions were pushing. The President of the CIO Packinghouse Workers, a Vice President of the ACWA-CIO, the Secretary-Treasurer of the Hosiery Workers, the President of the AFL Office Employees, a former braintruster for the Steelworkers —all of these national officials gained indispensable knowledge of and contacts in the relevant industries via advisory, administrative or research jobs with the NRA before moving into their unions. One respondent recalls this aspect of his transition from staff expert to line officer:

> I'd done research with the NRA code authority. I learned more about the industry that way than I could possibly learn outside. Putting that together with the field contact, I was in a good position to know the industry and the union. . . . I'd been up in [city] for the NRA. . . . Having been up there before, I was more familiar with the complex political problems, the personalities of the leaders, as well as the economics of the thing. So when we negotiated the contract I worked with [the top officer] on it. (10-2.)

Others gained the necessary knowledge and contacts in some unit of government promoting unionization in the Depression, e.g., the WPA Workers' Education Program, or the LaFollette Civil Liberties Committee.

The Wartime Crisis.—Some unions were barely off the floor when mobilization hit them in the forties. During the confusion that followed, several cases made contacts and gained experience which formed the basis of one of the four executive positions. A typical comment about such a case (from a respondent hostile to the man in question):

> He'd been important in all negotiations nationally and he'd gone into the locals to assist, too. [The top officer] depended on him heavily. His supporters felt nobody could know the industry as well as he could. . . . During the War Labor Board days, because of his training as a lawyer, he'd been able to see lines of progress no one else saw. While you stewed around, he found a way out. (909-2,3.)

Instances of legal or even economic consultants who became Braintrusters or line officials at a local or regional level during this period are also common. The comment "There was a vacuum and he [or I] filled it," appears as a frequent characterization of these cases.

Schism or a Push into New Territory.—Another of the crises out of which some men of knowledge have emerged as men of power or authority is the creation of new units of the labor movement through secession, or through an organizing drive into unorganized industries, occupations, or areas. This may duplicate labor's early organizing struggles, with a similar demand for leadership talent and a similar disregard for its social and occupational origins. Today, organization in white-collar occupations, in the communications industry, and in the South has provided circumstances for the rise to power of a few men of knowledge.

The factional battle, even if it does not lead to secession, may also provide a fluid situation into which a man may move. Both sides in an internal war need program ideas, propaganda and organizing talent; both need all the manpower they can recruit. The willing intellectual is sometimes among those who can help.

In one prominent case, a factional battle became deadlocked and a staff expert who had proved indispensable rose to power as the reconciliation candidate. Union people often cite this case, President Ralph Helstein of the CIO Packinghouse Workers, either as the exception that proves the rule (that a staff expert can never achieve power), or as the horrible (or encouraging) example that shows that technical indispensability inevitably means power in the era of the managerial revolution. As we have seen, neither view is tenable. President Helstein's career does, however, confirm the picture above in a striking way.[9] A fervent New Dealer, upon admission to the bar in Minnesota he went to work for NRA. His job was to enforce the minimum wage and hour provisions in the Act. When NRA died, he set up a private law practice. "Contacts he had made with union men as an NRA officer brought a good bit of union business to his office." His first major union job was to represent AFL Teamsters in St. Paul negotiations. "When the CIO began to take form in 1937 . . . Helstein found himself prac-

---

9. The facts that follow are well known, and were reported in the press. See, e.g., the profile by Keith Wheeler in the *Chicago Sun-Times*, June 9, 1950, p. 38.

ticing exclusively as a CIO lawyer. By 1940 when he negotiated the first major contract between the Packinghouse Workers and Hormel he was the CIO's general counsel in Minnesota. Two years later he was in Chicago as general counsel of the Packinghouse Workers international."[10]

Many of the union's leaders became convinced during the war period of General Counsel Helstein's indispensability and superior competence in bargaining and administration. At the 1946 Convention, which became enmeshed in a complicated factional battle, the President of the union, apparently with the blessing of representatives of the national CIO, agreed in a crucial caucus meeting to step down to Secretary-Treasurer and let Mr. Helstein take over as a reconciliation choice. The staff lawyer was promptly elected President, amid vigorous cries that the labor movement was bankrupt if it could not find leadership in its own ranks. At the 1948 Convention—in a bitterly contested election in which President Helstein was pitted against another staff expert, the union's Editor and Education Director—Helstein retained the post. He has held it ever since.

His rise to power thus involved all of the favorable circumstances I have discussed: Depression-born ideological conviction coupled with opportunity to learn the industry and the union before the big organizing push; a solidification of position via technical service and political contact during the war crisis; and, finally, factional fluidity which opened the way for his election to the top spot.

"Knowing Where the Bodies Are Buried"

One group of outside professionals, almost all lawyers, work their way into braintrust or executive posts at a local level. "There's hardly a business agent who comes in here," says a high national official, "who doesn't have a lawyer tagging after him." (16.2.) Similar comments call attention to the large number of consultants who play politics in local unions.

It must be understood that the local union is often a better

---

10. *Ibid.*

THE MOVING-IN PROCESS: MANAGERIAL REVOLUTION? *217*

target for the quick acquisition of influence, power and even high fees, than the national union. One labor lawyer observed:

> The X union has a General Counsel but he's nothing. The two-bit locals have more money than the International. I'm counsel for the locals. We have more to say about International policy than all the top officers. . . . I'd much rather represent them than the International which is broke all the time and has no power to do anything. (210-5.)

A few lawyers gain a hold over local union officers because of inside knowledge of clear-cut malfeasances. In the capacity of prosecuting attorney or regulating official of government, a lawyer may learn about a union official's illegal practices; upon leaving government, he makes this knowledge the basis of a large salary and larger powers in the local in question. Occasionally, the lawyer joins in the malfeasance. For instance, it seems clear that certain fee-splitting arrangements give the union official and the fee counsel a mutual hold over one another:

> A lawyer will handle a case that's worth $2,000 and he'll put in a bill for $10,000 and split the difference with the union leader. This is a common practice. . . . I don't know whether it's on the increase or on the decrease, but I know it occurs. The union membership sometimes worry about this, and a union leader will sometimes avoid hiring lawyers because he'll be suspected of fee-splitting. Others will go ahead and hire them and take their cut. (205-8.)

More frequently, the inside knowledge does not concern anything illegal; it concerns the political compromises made, the favors bestowed, the tactics of domination the leader has used to acquire and hold office. "He knows where the bodies are buried" is a phrase often used to designate this kind of knowledge and to explain why certain experts have moved in. A top officer describes the process:

> If the guy in charge is a little bit lazy and wants to slough off work, if the lawyer is striving for power constantly, then he'll do the old whispering job on you. The lawyer can manipulate the situation to boost himself. . . . And when the opposition takes over, they're indebted to the lawyer, so he's got control. . . . Some of these lawyers actually get contracts giving them four and five years guarantee. It's the goddamndest thing. Then they want to establish connections with the membership. They tell the officer, "Fix me up with a card. I ought to go to the convention to help you out." The average officer—he don't know any better. The lawyer can make a good speech, they have that

knack and he hypnotizes our guys. . . . They get a title, "Executive Secretary." [A lawyer in the X union] took over that way. Now he's got a contract, five years at $75,000 a year. He never worked as a wage worker in his life. . . . He watches the books, the officers are careless, he got information that makes it look like they was crooks and then he feeds it to the opposition. . . . (16, 2,3.)[11]

Rank-and-File Careers

There are two types of rank-and-filers who climb the union ladder via the expert route. Their means of ascension can tell us much about both the technical and the political imperatives in the moving-in process. The first type is the bona fide wage worker who acquires specialized knowledge and plays at being an expert. The second is the bona fide professional expert who gets some shop experience and plays at being a wage worker. Both may acquire high influence or executive authority. The top officers, for reasons to be discussed in Chapter XIII, take pride in the careers of both.

The Rank-and-File Expert.—It has been suggested that there are some things the expert does that the line official can do just as well. This has meant the emergence of many wage-worker union activists in expert positions—especially in lobbying, engineering, health, safety, compensation, some aspects of pensions and insurance, and sometimes in journalism, arbitration, NLRB, or general "research." In fact, some union people believe that the dominant source of recruitment of union experts in the future will be the rank and file. "Within five or ten years unions will be training their

---

11. Officer hostility to lawyers can be explained partly by the general anti-intellectualism and anti-outsiderism discussed below in Chapter XIII, but in part by experiences like the one this officer describes. Such hostility sometimes achieves formal expression in the form of convention resolutions or debate about the use of fee counsel. The 1947 Convention of the Chemical Workers, for example, adopted a resolution prohibiting the use of attorneys by local unions without prior clearance by the international. International Chemical Workers Union, AFL, *Proceedings of the Fifth Annual Convention,* 1947, Resolution No. 19. At the following Convention the Executive Board reported noncompliance, complained of "exceedingly large fees" which continued to be paid to local union attorneys. *Proceedings of the Sixth Annual Convention,* September 12-16, 1949, pp. 34-35.

own specialists on scholarships, in institutes and the like," said one outsider. "And it'll be tough for the outsiders to get in." (401a-5.) While there are many barriers to the full swing towards this rank-and-file source,[12] it is probable that the gross number of experts hired from the ranks, if not their proportion of the total, has increased somewhat.

The rank-and-filer who climbs through a series of elective and appointive offices into a staff-expert role can easily come to know the union and some of the companies, industries or trades under contract. But where does he get his technical skill? Two cases illustrate typical patterns:

Case 126: Ninth grade education. Some self-study in accounting and engineering. Active in organizing the union in a key plant in the Depression. Put on staff as trouble-shooter for top officer, especially in handling important last-step grievances. Began to specialize in wage rate problems, got to know thousands of jobs. Served as a member of the Labor Division of the War Production Board in World War II. Became successfully active in city politics, which boosted his prestige in the union further. When union moved into engineering program on a large scale he was ready for the top spot as staff expert. Careerist in orientation.

Case 83: High school education. Active in organizing union in Depression. Elected shop committeeman, then president of most powerful local in union. Took night courses in an Executive Training Institute, $5/lesson, emphasis on how to present ideas to groups. Heard union wanted to expand research department. Was ready with written proposal when it came up at the Convention. "I'd been studying Bureau of National Affairs reports and the like and I was really boned up for this thing." Feels his lessons in "pure psychology" were crucial aid in his presentation to the executive board, which won him the job as Research and Education Director. Moving from Careerist to Professional Service orientation.

The expertise is typically acquired both through varied experience in leadership positions and through periods of study, however brief, in night school, college extension programs, correspondence schools, union-run "institutes," radical party schools, and the like. Occasionally, union staff experts or even company officials encourage a rank-and-filer to develop specialized knowledge by lending books or suggesting courses. In the absence of this, the union activist's

---

12. See above, pp. 187 ff. and below, pp. 252 ff.

political or family connections may nevertheless get him a staff expert's job, in which case he may gain the necessary knowledge and skill through apprenticeship to a bona fide expert who arrived before.

Occasionally this type of expert is able to parlay his combined rank-and-file origin and newly acquired expertise into an executive post. In his orientation he may start as a Careerist or he may begin as a Party Missionary. Some of them acquire professional identification as they move up.[13]

The "Synthetic Rank-and-Filer."—The bona fide rank-and-file expert was in the workplace to make a living, then became a staff expert. The synthetic rank-and-filer, in contrast, is a man with considerable specialized training either in a profession or in college. He goes into the plant to achieve a brief identification as a wage worker, then becomes a staff expert or executive. One young college man just embarking on this type of career explained, "I'm in the plant as the best avenue for a staff job—probably as a technician —so I can live down the 'outsider' tag and my college past." (N954.) Why this should be necessary is discussed with reference to the institutional pressures and working climate of the international headquarters, in Chapter XIII.

Typically, the synthetic rank-and-filer is viewed by large portions of the union activist and leadership groups as a fraud because of his occupational or educational origins. However, the ritual period in the plant may convince some, especially if the man is able to don the manner of speech and the set of attitudes of the bona fide wage worker and make the necessary contacts with some strong political faction. That these last points and not the sheer length of time in the plant are what count is suggested by the fact that the time in the shop ranges from only four months to three and one-half years (for all cases for whom I have occupational histories) and yet the more proletarian of their fellows peg them all as ersatz. Despite this pervasive anti-outsiderism and anti-intellectualism, several of these cases have carved out truly remarkable careers via the synthetic rank-and-file route.

Case X: A college graduate, specializing in labor relations. "I did it

---

13. These changes in role orientation are discussed fully in Chapter VII.

by deliberate plan." Worked out plan with aid of professors with labor contacts. Wanted to get varied industrial relations experience. Went into plant, chosen for strategic position in the national union. Volunteered services to local leaders. At end of a month he had become special assistant to the local president—"on the basis of technical competence." What technical competence? "Command of the English language, a college education, broader knowledge of industrial relations positions so I could talk with company representatives on their own intellectual terms. In general, more rigorous training in logical thinking so I was able to pull the meat out of situations." In succeeding weeks he started campaign to call self to attention of national officer. "It was very complicated—working angles from several directions." At first he had "information-seeking conversations" with the top officer. He didn't let on he was after a job. Over a four-month period he had several people in and out of the union write letters or talk with the target official, calling attention to his talents and his presence in the union. At the end of the period, "he got the idea I was the boy. Then I told him I'd like to work for the international union—maybe as assistant to a field rep." The top officer hired him as his own special assistant. "It took a year as a trainee for the job to jell." Within one and one-half years of the date of entry into the plant, he had become a combination Braintruster-Administrative Assistant, "fully involved in the politics of the union." The pressures of a factional war aided his rise. (918.)

Can these career patterns—emerging in a crisis situation, "knowing where the bodies are buried," moving up from the ranks—be generalized?

Certainly my data show no invariant sequence of events in the careers of the experts who move into one of the four executive or quasi-executive positions. But on the basis of complete data on the twenty-one High Influence cases and more limited data on twenty executives (Braintruster-Confidantes, Housekeeping Administrative Assistants, elected officers), it is possible to delineate a few necessary conditions for moving in. The following features are general to all these cases, though they may occur in different sequence, be variously intertwined in any given case, and be of varying importance from case to case:

1. *Make prestigeful contact with the leaders of the unit into which one is moving.* Examples: A Socialist Party or CP activist or leader contacts union with Socialist or CP leadership as organizer, consultant, etc. A lawyer risks his practice to defend unpopular unions, fight their cases. A government bureaucrat sticks neck out

to fight for cause allied to labor's interests. A lawyer with good connections in a governor's office is hired as an area director in that state.

2. *Get sponsor by demonstrating loyalty, indispensability to, or power over a leader or group of leaders.* Examples: A staff expert, organizer, special assistant, etc., moves up with a leader rising to power, assists in overcoming opposition. A professional offers free advice in early organizing struggles, wins confidence of leader who found advice useful. An outsider learns "where the bodies are buried," or shares in some malfeasance.

3. *Become expert in the workings of the organization.* This is an accomplishment of all the successful experts.

4. *Seize opportunities to broaden influence.* Examples: leadership vacuums left by succession, or weakness of incumbents; war, depression, factional strife (each with their own heavy set of demands on officer competence).

Many of these men who moved in are people who sensed the moment, saw the possibilities of success, and seized the chance to climb aboard. From the ranks or not, "we took our lives in our hands and gambled on the union in the early days," says one. "And the officers know it." (519-5.) The interview explanations of how these men have moved in are replete with references both to "a good sense of timing" and a willingness to take a chance.

To say that the successful experts become "expert in the workings of the organization," is to point to the synoptic view that defines executive capacity. If the expert is a fellow profoundly immersed in his routine, a man whose intensity of vision destroys his sense of proportion,[14] then all of the successful experts have ceased being experts. The good labor editor, as we have seen, comes to know the organization in all its aspects; "he needs to know how this particular sentence would affect this particular local, this particular personality." (502-9.) The labor lawyer has to check clause IVB-3a for gimmicks; to do the job right he must know its relation to other clauses, the history of the bargaining relationship, and more.

---

14. " . . . *Expertise* consists in such an analytic comprehension of a special realm of facts that the power to see that realm in the perspective of totality is lost." Harold Laski, *op. cit.*, p. 9.

Even the most routine matter can provide occasion for spreading one's functions. "We do letter-writing, for instance," said one consultant:

Just plain letter-writing. These union officers are afraid of their grammar. They're afraid of not saying what they mean, so they bring in their letters or their speeches and want us to polish them up. So when you tell them, "Well, I wouldn't do it this way or that way," you have to tell them what way you *would* do it. . . . And pretty soon you're telling them what to do in negotiations, in all kinds of situations. . . . (205-3.)

The good specialist, in other words, becomes a specialist-at-large. By a gradual process, expert advice in one's area of special competence, if the action suggested is successful, evokes a demand for good advice in other areas as well. And the core knowledge required soon becomes a knowledge of the particular union—its personalities, politics, problems, traditions and routines.

The moving-in process may necessitate the acquisition of a stronger personal identification with the incumbent officials of the particular union, and a decline in the intensity of any previous professional identification. But it does not necessarily entail a loss of craft competence. Some of the most powerful union lawyers, for example, retain considerable skill as legal technicians despite the increased demand on their competence in politics and interpersonal relations occasioned by their emergence in executive roles. This coupling of technical and political skills—seen, for example, in the convergence of wage workers trying to become experts and experts identifying as wage workers—is a clue to the basis of "confidence" between expert and boss.

"Confidence" and Independence in Relation to Influence and Authority

We have seen that functional type, time of entry, and role orientation are good but not perfect guides to sort out the High Influence experts from the rest. However, all of the men of knowledge who have acquired some executive authority (including the High Influence experts) have some aspects of their career patterns

in common, wherever and whenever they start and whatever position they move into. They make prestigeful contact with union
people; they demonstrate loyalty or indispensability to, or acquire
some hold over, a sponsor; they seize opportunities to broaden
their influence; in general, they become expert in the workings of
the organization. The typical phrase used to describe this process
is "winning the confidence of the boss." The remaining sections of
this chapter analyze the components of "confidence" in the expert-
boss relationship among the High Influence cases, and consider
dependence on the boss as a variable in expert influence. The lawyer and the private consultant are then considered in relation to
these questions of "confidence" and "dependence," because in some
ways they represent prime instances of the points I shall make.

THE ANATOMY OF "CONFIDENCE"

The picture of who moves in and how, presents a series of paradoxes. It is as if the top officer were saying to the expert who aspires
to high position: "(1) Develop talents identical to mine, but don't
offer me any competition: (2) be one of the boys, talk my language,
but maintain an aura of mystery; (3) don't bother me, but be sure
to pose problems and force decisions when necessary: (4) be 100
per cent loyal to me personally, be dependent on me, but retain
independence of judgment, and maintain prestige-laden contacts
in and out of the union."

The Contact Man is the expert most likely to acquire high influence. The man of knowledge who becomes a Braintruster-Confidante or a Housekeeping Administrative Assistant again is a fellow
with political and executive, as well as technical, capacities and
skills. All of them are men in the top leader's own image. But there
are some crucial differences (beyond those of occupational and
educational origins), which tend to disqualify the expert as a serious contender for the boss' job. Some ready examples come to mind:
the Jew in a union where a Jew is unlikely to win top office;[15] the
Protestant woman in a Jewish male leadership group; an obviously

---

15. Only seven of the twenty-one High Influence experts are Jewish, and
four of these are in unions whose top leader is also Jewish. But this is mis-
leading. The cases of experts with the highest influence ratings and especially those who have moved out of my sample into executive posts are more
often of Jewish origin.

intellectual type who would never try too much to be "one of the boys"; an expert whose job alternatives are so clear and so attractive that he is thought not to want a union leadership job. Occasional cases combine one or more of these disqualifying characteristics with physical disabilities. Other cases show a self-effacing modesty which carries the imperative of anonymity to an extreme.[16] To win the boss' confidence and move in, the expert must develop the talents of the union leader; but he must also exhibit differences in aspiration, opportunity, and even personality, differences rooted in his social origins, occupational, educational and religious background.

Simmel has said that "confidence is midway between knowledge and ignorance about a man."[17] The officer gets to know his high influence experts, braintrusters, etc., pretty well. He wants them to be congenial, realistic, easy to take in close, sustained personal contact. The technically indispensable, but personally unacceptable expert is viewed as a breed apart.[18]

But this is only half the story. The officer may want the man of knowledge to be "one of the boys," but he also wants him to be an expert. He wants to believe that his hired brain "knows what he's talking about," and he wants what he's talking about to have, at least at times, an aura of technical mystery. He wants to maintain a relative ignorance about some of these matters. There are two main reasons for this: the snob appeal of having an intellectual around (so long as he's not *too* intellectual); and the function of ignorance in shifting the moral burden of decision to those in the know (i.e., to the expert). Both operate in the case of nonlawyers as well as lawyers.

The third paradox in the anatomy of confidence has to do with pushing, but not pushing too hard:

> How you win a man's confidence—the [technical indispensability] is only the foundation. . . . It has got to do with the business of giving you trouble. Any staff man wins out who doesn't give trouble. When he walks in the boss' office it's a fella who isn't pushing him. He doesn't have to say "No," when the man comes in the room. So it takes timing

16. All experts must "know their place," as Chapter XIII will show. But the cases I refer to here have almost developed this into a character trait.

17. *The Sociology of Georg Simmel*, trans. and ed. Kurt H. Wolff (Glencoe, Ill.: The Free Press, 1950), p. 318.

18. See Chapter V, pp. 68 ff.

and judgment. You're a staff man and you want to get the executive to do something. *When* you mention it, *How* you mention it—these are all "x" qualities. . . . On the one hand, the officer wants a guy who's no bother to him; on the other hand, he wants a man who'll help in making decisions and who's willing to make decisions when he wants to pass the buck. (916-3.)

The final paradox in the process of building confidence concerns the matter of loyalty and the expert's dependence on the boss. Personal loyalty to the boss is an imperative of survival for all the experts. In those experts who do not achieve an inner circle role, this imperative often makes for a "yes-man" mentality rooted in complete dependence on the boss for security and prestige. The really successful experts, however, are those who have not only demonstrated their loyalty, but have maintained enough independence to permit disagreement and objectivity. The components of this independence are complex. In part it consists of the mere weight of inside information: "He's taken me into his confidence so much," said one expert, "he's told me so many of his dreams, plans, his opinions of everyone—that he simply can't push me around too much. Besides, I tell him off." (522-10,11.) Inside knowledge is a help, but in the absence of some solid sense of security, the expert is not likely to "tell the boss off" so easily. For inside knowledge becomes relatively harmless if, by getting fired, the expert is removed from the political process.

SECURITY AND THE EXPERT'S DEPENDENCE ON THE BOSS

An expert's sense of security in an organization with no system of tenure, such as a union, is in part dependent upon his alternative employment opportunities, the replaceability of his skills, and his "connections" or "base" in or out of the organization. If these objective factors contribute to a sense of security, and if a sense of security is related to influence, we would expect the High Influence experts to be in a favorable market position.

A few of the High Influence experts (and several of the important ex-experts) clearly have acquired a "base"—a political following within the organization that could be mobilized in support of their continued service. Frequently, the rank-and-file base of the High Influence expert rests either on (1) his job functions (see Chapter VI); or (2) his political affiliation with a party or faction with strength in the union.

As for "connections" outside the union and replaceability of skills, there are two statistical clues to their relation to influence. The first is the predominance of Contact Men among those who rate high on influence. The second rough clue is in the data on how the experts got their first union jobs. The number using job-getting methods which involve outside contacts increases in direct proportion to increases in influence ratings. About three-eighths of those rated Low on influence, one-half of those rated Medium, and three-fifths of those rated High had government, business, newspaper, independent consultant, or labor relations specialist contacts who helped them to get their union jobs.

Finally, there is the question of alternative employment opportunities. Mobility-wise, many of the experts are locked up in the labor movement. Limited data on what became of 112 predecessors of the incumbents studied,[19] suggest that it has not in the past been easy to move directly from a union to industry, business, universities, or commercial publications. Almost half of the predecessors died on the job, retired, or moved to another labor job. Many of those in private consulting depend in good part on a union clientele; several of those who went to government and elsewhere have jobs which are filled by union nominees or which depend on Labor support. The engineers, lawyers, and pension experts find it easiest to move on to jobs in no way dependent upon Labor.

Assuming there is a lack of alternative nonlabor job possibilities, how would this be reflected in the mentality of the staff expert? A typical comment illustrates the sense of insecurity of many (in both stable and unstable unions).

> You become labeled as a union [expert], a union partisan. Your flexibility does decline. Your skills become bound up with the particular organization you're attached to and the range of alternative job possibilities narrows. . . . Hell, you never know what the future holds. I could get the axe next year. (306a-5.)

The sense of insecurity this respondent feels might continue, even if there *were* considerable chance to move into the nonunion world

---

19. There are 183 expert positions (Q Sample definition) now filled or once filled in the twenty-eight unions. I have relevant questionnaire data on 159 of these. Eighty-six of the incumbents had no predecessors. The remaining seventy-three positions (now filled or temporarily vacant) had 133 predecessors. I know what became of 112 of these predecessors.

at comparable salaries in similar jobs. In fact, there is some evidence that the present incumbents do have plenty of opportunity to sever the labor tie. Table 6 shows that the staff experts in the Main Sample have received a large number of industry-business and government job offers.[20] Many of the experts are evidently confined to the labor movement by a self-imposed rule. They find the prospect of cutting themselves off from the labor movement distasteful; the offers from industry, business, nonlabor consultant firms, government agencies, etc., are unacceptable. A few cases—especially among the Missionaries and Program Professionals—not only do not see any job outside the labor movement (save going into a plant, or back to college), but they also cannot see working for any union but the one they are in (see Chapter VII).

In terms of this analysis of alternative job chances as a factor in expert influence, what is significant in Table 6 is the picture of who admits to no job offers at all. Only one in sixteen High Influence cases admits he has had no job offers since he has been working for a union, but six in twenty-one of the Medium Influence cases and twenty-five in seventy-two (over a third) of the Low Influence cases so indicate. The proportion of all cases in the Main Sample who specify receipt of at least one job offer goes up as influence ratings go up—from about 57 per cent of the Lows to 71 per cent of the Highs.

Why this should be so is suggested in several interview comments. A staff expert describes a very High Influence colleague's opening speech to the Board as "a masterpiece":

> He said, "I want it clearly understood that I'm in a position to leave any time I want to." . . . He said, "You are my client and I'm your lawyer and I'm here to serve you in that capacity." (519-3.)

The expert who made this speech—a Professional Service type—explains his conviction:

> The greater degree of independence a top man can feel the better—he can speak up and offer his honest independent judgment. There's much too little of that. Staff people are too dependent on their jobs.

---

20. With increasing respectability of Labor, the union tag may be less of a bar to the present incumbents than to their predecessors. But since I cannot compare job offers accepted (by predecessors) with job offers turned down (by incumbents), I have no direct evidence on the trend.

Table 6—Relation of Job Offers Received to Influence Rating (Main Sample)

OFFERS*	INFLUENCE								TOTALS	
	High (6-10)		Med. (4-5)		Low (0-3)					
	N	%	N	%	N	%	N	%	N	%
1. Yes	15	71.4	15	60.0	47	57.3			77	60.2
a. Ind.-Bus.	6		7		29				42	54.5
b. Com. Pub.	0		2		5				7	9.1
c. Priv. Consult.	4		5		9				18	23.4
d. Government	5		8		19				32	41.6
e. Education	0		4		9				13	16.9
f. Misc.	2		1		2				5	6.5
2. None	1	4.8	6	24.0	25	30.5			32	25.0
3. No info.	5	23.8	4	16.0	10	12.2			19	14.8
Totals	21	100.0	25	100.0	82	100.0			128	100.0

* Several offers in one category are scored only once. "Yes" means one or more outside offers since working for a union.

The ideal situation is where you have staff people who know they're wanted and are in demand. They can then have security and be independent. Too great a dependence on the officer affects your judgment —no question about it. (227-4.)

Lack of *acceptable* alternatives, both cause and consequence of long immersion in a particular organization, appears to account for the middling influence (as well as middling salaries) of some old-timers of the "right" functional type (Contact Man), whose demonstrated loyalty is unquestioned. They have some security; they've become "fixtures around the place." But they are still very dependent upon the boss. One said:

I could go to work for the X industry tomorrow . . . for twice as much as I make here. But my heart wouldn't be in it at all. . . . I've been offered jobs with the industry. But when you've got a comfortable spot it's hard to move. I supose it may affect your willingness to stick your neck out. (522-10.)

PRIVATE PRACTITIONERS AND LAWYERS: A PRIME INSTANCE
AND A SPECIAL CASE

Many observers have noted the superior position of the outside private consultant relative to the inside captive. Many have also pointed to the lawyer—house counsel *or* private practitioner—as having a superior position relative to all other occupational groups among the experts. Are the private consultant in general and the lawyer in particular the real heavyweights when it comes to influence and authority? If so, are the reasons for their influence unique, or are they the same as those affecting the position of all the experts?.

Private Consultants in General.—Many union staff people wistfully point to outside professionals as the experts who carry most weight with their principals. These include lawyers, economists, university professors, and occasionally other men in public life (especially in politics and religion) who are noted for their labor-liberal political orientation and record. As we shall see in Chapter XII, the staff expert sometimes has to work through some friendly outsider a thousand miles away to reach his boss in the next room. Several people who have been both staff experts and private consultants note the marked contrast in their influence. A successful free-lance writer says he saw the boss only a few times in several years on the staff, but now, as an outsider, he has easy access. (G906-2.)

The chief thing that distinguishes the private consultant from the full-time staff expert is the diversity of his clientele. This gives him a relative freedom from dependence upon one union officer. From this basic fact flow many subtle differences in his relation to the boss.

The first consequence of independence is the preservation of a client-professional relationship, which the captive typically loses: "When I handled cases for X union," said one private practitioner,

I never worked there; they came here—here, where Smith [top officer] could never feel like Smith. I didn't come to them with hat in hand to worship at their feet. Much depends on where you're sitting —psychologically it counts. It may seem like a little thing but it's very important. (214-4.)

The union leader, as we have seen in our discussion of the "window dressing" function, typically wants to borrow prestige from his experts. The outside consultant is in a better position to deliver this prestige; his independence is rooted in his standing in the world outside the union he advises. His main claim to prestige in union eyes rests on (1) his contacts in important circles; (2) his high income; (3) his style of life. Union leaders face situations in which the respected outsider is needed as a "front"—negotiations in which a "big name" economist can assist in a public relations campaign, litigation in which a key law firm is needed to impress the judge, and the like.

In all of this, the prestige claim of the consultant is honored not only because of the "connections" and respect he is reputed to have in the groups with which the union must deal, but also because he charges high fees. If he costs so much, he must be better than the hired brain who comes for much less.[21] One top officer ex-

---

21. Median annual salary in 1951 for 122 staff experts on whom I have data is $7,500. The range is from about $3,500 to more than $20,000. Only twenty-five of these cases get $10,000 or more, only seven get $12,000 or more. See Appendix E, Table 10. Scattered data on the retainers and fees of consultants in the unions studied and on the annual incomes of a group of independent labor lawyers studied by Segal, *op. cit.*, suggest that their median income is very much higher than that of the captives in roughly comparable specialties.

plains why he is unwilling to save money by using staff experts:

> You got to pay for services rendered. If you pay one $4,000 you get $4,000 worth of service. If you need $10,000 worth of services, then you better pay $10,000. You get what you pay for. We had a case where we hired a distinguished judge. We paid him $25,000 for his appearance in court once or twice. . . . We needed something good. It was a top-level case—you can't leave it to amateurs. (17-4.)

A final aspect of this prestige-borrowing (or buying) process is related to the psychology of the newly arrived man of power, whose prestige rating in the larger society has soared less impressively than his position in the union hierarchy. "The union officer," explains an ex-expert, "loves to mix in intellectual company coming from the outside—that is, government officials or well-known attorneys. They love to bask in the social swim. You've seen the union man who can wear a tux as if he's been in it all his life." (915-4.)[22]

In sum: if a private consultant has a diversified practice, he can more easily maintain a professional-client relationship. Relative to the full-time staff expert, his prestige is high because he supplies needed contacts on the outside and charges high fees for his services. His contacts and his income in turn permit a style of life that enhances his worth in the leader's eyes. Sometimes the outside consultant successfully claims more prestige in union circles than his outside position really warrants. All of this adds up to an independence that permits greater objectivity and influence.

What I have said about the factors that give the outside consultant a superior position applies also to the staff experts. As we have seen, a staff expert with outside contacts or an inside base, easily transferred skills, and many acceptable alternative job chances, is in much the same position as a private practitioner—and this is reflected in his relatively high influence. The independent consultant, therefore, merely epitomizes the factors that maximize the influence of the staff expert.

Moreover, what I have said about the private consultant is not confined to the lawyer; it applies to all sorts of outside experts. What, then, accounts for the frequently expressed conviction that the lawyer is the fellow who has hit pay dirt in the unions?

---

22. See Chapter XIII for a fuller discussion of this aspect of the Union leader's psychology.

Lawyers in Particular.—Any list of the great names of modern history will include an impressive roster of men trained in the law: Robespierre, Danton, Lenin, Lassalle, Jefferson, Jackson, Lincoln. For the past sixty years over half (55 per cent) of the President's cabinet members in the United States have been lawyers (less than 1 per cent of the total labor force are lawyers and judges).[23] Between 1790 and 1930, two-thirds of the Presidents and of the U. S. Senate, and about half of the House of Representatives have been lawyers.[24] Many writers—from Tocqueville on—have noted the great power lawyers have acquired in American society in its private as well as public sectors.

In the union case, it is easy to exaggerate the influence and power of the lawyers. Only six of the twenty-one High Influence experts are lawyers. In ten of the twenty-eight unions in the Questionnaire Sample, lawyers are clearly less influential than some other occupational category among the staff experts. It is true, however, that (1) those staff experts with *very* High Influence ratings are mostly lawyers (five of the seven cases rated 8-10 are lawyers); and (2) many lawyers have moved into appointed or elective executive posts. Even in those unions in which the lawyer has become neither the braintruster nor the top staff expert, he is sometimes (a) paid more than other experts with as much training; and (b) viewed with some awe by the officers.

In explaining why the lawyers are in a better position than other experts, union people use phrases that either apply to all successful experts (the lawyer is "highly articulate," "good at problem-solving," "trained to give a dispassionate judgment," etc.) or apply to all Contact Men. Other explanations point to factors which, again, operate to increase influence of any expert, lawyer or not. One House Counsel, for instance, is described by a colleague in these terms: "He has more independence. . . . His status is higher —it's the status of an outside operator; he's sort of a consultant. It's as if he got 'fees,' not a 'salary.' There's more freedom of movement. Lawyers can always say, 'We could quit and make twice as much dough someplace else'—and they could! We couldn't."

23. H. D. Lasswell, D. Sterner and C. E. Rothwell, *The Comparative Study of Elites* (Stanford, California: Stanford University Press, 1952), p. 9.
24. C. W. Mills, *White Collar, op. cit.,* p. 127.

Here again the reference is to transferability of skills, alternative job possibilities, and, in general, degree of dependence on the boss —factors which we have seen affect all the experts. What is there that is unique in the role of the lawyer *per se* that can account for his favorable position?

1. *The device of the mystery.* Like the medicine-man of old who interpreted the supernatural, the lawyer of today sedulously cultivates the myth of the majesty and the mystery of the law. Ferdinand Lundberg—pointing to such metaphysical constructs as "corporate entity," "property rights," "fair value," "conspiracy," "proximate cause," "good faith, bad faith," and "malice"—observes that the law must still be classified with theology and lawyers as political theologians.[25] While the device of the mystery is employed by all experts in some degree as a means of building their prestige and influence, none has developed it as systematically as the lawyer. Many lawyer respondents cite instances wherein their special vocabulary impressed the boss—especially when the officer can see the lawyer at work in judicial proceedings. "The client has to have confidence in the law and the lawyer," said one. "It builds [top officer's] confidence in the lawyer when he sees us in action. He gets the idea we know what we're talking about." (217-3.) It is wrong to assume, however, that the union leader believes that the law has some fixed and inevitable meaning. Even the lawyer's legal review function is often a ritual; the officer shops around until he gets an interpretation that suits his needs.

Even though the officer may not really be mystified by the mystery of the law, he may nevertheless look for the lawyer's magic stamp of approval for proposed action. This fact points up an important function served by the device of the mystery: if the leader actually feels ignorance of the conceptual weapons of the lawyer or pretends to such ignorance, he can shift the moral burden of decision to the hired lawyer. He can say in the event of failure, "We did it on the best advice of our lawyer."[26]

The confidence the union leader has in the law and the lawyer —even if tempered by skepticism of their mystery—tends to spread

---

25. Ferdinand Lundberg, "The Priesthood of the Law," *Harper's Magazine*, 178 (Dec., 1938-May, 1939), 515-26, esp. 515, 519.

26. Cf. the "heat-taking" function of all the experts, Chapter III.

to confidence in all judgments: economic policy, though the lawyer may know nothing about economics; political policy, though he may know little about this.

2. *The fiduciary relationship.* "The traditional relationship of lawyer and client," a very influential House Counsel explains, "involves a feeling of confidence. There has to be the assumption he's talking to you and not somebody else. This is especially true in a political organization like a trade union. . . . The lawyer is accustomed to confidential communication; he knows how to receive without giving." (227-4.)

It is an aspect of the device of the mystery that many lawyers promote the myth that only lawyers are skilled in "confidential communication," only lawyers can keep a secret. The fact that it is embodied in the law reflects and explains the success of the profession in winning acceptance of this myth. The lawyer is, indeed, in a unique position on this matter of "confidence." He acts in a fiduciary capacity: "Just as a wife can't be compelled to testify against her husband," explains one lawyer, "I can't be compelled to testify against my client." (916-1.)

The constant analogies between the lawyer-client relationship and the doctor-patient, priest-communicant, husband-wife, lover-loved relationships further underscore the widespread image of the lawyer as uniquely equipped confidante. One non-lawyer sadly observes:

Legal services tend not only to solving problems in court but to solving problems in general. . . . The locals and the President define the role as a counselor. Maybe that's why the lawyers are paid so much. X in _____ union gets twice as much as the President of the union. . . . In our union, the President regards _____ as his private chancellor. He's more than a general advisor or administrative assistant. He deals not only with affairs of state, but love affairs, personal, financial and so on. . . . They influence bargaining decisions, too, unfortunately. (304-4.)

3. *The omnipresence of labor law.* An obvious reason for the unique position of the lawyer is the fact that union leaders become convinced that "the union is surrounded by laws" (see Chapter IV). The lawyer is a specialist in manipulating the rules that govern the political economy. And no union can get along without him. The union leader may be able to testify before a government board

and rely only lightly on his research man for the facts and figures. But when he goes into court he is entirely in the hands of his lawyer. Only a member of the fraternity can plead the case. This fact, in turn, makes the lawyer's services more visible, clear, and dramatic than those of nonlawyer experts. The lawyer has more frequent chances to deliver a dramatic oration in defense of the union and its leaders.[27]

4. *The lawyer's position in the larger society.* In the last analysis, whatever labor leaders think of lawyers, whatever skepticism they feel about the majesty, certainty, and mystery of the law, they are still forced to depend on the profession because of its great power and prestige in the larger society. If the average union member respects the lawyer as a shrewd or clever person,[28] if lawyers hold key positions in the companies, the legislatures, the investigating bodies, the government agencies, the courts, and the political parties with which the union leader has to deal, then the union is going to find the services of lawyers valuable, too. Contact Men of all sorts are likely to be influential; but if the contacts to be made are contacts with men trained in the law, the lawyer is the man to make them.

---

27. "The lawyer," says one lawyer, "is the kind of guy who's always got to be positive; as part of his professional demeanor he must exude confidence. That's how some of them arrive. They tell the union officer, 'We'll come in and beat the bastards with this angle.' The most successful lawyers —the ones with the most lucrative practices—are bull-throwing artists. . . . They'll put on a show—more histrionics than argument. The client pays through the nose, but loves it. Your lawyer is putting on a good scrap in court. So he's the kind of a guy who you'll look to as spokesman to tell the employer off. The lawyer is generally of some power in the building trades. It's profitable at a local level. I know one guy, e.g., who makes it a big operation. This attorney is a shrewd guy, a powerful character having to do histrionic-type pleading. The lawyer in the building trades is generally on the worst end of things—and you jaw a case when you can't win it. It takes an extroverted loud-mouthed character. . . . You get to be an expert on the rules of evidence—to extricate your client from untenable situations. . . . These lawyers kept the boys out of jail. Some of these unions can't live without secondary boycotts, for instance, and so the lawyer becomes crucial." (915-4,5.)

28. All the studies of occupational prestige find the lawyer ranks near the top. See, e.g., M. E. Deeg and D. G. Patterson, "Changes in the Social Status of Occupations," *Occupations*, 25 (Jan., 1947), 205-8; and Hatt and North in R. Freedman *et al.*, *Principles of Sociology* (New York: Henry Holt & Co., 1952), p. 206.

There's a lot of contact work. And a lot of debating. Who will they send—an economist? Who does the company send? A Vice-President who was formerly a lawyer! Then there are appearances before legislative bodies—changes in the law; you send a lawyer. The legislator himself is a lawyer. . . . Or say you want to throw a man out of the union. How shall the constitution read for that? You need a lawyer. You always come back to necessity. The lawyer is essential. (233-4.)

The union leader takes his cues from the groups he deals with and participates in. "There's a popular misconception which holds that the lawyer is the smartest guy in the world," says one private practitioner. "That's why the labor skates—especially the old-timers—tend to ascribe to the employer's attorney a great omniscience and power. . . . They figure, 'it takes a crook to catch a crook!'" (221-1.)

Summary and Conclusion: Managerial Revolution?

A "managerial revolution" is indeed going on in the American trade union, but it has not, save in rare instances, meant that indispensable technical knowledge is becoming the main basis for power. The managerial revolution in the union case occurs in these forms:

1. Unions have increased their employment of experts on and off the staff. Increasing use of experts, however, says nothing about their influence or power.

2. The trends in union structure, type of bargaining, degree of central control and involvement with government put increased demands on leadership competence. The expert's chance to move in depends in part upon how these demands are expressed in the officer's administrative style.

3. Most top union leaders—now professional managers with reasonably secure tenure—are acquiring some expertise in their own right.

4. Some men of knowledge are moving into four types of executive or quasi-executive position: High Influence staff expert, Braintruster-Confidante, Housekeeping Administrative Assistant, or line officer.

The staff experts who are able to make the most of the chance to move in are the Contact Men. They have the contacts and the political and human relations talents necessary to make maximum use of the informal channels for reaching the boss. The Facts and Figures Men, however technically indispensable the boss' deficiencies make them, are less likely to win high influence. The leader is more impressed by men in his own image, men skilled in the arts of negotiation, consultation, interpersonal relations.

Besides functional type, time of first service in the labor movement affects the influence position of the staff expert. The men who "grew up with the organization" have a better claim to a voice in its affairs, easier personal access to the boss. If they combine long service and the right functional type with a role orientation appropriate to the union's stage of development, high influence is even more likely—a point emphasized by looking at influence ratings of the Missionaries.

For a more dynamic picture of the influence, authority, and power of men of knowledge in the labor movement, however, the moving-in process was analyzed—with attention both to the high influence staff experts and to other men of knowledge who have made good.

"Emerging in a crisis situation," "knowing where the bodies are buried"—these phrases capture the career patterns of two groups of outsiders who achieve executive or quasi-executive posts in the labor movement. Two other types of careers begin in the ranks: the bona fide rank-and-file expert, and the synthetic rank-and-filer.

The man who can combine rank-and-file political experience with technical knowledge is in a good position to move in. Reasons for this can be seen in the features common to the careers of all those men of knowledge who have moved in, wherever and whenever they start and whatever position they climb to. The formula goes like this: make prestigeful contact with union people; demonstrate loyalty or indispensability to, or acquire some hold over a sponsor; seize opportunities to broaden your influence; in general, become expert in the workings of the organization. Why the successful expert must become "expert in the workings of the organization" is in part explained by the self-changing nature of the role of the expert: successful problem-solving in areas within his sphere of competence tends to peg him as a problem-solver in all areas. The expert who acquires intimate knowledge of the organization he works for can capitalize on this tendency of the role to broaden.

The imperatives in the process of "winning the boss' confidence" present a series of paradoxes. The expert must (1) develop talents very similar to the political-executive-human relations skills of the union leader, but not offer him any serious competition; (2) be one of the boys, but still play the expert and maintain an aura of mystery; (3) avoid bothering the boss, but still see that tough decisions are made; (4) give unreserved loyalty to the boss and be dependent on him, but not too dependent.

This matter of dependence on the boss is crucial in understanding their relationship and the expert's chances for high influence. The nature of his acceptable alternative job opportunities, which are a compound of his own role orientation, the number and kind of job offers he gets, and the transferability of his skills; the ease with which he can be replaced; his connections on the outside and his "base" on the inside—the data suggest that all of these affect the influence of the staff expert because they affect his dependence on the boss.

The special prestige and influence of the outside consultant, the lawyer in particular, underscore the importance of factors which promote a sense of security and independence. The private practitioner can be seen as an epitome of the conditions maximizing expert influence in general. The lawyer, though it is easy to exaggerate this in the union case, has in some respects a special position. He has developed the device of the mystery more systematically than other experts, he has a unique fiduciary relationship, and he profits from the omnipresence of labor law. Above all, his success in the labor movement reflects his great power and prestige in the larger society.

PART V

DEGREES OF BUREAUCRACY

CHAPTER XII

FORMAL AND INFORMAL CHANNELS
OF INFLUENCE: THE DYNAMICS
OF REACHING THE BOSS

THE EMERGENCE OF THE STAFF EXPERT in large-scale organizations, public and private, has been seen as the epitome of the bureaucratic trend in the modern world. Weber's classic account of the ideal-type bureaucracy emphasized these characteristics:

1. Minute division of labor and a clear-cut hierarchy of authority: the offices are clearly defined, have regular activities governed by impersonal rules, and are set off by fixed, official jurisdictional areas.

2. The offices are filled by full-time, appointed officials. The officials are recruited on the basis of technical qualifications ascertained through formal, impersonal procedures (e.g., tests).

3. The technical specialists who fill the offices are autonomous within their sphere of competence.

4. They are politically neutral professionals whose performance of duty is independent of personal sentiments and opinions.

5. Such faithful performance of duty is assured by the rewards of stable careers: regular salary, expectation of promotion, more responsibility, salary advance, secure tenure, and a pension.

To what extent does the modern union—as seen from the perspective of its staff experts—share these characteristics of bureaucracy? In what direction do typical patterns of union administration move?

Both from the objective side (the patterns of headquarters organization, the decision-making procedures) and from the subjective side (the work experience and role orientations of the experts), the data present a picture of slowly growing, but as yet embryonic bureaucracy.

Bureaucracy: Headquarters Organization

THE FORMAL CHANNELS

The fact that unions are big does not mean that unions are bureaucratized. The frequent reiteration of the old cliché that "the union is a political institution" attests to the fact that the forms of control and the bases of legitimation of leadership authority do not always conform to the Weberian model. There may be a world-wide trend toward rationalization of the means of administration; but the union leader is slow and sometimes reluctant to join. Still, he does join; some signs of embryonic bureaucracy are there. This section examines some of these signs in so far as they are relevant to a description of the channels of influence available to the staff expert.[1]

The bureaucratization process goes forward most clearly in the national headquarters of a few large unions. One clue to it is the frequent, sometimes nostalgic, recollections of functionaries who have been around since the early days. "The functions have been more clearly defined," says one. "More and accurate records are kept of the work of the Department." (Questionnaire.) An old-timer in another union: "In the old days . . . I'd get into everything. Now things are different. We're really big business—specialized. I wouldn't dare try to interpret a contract today—except my section of it!" (453-3.)

Scattered throughout my interview data is talk of problems of "clearance," "jurisdiction," "good departmentalization" (or bad), "overlapping activity," the need for "joint staff meetings," etc. "The union is no longer run on a Saturday night supper basis," says one expert in a big organization.

---

1. Consideration of recruitment, training, and career prospects and the question of political neutrality is reserved for later sections.

. . . The [President] is beginning to recognize bailiwicks and refers letters for drafting replies to appropriate department heads. It's no longer a group of stray people who meet at a bar or at a house party and decide on what the next move is. We're beginning to shake down organizationally. (401a-3,4.)

Even experts in unions only a few years old describe a process of routinization and specialization of their work.

Policy Meetings.—The increasing formalization of administrative behavior in these few large unions makes the formal channels of communication somewhat more prominent in the work of their staff experts. Regular department head meetings, executive board meetings, policy committee meetings, meetings of the "Braintrust," formal negotiation sessions, three-way phone conversations, "progress meetings," progress reports, inter-office memoranda—in a few unions these are places where the expert's voice is heard.

The Pressure Screener.—Aside from direct contact with policy-making boards, committees, and officials via memo or conference, there is in some unions a relatively new formal channel—or block, as the case may be. In large unions with highly developed departmentalization, the staff expert must cope with a series of functionaries assigned to watch over him and his expenditures: administrative assistants to the President, who channel important mail, pass out assignments, screen out the pressures (including those from the experts), do the follow-through work, the trouble-shooting, etc. They "smooth the situation over" when the situation gets out of hand; they apply the policy when the policy doesn't apply itself. They "try to make the job of the boss as easy as possible." They protect him from pressures and at the same time try to keep him from losing touch.

These men have more to do than watch the experts, but they constitute one of the principal formal channels for reaching the boss.[2] The expert may have a proposal he wants to put over. He can ask the boss' right-hand man what the boss would think of his proposal and get an accurate preview of his chances. For the administrative assistant works very closely with the top officer,

---

2. Sometimes they are officials from the line organization who are given department head titles, and assigned to act as liaison between the top officer and the staff people who do the work of the departments.

knows his problems and moods, understudies his administrative style. "In fact," comments one expert, "it's hard to tell where X [Administrative Assistant] begins and Y [top officer] ends. I sometimes find myself wondering 'Shall I take it to X or Y?'" (202-2.)

In a few unions, the "Secretary-Treasurer" or the "Executive Secretary" or the "Executive Vice President" or the "Executive Assistant to the President" combines the duties of administrative assistant and the duties of chief financial officer—in which case he constitutes a formidable check on the discretion of the expert, for "Housekeeping" plainly overlaps "Policy-making." For example, the Internal Communications Specialist wants to set up a program that requires staff work in the field. This costs money—per diem expense, travel allowance, etc. The financial functionary calculates the cost. He says, "You'll run way over." "So"—as the expert involved in this little drama states—"we sit down with him and discuss questions of the duration of field work, the kind of program possible—policy questions." (605-4.)

"Clearance".—Whether through an administrative assistant or directly, the mechanism of "clearance" is often a channel of influence and support for the expert. "Having decided on a policy," says one expert, "I wanted them to be identified with it. So I cleared." (607-2.) Several respondents report the conviction that some officer "doesn't give a damn for the program," but tolerates it because of careful "clearance" and a previous involvement in the planning stage.

The Ecology of "Experting".—Communication requires access; and personal accessibility is often a matter of physical proximity. In the big unions the floor layout, the simple office location, may be an important factor in (1) the expert's degree of influence; (2) his ability to keep in touch, and hence to know the channels and possibilities of influence. Several experts are convinced that their sheer physical distance from the boss is a limiting factor on their influence. One traced the changes wrought by expansion of the union's headquarters:

Because it was small, we ["professionals"] were involved in everything. . . . Now you can't possibly know everything that's going on—just the physical arrangements alone would prevent it. We have a standard joke around here: When we were [in a smaller] building you met [the top officer] in the john and could learn what's going on. Here we have a john on each floor! Actually it's more serious than funny. . . . There tends to be a tendency towards close contact by floors. The [nth] floor lunches together more and more. (602-1.)

Of course, physical distance, when coupled with a long and close personal association, high prestige and indispensability, may not lessen the expert's influence on important matters, but it does stack the cards against the kind of sustained, day-to-day influence achieved by some experts lodged in that office next door.[3]

THE INFORMAL CHANNELS

The beginnings of bureaucratization are there. But, as we have said, it is a process that comes to the trade unions only slowly. The examples above emphasize more what is in store for the unions than what is dominant now. Typically, the division of labor in the national headquarters is still not sharp, the hierarchy of authority not clear-cut. Jobs are loosely defined; jurisdictional areas, even if official, are blurred and shifting. It tries the patience of the participants to figure out the office hierarchy. I use the word "typically" advisedly—for whatever the size of the union, its age, its politics, or the length of time it has used experts, and whatever the role orientation of the expert, the picture seems to apply. Fifty-six staff experts of all types—over 43 per cent of our Main Sample—reported frustrations due to the absence of clear-cut or uniform administrative procedures, policies, hierarchy of authority or jurisdictional areas; or complained of clogged lines of communication.[4] Many more described a lack of rational, efficient, impersonal bureaucratic organization, but did not find it distasteful. This picture of "administrative chaos" is given emphasis by the fact that it applies in every respect—ambiguous and loose definition of job, division of labor, hierarchy of authority—to the union with the most thoroughly de-

---

3. Speaking of the problem of co-ordination and control in corporate bureaucracies, Dimock and Hyde in their TNEC study recommend close attention to the location of offices: "It is surprising how physical distance augments mental distance, and correspondingly, how helpful to co-ordination a decrease in physical distance may be." *Op. cit.*, p. 77.

4. All comments were either unelicited or in response to general open-ended questions on "what gets in your hair"—so this response is impressive. The comments were so distributed among role orientation types and unions that they may be assumed to reflect typical patterns of union administration.

veloped departmentalization.[5] "It's a very loose arrangement," says one functionary in this union.

> It depends on . . . an inexplicit mutual understanding which is thoroughly ambiguous. Some [union functionaries we can't deal with] without explicit instructions . . . others we can deal with without checking with anybody. A guy like Y will know which are which. You have to live in it, get absorbed by it, know it inside and out. . . . It's a labyrinth with respect to the chain of command. So many traditions have grown up—so many shared experiences—that ways of working together have evolved that can't be pinned down. (752-3.)

In the absence of clear-cut job duties, fixed jurisdictional areas and neat lines of authority, a premium is put upon skill in the use of the informal channels of communication and influence. "Guys in the national office in this organization," one expert observed, "have to make their own way. . . . You carve out what you can and reach who you can reach." (318-1,2.)

The Personal Relationship and Direct Access.—There is no more widely and strongly held conviction among the union staff experts than the idea that their personal relationship with the boss—the "confidence" the line officials have in them, their informal contacts with key officers on and off the job—is the crucial determinant of their influence. Typical comments from functionaries in a variety of unions, new and old, large and small, indicate this.

> *A Contact Man:* There's a great amount of that stuff that's not formalized. It's "pre-policy" discussion. . . . For [years] I've had lunch with [the top officer] 95 per cent of the time when he's in town. Much of the conversation is [the top officer] asking, "What do you think about this?" (519-2.)
>
> *Facts and Figures Man:* [Line officials] come in and want a curbstone opinion. I've traveled all over the country and know most of the staff and many local union people. . . . They'll stop in and kick around their problems; they use me—just as another guy to talk to. (209a-2.)
>
> *Ex-expert:* I had [the top officer's] confidence for years. We'd make policy decisions whenever we talked in a sense. He'd think things out with me. (910-3.)

Many experts, to be sure, are not so favorably situated—either in

---

5. For example, all department heads in this union were asked for the kinds of things they clear with X. Everyone felt he had to clear expenditures with X, but no two respondents agreed on "expenditures above what figure" and several named a top figure beyond which they would go to someone else.

personal resources or opportunity—that the boss "thinks things out" with them:

> I'll be damned if I'm going to kill three afternoons a week at _____'s bar drinking whiskey with [a line official] or working on all-night poker games. I just couldn't do that—not only because I don't have the "technical" skills required but because I couldn't do it and my job at the same time. (401a-5.)

But attempts to deal with lower officials or the rank and file according to the impersonal norm are met with resistance. For instance, the staff expert just quoted—used to administrative procedures in government—describes his effort to maintain formality in his work relationships in the union setting:

> The old-timers in the union don't know what to make of it. When they call in here and ask for Mike they get, "Just a moment, sir, Mr. _____ handles that problem," or they get the answer, "We'll have to check policy on that problem—as soon as we take it up in Thursday's staff meeting we'll let you know." They're used to a personalized service. They know Joe Blow in a department in the International; they want the answer from Joe. (401a-6.) [6]

This case—since departed from the union—later said he was working at this personal relationships problem by eating about three lunches a week with the proper people. Whether they find the process comfortable or not, the experts recognize the importance of the thousands of casual deliverances of opinion in sustained, direct, informal contact with the boss and other line officials.

Indirect Informal Channels: the Use of a Third Party.—Some of the most effective informal channels of expert influence are indirect. If you can't reach the boss with a memo or through direct conversation, reach him through a third party.

The first channel is obvious:

> You plant your ideas with one officer rather than another—and expect him to carry the ball for you. [Officer No. 2] is less harrassed by broader union problems than [officer no. 1]. He's also less conservative on some things. . . . There are times where it's best [no. 2] instead of [staff expert] present the case to [no. 1]. (320-6.)

6. Informal sanctions such as kidding are directed against efforts at depersonalization. Headquarters colleagues say they needled the case quoted above: "Most other union people don't operate that way; why should we let him?"

The use of a more influential staff expert—e.g., one who is temporarily in favor, or has not recently bothered the boss—is also common. When the expert has much contact with the local activists and lower line officials, he is also in a position to build up pressure from below if he encounters resistance in headquarters. "I get what I want, anyway," says an Internal Communications Specialist, "by nurturing a demand from the field. . . ." (523-2.)

Less obvious are the expert-fostered pressures from the outside. Plant the idea with a government bureaucrat, a college professor, a politician who sees the boss in his more receptive moods. In return, feed him a little harmless "inside dope" that will help him in his work or prompt him to bring up the problem when he sees the boss.

Another *sub rosa* area of influence stems from the demands the third party may put on the expert. How often this occurs is an open question, but these two examples illustrate the point. The first concerns government policy affecting the union:

> Someone in the White House wanted a real feel as to what's going on; they called in [union staff experts] informally. . . . The way they figured [in the White House] is why take it up with the officers—the kid is going to write it anyway. There are situations where the office boy is a more efficient source! (335a-3.)

The second example concerns an arbitrator who similarly used the staff expert to feel out the union's position. Reams of data had been submitted, lengthy written testimony and argument concluded. "Nobody could go through this tremendous pile . . . nobody," reports a participant. So——

> Two or three days after the hearings were concluded, the arbitrator came to me [expert] and said, "I want to ask you to clarify this table for me" (it was the critical table—one on productivity). "Would it be right if I said you had an increase of productivity of 15 per cent?" Then, I happen to know, he went to the employer and asked if he would clarify this table. "Would it be right if I said there's been a 10 per cent increase?" After having felt us both out he gets the difference between 10 and 15 and he splits it, awards 12.5 per cent. Is that economic interpretation I made a matter of research or of policy? The fact is, it's a policy matter! . . . That's an area of decision on the part of the [staff expert] that never appears in the record. He'd never admit he's feeling us out. He's not going to [the union officer] and say what will you take; he goes to the [staff expert]. He's an honest man. I knew he wouldn't

betray the fact that I didn't read the table for him but on the basis of what observations I could make, interpreted the officers' limits for him. In that brief moment and within those narrow limits, I as [staff expert] had an effect on the outcome. (313-5,6.)

Another third-party channel of influence—more important and more pervasive than the friendly outsider—is the female contingent in the headquarters building and around the boss. The well-known "office wife" who protects the busy executive from unimportant people, picks up after him, shares his secrets, knows his weaknesses —this figure is not confined to the business world.

His secretary was one of my principal problems when I came on— creating a good relationship with her. She figured like most private secretaries, "If you don't tell 'em anything you can't get in any trouble." I had a helluva time finding out what was going on. It took her and me two years before she became convinced I could be trusted.

The union leader's private secretary can be a source of much grief for the staff expert, or she can be a powerful support. For it is her job to decide whom the boss will see, whose memo gets on top of the pile, whose problem gets mentioned at the most propitious moment. The secretary is a key point of transmission on the grapevine, and can slant the content of the rumors that pass along it. But the crucial facts that make her a force for the expert to contend with are these: (1) the white-collar girls in the union are typically among the few females on an almost all-male payroll; and (2) unions often recruit the wives and relatives of loyal unionists for the clerical jobs. These white-collar girls easily establish liaisons of friendship or marriage—if they don't already have relations of blood—with visiting line officials. They sometimes acquire a better "base" than the staff expert can build. In fact, there are cases in which the office girls have been able to invoke the ultimate sanction against a staff expert, i.e., get him fired.

Not only the office wife, but the wife at home—the expert's wife and the officers' wives and the wives of one's colleagues—may play a role as a channel of influence. This occurs where the off-the-job social life of the inner staff and line officials is close-knit. The expert's position may be much affected by the performance of his wife in these off-the-job cliques.[7]

---

7. Compare the role of the business executive's wife as reported by William H. Whyte, *Is Anybody Listening* (New York: Simon and Schuster,

Smooth channel or rock-like blockade, the females with steady access to the boss must be counted as an important part of the communication system in the modern union; they often comprise for the expert an important indirect way to reach the top man.

In sum: the formal channels of influence are increasingly prominent in the work of staff experts in the larger unions. But typically, the aspects of bureaucracy we have discussed are not yet well developed: the division of labor, the definition of the job, the jurisdictional areas, and the hierarchy of authority remain fluid and loose.

As for autonomy within his sphere of competence, this is the exception, not the rule. In fact, the expert who moves out of his sphere of competence is more likely to acquire maximum leeway and autonomy (see Chapter XI). Hence the great load on the informal channels and ways of influence. To reach the boss, you cultivate his confidence in informal, direct contacts on and off the job; or you work indirectly through a third party who has his ear —other labor functionaries, local union activists, prestigeful outsiders, the female contingent at headquarters or in the inner-circle social clique.

Bureaucracy: Recruitment and Training

A similar picture of slowly growing, but still embryonic, bureaucracy emerges from analysis of recruitment and other personnel practices. Data on how the experts got their jobs suggest that, in a substantial proportion of the cases, the method of selection involved no necessary demonstration of competence in a "technical" specialty (broadly defined).[8] However, the trend seems to be

---

1952), pp. 146-205. Though the dilemmas posed by the social correlates of career climbing in industry are absent in the smaller staff hierarchies of the union world, the "union widow" must have many of the qualities Whyte finds in the business wife: adaptability, discretion, gregariousness and corporation [labor] identification. For a penetrating essay on the private secretary's relations with the union officer, see Kermit Eby, "In a Man's Shadow," *Mademoiselle*, 35 (Sept., 1952), 100-1, 161-63.

8. Of 156 cases, some previous demonstration of competence was indicated in 51.2%; no such demonstration in 30.9%; no information in 17.9%. The most frequent ways to get a staff expert job are: (1) general activity in

toward less casual recruitment. This is reflected, for example, in the fact that the Facts and Figures Men hired in the postwar period have more previous training and relevant occupational experience than those hired before 1945 (see Chapter IV). The emergence of the synthetic rank-and-filer and the increased number of officers with "sea lawyer" inclinations or college background parallel this development.

Similar, too, is the picture of changes in the outlook of the experts recruited. Data in Table 2 suggest broadly that the rising labor movement attracted both Party Missionary and Rank-and-File Careerist types from the beginning; the Legislative-Liberals and Outsider-Careerists came along a bit later (over half in World War II or later); the Professional Service types were recruited when the movement had matured and organizational stability had been achieved.

The trend in recruitment is also seen in (1) the comments of union leaders and other union people, and (2) scattered instances where hiring and training practices are approaching the bureaucratic model.

Several top officials note the drying up of some old sources of union staff people—the labor schools such as Brookwood Labor College (which in its dozen years turned out scores of men who moved into union jobs, both elective and appointive), the Rand School, Commonwealth College, etc.; the radical youth groups or political parties (ex-YPSL's for instance, constitute a large number of my sample of staff experts); various units of the workers' education movement on the periphery of the labor movement (American Labor Education Service, the WPA Workers' Education Service, the Wisconsin School for Workers, Hudson Shore Labor School, etc.). Fifteen years ago young men drawn from these sources would go to work for a union with much enthusiasm and little pay. Today the top officers say they are not so sure they can depend on "idealism" to attract and keep either their staff experts or their line officials. A hint of things to come, perhaps, is seen in advertisements recently run by the ILGWU-AFL: *"TRADE UNION CAREER*

---

local union or radical party politics (excluding specialized work); (2) contact through a government labor agency; (3) demonstration of "technical" skill in union work, usually at the local level; (4) contact as an independent consultant serving labor.

with *POSITION GUARANTEED*. Free Tuition. The International
Ladies Garment Workers' Union Training Institute offers an opportunity to men and women interested in making service to the
trade-union movement their life work. . . . Applicants must be
in the 21-35 age group. All students completing the year's work
are guaranteed a position with the ILGWU. . . . *ACT NOW!*"[9] This
training Institute, established in its fiftieth year by a union once
staffed largely from the ranks of the socialist movement, aims to
train future organizers, business agents, managers, officers as well
as staff experts.[10]

Comments of various functionaries in the union about the new
Institute illustrate again the pattern of change in recruitment:

> The old way was to chisel your way in and make yourself indis-
> pensable. With this new training program it's put on a practical, effi-
> cient basis. . . . It takes the guesswork out of it. There's careful selection
> and a specific preparation. The Training School is the modern equivalent
> of the YPSL and of course more . . . orderly and fair. (600-1.)
> Twenty to thirty people a week come here looking for a job. That's
> a haphazard way of recruitment. There's no organized channeling and
> control. (100-3.)

The ILG Training Institute represents a highly developed symp-
tom of a slow but general tendency toward more bureaucratic ways
of recruitment. Labor lawyers connected with other unions comment about the applicants who come asking for union jobs: "The
people who go into labor law today are the people who want to
get into our type of labor law; police-court stuff doesn't appeal
to these bright young Yale students. They flood into the specialized practice." (G225-1.) "I get applications from many more
than I place. . . . [Instead of worrying about labor agency ex-
perience], I myself pick them for overall competence as a lawyer:
do they have legal ability and are they interested in what they
are doing." (227-3.) The young man who wanted a starting job
as a Facts and Figures Man a few years ago was told to go into

---

9. Advertisement in *ADA World*, Vol. 8, No. 1 (Jan., 1953), 4.
10. International Ladies' Garment Workers' Union, *Report of the General
Executive Board to the 27th Convention*, May 23-June 1, 1950, pp. 226-27.
For general description of the Institute see Arthur Elder, "The ILGWU
Training Institute," *Industrial and Labor Relations Review*, 3 (July, 1950),
627-29.

the shop, get some union experience, volunteer on a picket line. Today, though the probabilities are still high that he would get that advice, in at least two unions he might be given a formal written examination as a preliminary screening. A few years ago no union would think of using the want ad columns for recruitment purposes. But recently, the ILGWU offers of "union careers" with "position guaranteed" have been matched by other unions: the TWUA-CIO has advertised in commercial papers for auditors, the Airline Pilots-AFL for a statistician and research director ("University graduate. Must be an aggressive, capable, responsible, individual. Steady employment with progressive organization."[11]); the UAW-CIO, anticipating expansion of its negotiated health and disability insurance programs, circularized for "Group Insurance Consultant" and "Health and Welfare Program Administrators"—with the accent on persons with "transferable training and experience" who seek "advancement and professional growth." One union executive has even used a regular employment agency to recruit staff representatives.

While these attitudes and practices presage a new look in recruitment patterns, there are very strong resistances to bureaucratic ways, and the less systematic, less formal methods are still dominant, though the criteria of selection are clearly changing. In brief, the resistances include: (1) favorable union views of nepotism; (2) traditional requirements that union payrollers have shop-experience—and the attitudes these reflect; (3) traditional political criteria for selection of all staff; (4) the problem of what to do with incumbent old-timers when union needs change. The weight of their past character as a protest movement is very much with the unions. The barriers to bureaucratic ways of recruitment are similar to the resistances to bureaucratic behavior in other aspects of union administration and have a common root in the institutional pressures to which all union functionaries are sensitive. Discussion of them is therefore reserved for a final chapter on the psychology of union leadership.

---

11. *Chicago Tribune*, November 16, 1947.

The Bureaucrats: Role Orientation,
Career Prospects and Influence

If bureaucratic tendencies are growing but slowly in headquarters organization and recruitment, what of the subjective side
of bureaucracy—the mentality and outlook of the bureaucrats themselves?

The central tendency, as was evident in the discussion of role
orientation, is towards the Professional Service type. But this professionalization process, pointing toward a future where most
union experts will fit the image of the politically-neutral, techni-
cally-equipped bureaucrat, should not obscure the fact that as yet
most of the incumbents deviate significantly from the Weberian
model. Of the 126 typed by role orientation, only thirty-one are
Technician Professionals and share neatly the characteristics of
the professional bureaucratic type. The twelve Politicos and thirty-
two Careerists are also means-centered, easily adaptable to shifting
organizational goals, but they lack any dedication to the professional
norms of objectivity and independence. Most important, however,
are the fifty-one cases—twenty-nine Missionaries and twenty-two
Program Professionals—who see the union as a vehicle for the promotion of some strongly held ideas; though the focus of the latter's
interest in program impact is relatively narrow, both groups are
policy-oriented. Moreover, when we examine the influence ratings
of the staff experts, the relatively high influence of the Missionaries
and Politicos suggests a low degree of bureaucratization—on the
assumption that the character of a social group is reflected in the
orientations of its successful men (see Chapter X). Thus, on the
subjective side, the bureaucratization process has begun, but its
progress is still slow.

What about the rewards of bureaucratic compliance—can the
union employee look forward to a stable career? What are the
practices and expectations on promotion and tenure? Here is one
of the sharpest deviations from rationalized bureaucratic procedures. A change in top union leadership typically brings a shake-up
all the way down the line. The personal loyalty imperative makes
the staff man's tenure dependent largely on the tenure of the man

who hired him. An officer reaction to the suggestion that things might be different illustrates the general expectation in unions where factionalism exists:

LO: A Civil Service for technicians. Who the hell ever said he wanted that? That's a joke! Why, what security is there for any of us? Every convention—you ought to see the heads fall. _____! Who does this technician think he is? If he's going to work for a union, he'd better get rid of ideas like that. It wouldn't be desirable. It wouldn't be politically possible. (8-6.)

As for incremental salaries and regularized promotion procedures—these are typically missing. For one thing, the staff-expert hierarchies in unions using many experts are flat—with little possibility for the assistants to move into the departmental directorship, and nowhere else for the department director to go. Many of those interviewed in the lower positions called attention to the relatively high turnover among professionals below department head in several unions and attribute it to low morale among them. Not only are they confined to the less challenging work, but they typically see little chance of moving up within the union. Mobility for the subordinate, as for the department chief, tends to be horizontal —with "promotion" taking the form of a move to a more desirable union. And both the top expert and his subordinates are, with some exceptions, limited to a salary ceiling set by the top officer's Convention-determined level, which seldom matches the corporation counterpart. The distance between top and bottom salaries for professionals in unions tends to be slim, with good starting salaries but small prospects for salary advance and no system for increases.

This does not mean that there are no exceptions to the rule of unstable tenure or that no unit in the labor movement has a civil service mentality on the matter of promotions. One staff expert got himself a four-year contract with an arbitration clause attached to protect against an impending shift in leadership. Some of the older stable unions with no factionalism on a national level provide reasonable expectation of lifetime tenure for their staff—and in some cases, never fire anyone who has long service (new positions may be created to take care of the loyal aged).[12] If we include consideration of nonexpert staff and line employees, the

---

12. Yet—even in these stable unions—some of the staff experts are convinced they'd be the first to go if the union faced hard times.

exceptions grow numerous—and the trend is clearly toward more bureaucratic administration. The large clerical and subprofessional staffs are typically organized into unions and operate under contracts comparable to those in corporate bureaucracies, with formalized salary structures, promotion systems, pension and insurance arrangements, etc. Lines of promotion for the administrative and organizing personnel may also be fairly clear. Unofficial organizations among the international representatives sometimes exist to regularize employment relations with the union. In one union, the spokesmen of such a group actually bargain on key issues with the top officer and present demands at union conventions. At a recent convention they demanded an increase in their home base per diem in return for a decrease in their out-of-town per diem, and got it.

Whatever the trend, and despite the exceptions noted, the career outlook of the staff expert—his expectations on promotions, salary advance, security of tenure and the other marks of bureaucratic reward—is still typically uncertain, and his role orientation in most cases deviates significantly from that of the bureaucratic professional. And the role orientations of the most successful experts do not reflect a bureaucratic mentality.

In sum: whether we consider objective patterns of organization, recruitment, and reward (tenure, promotion and salary practices), or the subjective orientations and career expectations of the staff experts, or the characteristics of those who are selected for high influence, the picture is one of slowly growing, but as yet embryonic bureaucracy. Much of the explanation for this picture lies in the social psychological content of the trade union leader's role as it develops through time, and the kind of working climate the pressures on him foster. This working climate cross-cuts all functional and role orientation types, all influence positions.

CHAPTER XIII

THE WORKING CLIMATE
OF UNION HEADQUARTERS

THE WORKING CLIMATE of the national headquarters is set by the social origins, career lines, and dominant preoccupations of the top leaders—by the organizational purposes and codes to which their past histories and present roles have made them sensitive. The problem of the staff expert, as I have said, begins and ends with the problem of the executive.

Organizational Purposes and
Leadership Career Lines

In all of my decision-making analysis the overwhelming importance of collective bargaining as it relates to organizational survival and growth was clear. "Delivering the goods" in the short run via successful collective bargaining with employers under contract is a leadership imperative, whatever the leader's politics, past or present, whatever his style of leadership. Relations with the rank and file, government, other unions and various publics tend to be shaped by the dominant preoccupation with collective bargaining and the problem of organizational survival—and organizational survival tends to be identified in the leader's mind with his personal advancement. Whatever the partly divergent purposes and loyalties comprising the role orientation of the staff expert (or the officer),

259

they tend to be shaped by these central organizational purposes, which in turn are shaped by the leadership interest in maintaining tenure.

As the top union leader has climbed to national power from modest beginnings he has acquired heavy responsibilities, a vastly more complex job of collective bargaining and internal control. His increased involvement with government contributes to a vision of himself as a statesman moving on a world stage. In general, his rise has been accompanied by a dramatic change in his style of life and work. While the labor movement may be a source of great mobility chances for wage workers, the top leader's tenure problem looms especially large, for he knows of others who have had to make the trip all the way down again. Unlike the staff experts whom he has found indispensable in his new role, he can seldom make horizontal job moves; his skills are bound up with his particular organization even more than those of his experts, and labor career patterns are such that he cannot easily set up shop in another union. Therefore he cherishes the privileges and rewards of office all the more.

Social Distance in the Expert-Boss Relationship

Typically, there is a large contrast in the occupational and educational backgrounds of the top officer and his staff expert. These differences are often accented by differences in family origin and religion.[1] The contrasts between boss and staff expert—especially

1. On the occupational, family, and educational background of labor leaders see C. W. Mills, *New Men . . .* , *op. cit.* Cf. Eli Ginzburg, *The Labor Leader* (New York: Macmillan Co., 1948). While only four of the top executives in my twenty-eight priority unions (and none of the top men in my five "extras") are Jewish, at least 35 per cent of the 156 experts in the sample who work in these unions are Jewish (33.3 per cent are Protestant; 12.2 per cent, Catholic; 13.5 per cent say "no religion"; 5.8 per cent are unknown). The general picture is one of college graduates with white-collar or professional backgrounds, working for leaders with little formal education whose occupational experience has been in working-class ranks. Often the expert's family origin (as shown by father's occupation) is also higher. While eight of the top executives in the twenty-eight unions had some college or college extension courses (two of them leaders of white-collar unions), only three graduated. It is significant for my analysis that seven of these eight unions have low membership-expert ratios (at least one expert per 28,000 members). The less the social distance, the more the leader's tolerance for experts.

on educational and occupational background—are usually much sharper in the union setting than in industrial or governmental organizations. Such disparity in life experience fosters an awareness of social distance on both sides which has some crucial psychological consequences.

The labor leader looks at his own lowly origins and is struck with the immensity of his present position. He tends to have a sense of inferiority in his relations with other men of power in government and business whose prestige is more secure. This sense of inferiority easily takes expression in his relations with his hired brain, whom he views with a strange ambivalence—alternating between pride and resentment, respect and arrogance, admiration and envy, trust and suspicion. He is anxious to appear administratively modern and up to date, so he keeps the expert as "window dressing" (see Chapter III). He may have an awe of academic degrees. But he is also conscious that he's the boss, sitting right on top of those degrees: "I'll tell you," said a top officer, "actuaries and statisticians come a dime a dozen—just like lawyers." (19-1.) An ex-expert tells of his exit interview:

> I told him off. He wanted to know why I'm leaving. I told him, "I'm an errand boy. I run a forum, a class, I write speeches. But . . . this is phoney—it's your front, your window dressing. . . . I'm not going to spend the rest of my life as an errand boy." I said, "You've got lots of young and eager people working for you. . . . You know Smith?" I asked him. He wanted to know what I think of him. I told him he's a genius. He said, "Genius? So he's a genius. You couldn't name two places he could get a job if he didn't work for me!" (G 906-1.)

The labor leader, as this suggests, sometimes exaggerates the characteristic officiousness of the newly arrived, the insolence of the parvenu.[2] His arrogance, however, is often tempered by respect

---

2. A flamboyant example of this appears in a report by the late President A. F. Whitney, of the Brotherhood of Railroad Trainmen, in which he recounts his experience with Dr. J. H. Cover, whom he describes as a "so-called economist" hired to present the union's wage case before a government Emergency Board in 1941. "The learned doctor," it seems, "proved himself a traitor to the Brotherhoods," "made a pitiful figure cowering under the attack" of the "clever Mr. Fort, attorney for the carriers." "Mr. Hay, attorney for the brotherhoods," notes the labor leader, ". . . appeared equally ignorant. . . . It remained," he continues, "for the 'non-experts' to finish the job. At this unfortunate juncture, I was recalled, following in the wake of the fiasco left by Dr. Cover. This time," he modestly reports, "I concen-

for the expert's skill in symbol manipulation, his mastery of words.
He may cherish the conviction of the natural superiority of the
amateur, but at the same time be impressed by the brilliance of
the professional.

One top officer who began an interview with the proud boast,
"I was educated in the school of hard knocks," and followed this
up with complaints about his lawyer's high fees, ended it with the
equally proud announcement that "I've told my son to take up
labor law in college!" (19-2.)

The union leader senses the indispensability of the man of
knowledge, but he typically resents it. An expert explains:

. . . A guy comes up from the shop and his whole future depends on
successful bargaining. And he has to call me up and have [a complex
issue] all explained. I'm not naive enough not to see that this doesn't
earn me the gratitude of this man. The opportunities for hostility are
huge. Yes, the expert is indispensable and more so as time goes on.
But we're not liked any better. (315-4.)

The staff expert, on his part, sometimes invites this resentment and
hostility. He may look at his own broad experience, education and
professional equipment, compare them to those of his boss, and
figure he could run the union a lot better. The boss, after all, seems
to him a man of limited understanding and narrow horizons, less
trained in disciplined thought. Said one expert: "We do things
so much more intelligently since I came on!"[3]

The Anatomy of "Anti-Intellectualism"

The union's organization purposes, the nature of the officer's

---

trated my attack on the financial operations of the railroads. I set the big
boys by the ears." Report of the President, Brotherhood of Railroad Trainmen, *1941 U.S. Railroad Wage Movement*, pp. 58-59.

3. Some experts attribute the boss' hostility and suspicion to his experience with experts on the company or government side: the labor leader has
become convinced by past encounters with antilabor lawyers, engineers, arbitrators, etc., that nothing good can come from the man of knowledge.
This is insufficient as an explanation, however, for the officer is at the same
time aware that many an expert has given long and devoted service to
labor; moreover, the leader often finds it easier to deal with educated industrial relations staff men than the company's line officials. The contempt-envy
complex has deeper root in the social distance between the leader and his
hired brain.

career line and tenure problem, the social distance between leader and expert—these result in an all-pervasive anti-intellectualism, which helps explain some of the nonbureaucratic aspects of the labor movement described above. The components of this anti-intellectualism include: (1) hostility to anything reminiscent of Marxist ideology; (2) suspicion of the "theoretical," i.e., new ideas, Marxist or not; (3) resentment of the outsider, which is often a product of (4) job envy.

The image of the Marxist radical of middle-class origins infiltrating the labor movement is very much alive in the consciousness of the labor leader as he deals with the men of knowledge on his staff. Historically, such men were associated with secession movements, and "dualism" has always been the cardinal sin in trade union circles. The tirades of Gompers and his followers against the "intellectuals" stemmed from their experience with Marx, Sorge, Daniel De Leon, and other radicals of bourgeois origin and secessionist bent.[4] This hostility to Marxist ideologies soon expanded to include the holders of any new idea, Marxist or not, middle-class in origin or not. Today, if a worker on his way up the union ladder acquires an ideological or even a professional orientation he, too, becomes an "outsider," a "longhair," the target of anti-intellectual criticism. He may have been in the shop for a decade, he may have been through the early struggle to establish the union, but he can still get tagged. With the elevation of "pragmatism" to a rule of union life, one finds at all levels of the hierarchy resentment against superior knowledge and competence, against new approaches to new problems (or new means of meeting old ones), against anyone—home-grown or imported—who wishes to put an unorthodox stamp on the pure-and-simple union.

Sometimes what may be labeled "anti-intellectualism" is nothing more than "anti-outsiderism"—the disdain of the old-timer for the

---

4. See Chapter II. Norman J. Ware points to a significant incident at a national convention of the AFL in which some old-line labor leaders expressed much fear and distrust over the accrediting of a Yale University Professor as delegate, on the grounds that he might "start something!" *Labor in Modern Industrial Society* (New York: D. C. Heath & Co., 1935), p. 151. For a perceptive analysis of the cleavage between unionists and socialist intellectuals see De Man, *op. cit.*, pp. 219-37. Cf. S. Perlman, *op. cit.*, and Egbert *et al.*, *op. cit.*

newcomer, of the initiated for the uninitiated. The political contingencies of a union leadership career, however, complicate the anti-outsider component of anti-intellectualism. The local or middle-level official who aspires to higher position looks at the staff expert in the national headquarters as a man who takes away what rightfully belongs to him. Fewer and fewer staff expert appointments are made solely as political payoffs, but the tradition that union jobs should go to loyal machine supporters remains strong. This job envy is strengthened by an idealized view of brain work.

> LO: . . . Many's the [line official] who's told me, "Why, that S.O.B., he's got the soft job. Why . . . should he get the same money as me? I knock myself out taking crap from the rank and file, I gotta go out to local meetings night after night while he sits behind a desk and writes up all that stuff."

Such job envy may even appear among the top officers in the national headquarters. "It's funny," observes a staff expert. "If you leave the union—no matter where you go, there's the feeling you've sold out. Part of this is due to a certain jealousy. The officer himself doesn't want to go back to the industry, but where can he go if he gets defeated? He sees that his hired technicians can go get a job with the Labor Department or go teach in a university. It's jealousy." (G 334-2.)

These components of anti-intellectualism—hostility to the ideologue, resentment of the "theoretical" or the new, anti-outsiderism and job envy—take varied forms in the modern trade union. The forms of expression of anti-intellectualism, and the means by which the staff expert becomes sensitive to it include two interrelated myths, which function to celebrate and legitimate the leader's authority in his staff relations: (1) the "Practical Experience" Myth; and (2) the "From-the-First-Hour" myth.[5]

---

5. These are "myths" both in the sense that they are only partially true; and in the sense that they are traditional stories or propositions which symbolize and validate a collective sentiment. They may function to preserve group values; or rationalize dissociation between culturally prescribed values and socially structured means for realizing those values (e.g., in a social structure where success goals are glorified but promotion is rare, there will be myths which rationalize failure to climb); or they may be fabricated consciously by leaders to achieve given ends. For examples, see Richard R. Myers, "Myth and Status Systems in Industry," *Social Forces*, 26 (1948), 331-37. Cf. Bronislaw Malinowski, *Magic, Science and Religion* (Glencoe,

The Practical Experience Myth is the proposition that political, organizing, negotiating, and administrative talents and ideas are the exclusive property of line officials from the rank and file and can be acquired only through direct experience at the workbench and/or in local union activity. To be of practical value, experience has to be first-hand, direct—had by the man who's going to make use of it. True knowledge and understanding of the union and the industry cannot be attained vicariously.

The From-the-First-Hour Myth is the proposition that no one can understand the worker's psychology unless he was a bona fide on-the-spot participant in the great events of the early days, the struggles to establish the union. Long suffering in Labor's cause, first-hand participation from the very first hour of the battle, gives a man a feeling for the aspirations of workers and makes him especially qualified to rule. It is the line official who was "there" who has the right to lead.

Both these myths, of course, are found in successful social movements everywhere and in a wide variety of occupational and institutional settings.[6] In the modern union they are embodied in and help explain: (1) constitutional requirements that all pay-rollers have been workers in the trade or industry and/or members of the union; (2) convention debates and resolutions directed against staff intellectuals; (3) top officer pride in the careers of rank-and-file experts, both bona fide and synthetic; (4) the belief among some union people that some day Labor will train all its own experts; as well as such nonbureaucratic features of union

---

Ill.: The Free Press, 1948), pp. 119-24, for the function of myth in primitive psychology.

6. On the Practical Experience Myth see, e.g., V. Thompson's complaint that OPA administrative units gave too much attention to the need for "the practical, experienced representative from business," who, he found, "seldom had the needed knowledge of the whole industry," and whose knowledge of current practices was not difficult for others to acquire. Op. cit., p. 426. Parallel to this is the belief in the superior wisdom of "the man who has had to meet a payroll," which has had so great an effect on the recruitment practices of the Eisenhower administration. Myers' discussion of the "myth of the boy apprentice" among building tradesmen contains elements of both "practical experience" and "from-the-first-hour." Op. cit., p. 332. Phenomena comparable to the From-the-First-Hour Myth in institutionalized social movements are discussed in Hoffer, op. cit., pp. 148-49; and Lasswell, The Analysis of Political . . . , op. cit., p. 169.

administration as (5) nepotism in recruitment and the reluctance
to retire some superannuated old-timers; and (6) the unexpectedly
high influence rating of the Missionaries.

Several unions have constitutional provisions which direct the
top officials to hire for all headquarters staff or specified portions
of the staff only persons with a certain amount of time in the trade,
shop, industry, or union. This expression of the Practical Experience Myth is dictated by an ideology common to many democratic associations, which holds that the man who leads and serves
us should be one of us. Such requirements are typically stretched
in practice, officially or unofficially, to make room for indispensable
outsiders—lawyers, editors, economists, etc. In some unions, periodic
objections to the presence of these outsiders are heard on the convention floor and elsewhere. These objections are sometimes met
by special resolutions or administrative rulings which allow the
outsider to purge himself of his illegitimate social origin by joining
the union. Sometimes a brief stint in the factory to get a union
card will serve the same purpose.

Convention oratory occasionally focuses on the hapless intellectual in less casual ways. The use of epithets like "longhairs," "intellectuals," "outsiders," "Johnny-come-lately's" against factional
opponents has been a feature of several serious internal wars in
the labor movement.[7] Occasionally, one sees the spectacle of both
sides in an all-out war claiming the least contamination by education—either through the use of outside intellectuals or through
line officials' record of public school attendance:

SE: When things were dull, and someone wanted to get a rise out of

7. Excerpts from the CIO Rubberworkers Convention Proceedings: Delegate Robert Hill: "Your whole thinking on this matter . . . is fantastic. You
are a legal mind; you are from Harvard, or Yale, or some other place like
the rest of the guys up there, and you don't understand the thinking of the
workers." Executive Board Member Samuels: "You know it is a very nice
thing to have a staff of . . . high salaried assistants. It is a good thing if you
can get it. Now I don't disagree too violently on the issues with the President. I violently disagree with the way . . . he presents them. And he is
clever at it. Look at all that talent he has got behind him there: $12,000 a
year, $5,000 a year, $4,000 a year. Darned near $30,000 a year he is paying
for. I mean you are not paying for it. You aren't. He is not our attorney. He
is the . . . President's attorney. The lad from Harvard there is not our assistant. He is Buckmaster's assistant." URWA-CIO, *Proceedings 13th Convention,* September 20-25, 1948, pp. 102, 115.

the crowd, one thing was sure fire: make a speech about how the union has been turned over to a bunch of outsiders in the national office. End it with, "We want to give the Gadgetworkers Union back to the gadgetworkers!" and it'd bring the house down every time. (506-2.)

SE: Someone commented to me . . . that if the debate goes on, they'll wind up claiming we're all imbeciles.

HLW: Yes, I understand it became a badge of honor to say that you didn't have any education.

SE: Yeah, X said he only went through grammar school. He was boasting about it. When Y [factional opponent] stumbled over a word he stopped and said, "I can't even spell it!" What a faker! 501-12.)

The strength of the Practical Experience and From-the-First-Hour Myths—and hence of anti-intellectualism in general—is further illustrated in their impact on trade-union recruitment and personnel practices and attitudes. There is the pride the officers take in the careers of rank-and-file experts. There is the illusory belief of many union people that labor will eventually recruit *all* its staff experts from the rank and file, training them either through "colleges" of its own or through University extension programs.[8] More important is the persistence of political criteria, of nepotism and of chance in the recruitment of both experts and other staff functionaries. Political reliability as a criterion of selection—even in unions not torn by factionalism—is still obvious, though the importance of other criteria of competence, as we have seen, may be increasing. A top officer indicates several such criteria—vague and political—in his recruitment methods:

We don't recruit. You can't learn it from books. There's no substitute for experience. . . . [Staff expert?] I happened to know him. We happened to meet on the street cars. . . . [When hiring my staff specialists] I looked for what people they were connected with. What reputation they had; their family background; and especially whether they're tinged red or not; but not reactionary—I don't want that either. (17-2.)

---

8. What evidence we have indicates not only that the recruitment trend has actually been in the opposite direction, but that barriers to the full swing towards the rank-and-file source are very strong. For example: Several union people complain that the products of university programs come out corrupted—they think they know more than they do and "get creamed" by corporation experts, they create dissension because of their airs ("He split the local and had to be expelled!") or worse, they take management jobs.

It is in union views of nepotism, however, that we see the clearest expression of the two myths. Nepotism in unions, in contrast to many other private associations in our society, is often regarded as a virtue, not to be apologized for. "The relatives and sons of our members should have preference" (21-2,3) is announced as a general principle for fair selection. Though very few of our top staff experts owe their jobs to nepotism, several of the functionaries at lower levels, several consultants, and many nonexpert staffers were hired on this basis. Note, however, that the union leaders in my sample who held strongly favorable views of nepotism are not of the new rising generation.

The various expressions of the Practical Experience and From-the-First-Hour myths—especially this view of nepotism as a legitimate recruitment method—can be seen as a hangover from the days when the union was a protest movement. Memory of those days is still vivid and deeply affects the leader's personnel attitudes and practices. Any movement which sets itself against the existing order and views the environment as hostile to its purposes, is faced with acute problems in recruiting and maintaining a loyal leadership core. If it is not to disintegrate, a protest group must give especially close attention to the loyalty of the men in its inner circle. Where is there a more reliable source of loyal personnel than one's relatives and relatives' friends? Even after the union has "arrived," the practice may linger on. Despite the changed motivation, the leader can justify nepotism by continuing to invoke the image of hostile encirclement. Thus do bureaucratic and patrimonial ways of rule become intertwined—and we find staff men recruited on the basis of technical competence serving side by side with men who are in a state of dependency on the chief through kinship.

In all of this discussion of the working climate of the staff expert, bureaucratic and nonbureaucratic aspects of union administration have appeared intertwined. If we analyze the top leader's authority in his staff relations in terms of his claim to legitimacy, we sometimes find aspects of three types in one leader: rational-bureaucratic authority, which rests on a belief in the legality of the leader's commands (authority is exercised impersonally within a framework of rules, and the rewards of compliance consist of stable career expectations); charismatic authority, which rests on devotion to the leader (whose disciples regard him as the possessor of extraordinary qualities of personality and obey him because of his mission); and "bossism" or patrimonial authority, which rests on a personal political machine (where the boss views his authority as a personal prerogative and the members are bound to him by material interests). One or another of these types of authority may predominate in a given union; typically we find an intricate admixture of all three—once again reflecting the protest movement hangover, the bureaucratic tendencies promoted by practical problems of routine union administration, and the political contingencies of the leader's career.

These aspects of union administration are best seen in the survival imperatives of the staff expert. These imperatives are a consequence of all the features of union headquarters life discussed above: the central organizational purposes of the union; the career line and tenure problem of the top officer; the social distance between expert and leader; the pervasive anti-intellectualism, expressed in the Practical Experience and From-the-First-Hour myths.

The Staff Expert's Survival Imperatives

Whatever the expert's functions, role orientation, or influence rating, he accepts in some degree the imperatives of (1) personal loyalty; (2) being "pro-labor"; (3) anonymity—"knowing his place"; (4) perseverance and flexibility in the face of crisis.

The Personal Loyalty Imperative—Nowhere is the interweaving of charismatic and patrimonial forms of organization with bureaucratic forms in the modern union so clearly illustrated as in the injunction, "Be 100 per cent loyal to the man who hired you or out you go." The workings of this imperative are, of course, most clear in factional crises where the staff men active on the wrong (i.e,. losing) side are fired. A change in top leadership, as we have seen, typically results in a shake-up all the way down the line. The method of elimination may or may not be outright dismissal.

For [decades] I served. They had an election. The new crowd had different standards. . . . My ideas didn't fit their way of operation. They couldn't fire me outright—it wouldn't look good. So they lowered my pay. . . . (910-2.)

In some offices, such as that of editor, even neutrality in an internal war is impossible and can result in dismissal by incumbent leaders (see Chapter VI). Aside from factional turnover, there is another clue to the personal loyalty imperative: interview comments about those staff experts fired outside the context of factionalism:

He didn't play it cagey . . . took credit for setting up conferences instead of building up the officers. (205-4.)

He was fired because he was an independent sort of guy and was meddling in the politics of the union. . . . He embarrassed the boss in his relations with [important union leader]. (524-3.)

The main thing is that I couldn't pretend to respect people I didn't like. . . . Around your 45th birthday—by then you have to ask, "If I stay in, what am I brown-nosing for?" I didn't mind brown-nosing for history; but to brown-nose for some S.O.B. is a different thing. (914a-3.)

We have seen that political reliability is often a necessary and sometimes a sufficient criterion in recruitment. Similarly, in the day-to-day expert-boss relationship the expert (along with other staff men) feels compelled continually to demonstrate his loyalty, and the leader, in turn, is continually alert to possible deviations from that loyalty. Elements in the staff experts' concept of the ideal expert underline the loyalty imperative. Cross-cutting all role orientation types is an emphasis on the necessity of (1) knowing and understanding the personalities, politics, or policies of the particular union, etc.; and (2) having the "right" type of personality.[9]

The emphasis on studying the boss' personality and developing an acceptable personality of one's own is an index of the continued strength of charismatic and "bossist" ways of rule in the union. At best my data here are merely suggestive, but interview comments on leadership styles of administration seem to point to the conclusion that union headquarters life more directly reflects the personal idiosyncrasies of the top officer than in more fully bureaucratized structures.

Union X: Staff social life illustrates the Byzantine character of the group. . . . There's the apparatus and attitude of a Court. [Top officer]

_____

9. Code 9 (know union personalities, etc.): Missionaries, 10/29; Professionals, 20/53; Careerists, 11/32; Politicos, 7/12. Code 12 (right personality): Missionaries, 11/29; Professionals, 19/53; Careerists, 12/32; Politicos, 6/12.

buys a house on Smith Street; now everyone is trying to buy houses there. The status of women captures the essence of the situation. [Describes close personal relationships of union wives which were abruptly shattered when they no longer served the purpose of entree to the inner circle]. . . . They're conniving with their wives to get close to the throne. . . . It's considered a terrific honor being invited to his home and everyone vies for the privilege. . . . The funny part of it is, I think there's no consciousness on [top officer's] part of being at the apex of that pyramid. (507-3,4.)

Union Y [Top officer speaking of how much and what kind of staff supervision is necessary]: They won't get out of line if you know how to run a union. What you got to do is develop staff. . . . I'm an executive, not a hired hand. I make policy. I hold a staff meeting when I get home and I tell 'em what's happening, what commitments I made. . . . Then they do the leg work and the details. They'll ask me directly if they're in doubt. . . . Of course the best regulated family gets out of joint once in a while. Generally they've been around me long enough so they know what's right. I keep them oriented. I go off on a trip. I make sure they know what the latest developments are when I get back. We work together like a team. (22-4.)

References to the "team" and the "family" are frequent, and reflect patrimonial ways of rule. Elements of charisma, however, are also present. Several staff experts note the "hero worship" among their headquarters colleagues: "You have to make a distinction between boss and superman. He's got personal appeal. . . . You get imitators of [top officer]—even imitators of imitators of [top officer]!" (315-7.) Another, more decisive indication of the persistence of charismatic authority is the human interest stories some staff men tell about the top man. In brief, they either indicate wonderment when he shows ordinary human qualities, or they indicate a belief in the almost mystical force of his personality.[10]

The "Pro-Labor" Imperative.—The demand for diffuse loyalty to the leader's person easily becomes fused in the leader's mind with loyalty to the particular union and its policies, and this becomes merged with loyalty to Labor in general. The imperative that the staff expert be "pro-Labor" is thus another aspect of the

---

10. E.g., one story repeated by several informants concerned the testimonial of an alcoholic who, because the top leader stopped and talked over his problem with him in the hallway, reformed his ways completely and is now on the wagon. This is told to illustrate the personal magnetism of the leader—who, with one stroke, cured a sick man, where ordinary mortals had failed.

personal loyalty imperative. The typical statement of it: "You can't have any reservations about being an advocate—full-fledged —for Labor. If you have reservations, you're in the wrong Church." (217-6.) Of course Labor speaks with many voices, so this imperative constitutes no clear behavior directive unless translated into terms of loyalty to the particular union.

Aside from the diversity and variability of union policies, the idea that the staff expert must have no reservations ("to be convincing, the first man a propagandist must persuade is himself") is belied by the thoroughgoing cynicism of many cases—and the relatively high influence of the most cynical. What the pro-Labor imperative does imply is a reasonable amount of lip-service to the notion of Labor as a cause—similar perhaps to the demand on higher business executives for expressions of loyalty to both the business community and to enterprise purposes. This is revealed in two ways. First, there is the widespread feeling among line officials that a man has deserted when he moves to a non-Labor job— or even to another union. One top officer expressed the general view: "You can never tell when [the intellectuals with college background] will pack up their bag and fold their tent and leave the union for some other adventure. We had a lot of bitter experience with that. . . ." (13-1.) Second, there are the frequent interview comments of the line officer which indicate both his expectation as employer that his employees produce and his demand that their motives in producing go beyond mere porkchops.

The own-union, own-boss focus of the pro-Labor imperative is also seen in the effort of all staff experts to justify their activity in terms of the central organizational and personal goals of the top leader. Those experts on the fringe of the union's job-control function and those whose contribution to the tenure of the officer is intangible feel strong compulsion to demonstrate their practical utility: "There's more resistance to an appropriation if it isn't close to the main function of the union. It has to look useful for the problems the union faces here and now." (302a-2.)[11]

---

11. See Chapters IV-VI for examples. It is significant that while Satisfaction Code 4 (rendering service in terms of straight trade union gains) cross-cuts all role orientation types, the Politicos (who lead in influence) cite it relatively most often (four in six as compared with about one in six for the other main types).

"Know Your Place": the Imperative of Anonymity.—The third major imperative of survival for the staff expert can be stated like this: know your place and stay in it—a staff expert is rightly a mere hired hand; he should remain anonymous, keep out of the officers' hair, offer no threat, no trouble, accept the subordinate importance of his functions and the natural superiority of the line official. This imperative of anonymity takes the form of (1) vigorous expressions of anti-intellectualism by intellectuals—best seen in their adherence to the Practical Experience and From-the-First-Hour myths; (2) an exaggerated humility, typically stated in the form of the Staff-Line myth.

Like self-hatred among Jews and other minority groups,[12] the anti-intellectualism of our staff experts is prompted by feelings of fear and inferiority rooted in the acceptance of negative valuations of the dominant group. It's a protective device, a means of dissociating themselves from the epithet "intellectual." One way to "live down your college degree" is to proclaim a strong belief in the superiority of the untrained man. Thus some of the most vigorous statements of the Practical Experience myth come from staff intellectuals who themselves have little or no practical experience, or from line officials who are self-conscious about their distance from the shop. This self-flagellation is even more marked in the earnest espousal by wartimers and newcomers of the From-the-First-Hour Myth:

SE: It seems to be a characteristic of these intellectuals that they have all the answers. . . . _____! They don't know what it's all about. Mostly these people were never actually in the labor movement when the going was tough. They don't know what it means to organize workers, to . . . bat your head against a stone wall. They have no idea of the thousands of practical jobs you do day-to-day to keep the union going. . . . It compares with the Fabian intellectuals trying to set trade union and Labor Party policies in England—and it has the same disastrous results.

HLW: You speak of "these intellectuals." You've done some graduate work yourself, haven't you?

SE: Yeah, they kid me about it. In fact, [top officer] calls me a longhair. But I'm accepted as one of them. (750-2.)

The young intellectual who never got the chance to participate in

---

12. See Kurt Lewin, *Resolving Social Conflicts* (New York: Harper and Bros., 1948), pp. 186-200.

those great events of the "early days" sometimes lives them in his imagination and idealizes them. These events may come to have a greater symbolic meaning for him than for his older colleagues who lived through them and who, in the press of more recent staff responsibilities, let them lie dormant in the depths of dim memory. Thus we find a young staff intellectual looking up to a long-service staff expert as a man who was "there" and who is therefore a more bona fide member of the labor movement than he—while the old-timer views himself as an outsider and views the youngster's admiration with amusement.[13]

The staff expert's effort to emulate the practical man of affairs in his anti-intellectualism leads to a tension between "being one of the boys" and "being all expert." The expert who achieves high influence is likely to be a man who has struck a neat balance between the two, a man who can "talk their language" but at the same time skillfully employ the device of the mystery (see Chapter XI).

The "know-your-anonymous-place" imperative shows up not only in the intellectual's low rating of intellectual skills, but in an exaggerated humility in his manner and his rhetoric. Experts of all types must try to live up to the ideal of a man who knows he's subordinate to the line official and has no power strivings—or at least gives the impression he has none.[14] This finds its typical expression in the Staff-Line myth: "A staff man never makes—or even influences—policy; that's the officer's job. We carry out the officer's policy. The trick is to keep in touch with that policy, and not have to be told what to do. We give our opinions only when asked for them in an advisory capacity." The workings of this myth can be

---

13. A few old-timers, like this one, show little or no self-hatred: "I went to college, then into the labor movement. . . . I was in the .... strike, worked in the shop [many months]. I don't pass myself off as from the industry. I don't tell 'em 'I've sweated beside you.' Some of these guys have a martyr complex: 'You're no damn good because you went to college.' You know what I tell 'em? 'I was going to college and working my ass off while you were on WPA drinking beer!' A lot of these intellectuals take an awful lot of crap. They think they missed an experience, not going into the shop. . . . What the hell. In this crisis situation no one knew what they were doing! A few Socialists maybe." (405-3.)

14. Though Professionals accent it more and Careerists less, the distribution of Ideal Expert Code 10 (humility) does suggest this as a possibly cross-cutting pressure: Missionary, 7/29; Professional, 22/53; Careerist, 3/32; Politico, 4/12.

seen in several cases where experts were fired for violating its spirit.

The fact that this Staff-Line notion is myth and not reality is suggested in interviews where its strong expression is followed with reports of expert policy impact. In one breath:

> The staff man should be seen and not heard. . . . He can't push too much. The less anyone knows about what I do, the better I get along, the happier everyone is. (306-1.)

In the next breath, a description of ways of influence, direct and indirect, formal and informal, of activity that cannot conveniently be called anything else but policy-making (see Part IV). The Staff-Line myth functions, like the other myths, to celebrate and justify the leader's authority in his relations with staff men whose competence to deal with certain problems may exceed his own. For the staff expert it functions to make what policy impact he has tolerable to the line organization.[15]

Again there is a paradox: the staff experts who are most successful in winning the boss' confidence, while they know their place, obey the imperative of anonymity and adhere to the Staff-Line myth, also have to be ready to fill the policy vacuum when it appears, make quick definite decisions on their own and take any resulting "heat" where necessary (see Chapter XI).

The Crisis Atmosphere: the Imperative of Perseverance and Flexibility.—All staff experts, of high influence or not, must make some adjustment to the crisis atmosphere typical of the trade union headquarters. The union is still basically a conflict organization. It must be geared for quick decision in a fast-changing environment. Its leaders, given their career patterns, tend to be more skillful in political combat than routine administration.[16] Leader-

---

15. For description of the Staff-Line myth at work in a government agency, see V. Thompson, *op. cit.*, pp. 285-86, 430-32; in private industry, see Melville Dalton, "Conflicts Between Staff and Line Managerial Officers," *American Sociological Review*, 15 (June, 1950), 342-51.

16. Union people cite many examples of administrative bungling: the use of high-priced labor for routine tasks (e.g., a Research Director doing the work of a statistical clerk), lack of liaison between departments, the absence of rational financial management, etc. Leadership practices in investment of union funds also reflect a characteristic disinterest in routine administration. See Nathan Belfer, "Trade Union Investment Policies," *Industrial and Labor Relations Review*, 6 (April, 1953), 337-51.

ship hostilities and ambivalences toward the staff expert mean that the latter is typically understaffed and overworked, as well as unappreciated. It is easy to understand why the question, "What do you do—what's the job consist of?" is so often met with the initial reaction: "It's quite a scramble," "it's a fireman's proposition," "it's like a combination city desk, fire station and library," "it's unpredictable," "continual hysteria," "the pace is fantastic," "a situation is normal for the boss only if it's a crisis," and so on.

Thus, it is an imperative of survival that the expert acquire the ability to persevere in the face of adversity, be flexible and adaptable in the face of constant confusion, and come up with answers quickly when they are needed.[17]

Conclusion

In so far as an analysis of the leader-expert relationship can serve as a guide to typical patterns of headquarters administration, the large modern trade union represents an intricate admixture of charismatic, patrimonial, and bureaucratic forms of organization and ways of rule. The union is at once a bureaucratic hierarchy, and a body of faithful followers sometimes tied to the leader by a belief in his extraordinary personality or his mission, or more often by material interests. Political criteria and nepotism in recruitment; the absence of regularized salary structures, tenure systems, and promotion procedures; the fact that the role orientations of most experts deviate significantly from the model of bureaucratic professional; the unexpectedly high influence of the Missionaries; an all-pervasive anti-intellectualism; the personal loyalty and "pro-Labor" imperatives, the crisis atmosphere and the demand for flexibility—these appear side by side with practices and attitudes that point to increasing formalization and routinization.

While competition for access to the inner circle takes the form

17. Ideal Expert Code 11 (naming these qualities) cross-cuts all types: Missionary, 8/29; Professional, 16/53; Careerist, 7/32; Politico, 4/12. Similarly, Frustrations Code 10 (no clear-cut administrative procedures, etc.) and 11 (clogged lines of communication) also seem to reflect typical patterns of union administration.

of constant demonstrations of the purity of one's loyalty to the union or union policies (which is equated with loyalty to the person of the boss), those who acquire highest influence must mix 100 per cent loyalty with some degree of independence. In a personalized bureaucracy such as the modern trade union it is true, as Hans Gerth suggests in another connection, that ". . . the confidence and favor of the leader alone determine who belongs to the inner circle. . . ."[18] But such confidence is in part a function of a man's market position. Influence for the staff expert is more than a matter of "the changing personality preferences of the leader . . . institutional entrenchment . . . personal propinquity . . . comradeship during the struggle for power."[19] It depends also on the nature of his acceptable alternative job chances, which are a compound of his own role orientation, the number and kind of job offers he gets and the transferability of his skills; the ease with which he can be replaced; his connections on the outside and his "base" on the inside. Moreover, with the transformation of the staff expert's role orientation toward the Professional Service type, the trend toward recruitment of better trained specialists, the rise of better educated, more efficiency-minded labor leaders—at once reflecting and strengthening the integration of labor into American society—we can expect a devitalization of the charismatic and "bossist" aspects of union administration and an accentuation of the bureaucratic ones.

It is probable that the present low degree of bureaucratization of the labor movement makes life hard for the staff experts who serve it, but at the same time makes the union a more efficient instrument for the accomplishment of its central tasks.

For the expert, it means little security, difficult working conditions, and little understanding from his boss of the technical aspects of his work; if he develops self-hatred as an adaptation to

18. Hans H. Gerth, "The Nazi Party: Its Leadership and Composition," in *Reader in Bureaucracy*, ed. R. K. Merton, *et al.* (Glencoe, Ill.: The Free Press, 1952), p. 102.

19. *Ibid.* Compare Gerth's picture of the Nazi Party as a fusion of charismatic and bureaucratic domination and Burin's discussion of "ideological bureaucracies," *ibid.*, pp. 39-43, with Franz Neumann's similar analysis in *Behemoth* (New York: Oxford University Press, 1942), p. 81.

anti-intellectualism, it also means considerable tension and anxiety. At best he can hope to win toleration and a grudging recognition of his growing indispensability.

For the union, however, a low degree of bureaucratization may spell greater flexibility in the accomplishment of organizational goals. Devotion to the leader rather than to rules of procedure; partisanship rather than political neutrality; personal loyalty in staff-line-rank-and-file relations rather than depersonalization; loosely defined jobs, rather than airtight spheres of competence—these mean less pressure for conservatism, overconformity and technicism.[20] For the large tasks facing it in a world crisis and in a country with many millions of workers as yet outside the ranks, the labor movement may gain in flexibility what it loses by its careless treatment of its hired brains.

---

20. See Merton, *Social Theory* . . . , *op. cit.*, pp. 156-59.

METHODS OF THE STUDY

SOURCES OF DATA

THE MAIN SOURCES of data for this study were: (1) intensive interviews; (2) questionnaires; (3) documents; (4) observation of meetings; (5) participant observation.

Interviews

The most important source of data was interviews with (1) the incumbent experts and their assistants; (2) former experts; (3) elected and appointed union executives; and (4) other people who have intimate contact with the experts and their work. The interviews were relatively intensive. Interview guides were drawn up at the beginning of the study for experts, ex-experts, and officers, and elaborated as the field work progressed. Most of the questions were open-ended. The interview guides as amended after the first ten interviews appear below.

Approaching the Respondent: the Problem of Rapport.—The problem of rapport, of securing the respondent's acceptance of the goals of the study and his active co-operation in reaching those goals, was complicated by the great range of union types and types of respondents. Obviously, my university connection and my past work with unions meant different things to different respondents. To get full co-operation it was necessary in most cases to (1) get an introduction from a friendly source; (2) emphasize different aspects of the study and of my background in making contact or

281

beginning the interview. Accordingly, various people with good labor contacts, principally from the University, were asked to write letters describing the study and the researcher and/or asking entree as a personal favor. These went to at least one key person in each union. In some cases more than one letter converged on the respondent. Some I wrote myself. People not in the sample who might offer resistance were informed of the nature of the project. Once clearance was secured from a responsible official in the line organization or firm rapport established with one or two staff functionaries in a position to line up interviews, the other contacts were easier. In only rare cases did I go in "cold."

In approaching the respondent my role varied: in some cases the university connection was emphasized (one intellectual to another, or one agent of a large research organization to another); in others, the labor sympathy and background were emphasized (staff man on Union Leadership Training Project to staff man in unions). In some cases it was necessary to play down the university connection. In some cases the focus on "some problems of union administration, etc." was emphasized; in others the focus on "the problem of the intellectual in modern society" was emphasized. A few people got a complete briefing on the study design.

In most cases, getting sent by the proper friendly source was sufficient. In a few cases the respondent made calls to check up on me before beginning the interview. The two direct staff expert refusals did not interfere with interviews with other respondents in the same organizations. A third "refusal" (who explained his reasons for half an hour) months later consented to a long interview.

In all cases anonymity was assured; identification of persons was to be ruled out unless permission was granted. In rare cases the respondent asked that quotations not be used, anonymous or not. Since the most private or emotion-laden material came both from men who did not care about the use of the data and those who did, illustrative quotations on almost any subject could be used.

In descending order of frequency, the interviews took place in (1) their private offices; (2) restaurants, bars, hotel rooms, etc.; (3) their homes; (4) miscellaneous places (cars, taxis, walking on the street, conventions, my office or home, etc.). The main effort was to assure privacy, though in some cases a group interview proved very useful.

Interviews ranged in length from thirty minutes to more than eight hours; most were over two hours. Many cases were interviewed more than once (there are fifty-six repeat interviews). The most time spent interviewing in and around the headquarters of one organization was three weeks.

The Interview Procedure.—The interview guide for the staff expert was used to get the respondent to talk about his job activity, the meaning it had to him, and how both his activity and role definitions had changed through time. Alternative phrasings and frequent probes were used where necessary to get coverage of the area. The data were elicited by both indirect and direct questions. Occasionally, where penetration of clichés was difficult, a change of tone and pace was successful—e.g., I might offer an outrageous opinion or allegation of fact, or suggest in some casual way the possession of inside information which might encourage the respondent to abandon evasive verbalization and "level" with me, etc. Often the respondent knew whom I had seen before him and assumed I had knowledge—and this in itself facilitated fuller expression of opinion.

Interviews with all respondents were generally focused on the top staff experts in my sample—to provide cross-checks and fill in gaps. Thus, a whole interview might consist of a play-by-play description by a consultant of his and others' participation in policy formulation on a given problem. Another might be a clean-up interview with a key person in a union to check facts, official union policy, salary structure, etc., indicated in other interviews. Still another might be designed to get reputation data on role orientation of several key experts well known to the respondent, or rankings, by a person with an overview of the organization of the relative influence of several cases. An initial interview in each organization usually consisted of a check of my list of staff experts and a description of where they fit in the organization, along with a discussion of borderline cases.

Extensive notes were taken throughout most interviews on 4" by 6" pads. These notes were reconstructed at the first opportunity after the interview. Immediate reconstruction was attempted also where no notes or only brief notes were taken during the interview. While the extensive use in note-taking of symbols for standard questions and abbreviations for recurrent phrases and words in the replies permitted nearly verbatim records for the slow talkers, there is no claim that the interview data are verbatim—or even that half of what was said was written down. Forty-seven of the 306 interviews have less than two single-spaced pages. Many devices were used, however, to get the relevant material down for the fast talkers: inserting an irrelevant question or asking for useless elaboration to allow time for writing previous responses, writing only a phrase to indicate clichés along a stereotyped political line, etc. In a few cases where rapport was extremely good, the respondent could be asked to talk slower while I wrote it down.

Ultimate reliability of interview data gathered from functionaries in large-scale organizations rests not only on the investigator's ability to establish "rapport," but also on his knowledge of the structure, history, traditions, interests and current problems of the particular organization. To maximize reliability of interview data I tried to get (1) a large number of interviews focused on a small number of top staff experts in the international headquarters of each organization—to permit some cross-checking; (2) a pre-interview grasp of the structure and problems of each organization, by reading their official organs and by contacting where possible former staff experts (or even experts about to leave) before approaching the incumbents. Talking to former union staff experts in the preliminary stages of research provided a base of opinion and information from which to interpret and probe the comments of the incumbent functionaries. Some of these recently departed ex-experts—despite occasional bitterness at various unhappy union experiences—have achieved a greater degree of "objectivity" about their union roles than their successors. Their use as informants has its parallel in the "method of the casual breakdown" described by J. S. Plant. The crisis that occurs when a member of an institution breaks away from its controls provides the basis for a conscious examination of his role in the institution. As Plant suggests, "It is . . . the angry husband slamming the door, 'never to return,' who assays in heightened lights and shades what marriage has meant to him. . . ."[1] The "ex-experts" recently departed from the unions do not meet all of Plant's criteria for the "casual breakdown," but their advantages as informants are much the same. Used, with awareness of the dangers of distortion, as background on each organization approached, this material can be invaluable both in planning interview approaches to the incumbents and in interpreting what they say.

Questionnaires

Questionnaires supplemented the interviews. In most cases these were either administered in person, or handed to the respondent and returned by mail. Others were mailed both ways. Table 7 shows a breakdown of returns and nonreturns. The questionnaire was first hectographed and used in the first two unions contacted. With slight modifications (a different way of asking for occupational history and the elimination of some questions) the original questionnaire was printed and used for all subsequent interviews and for mailing. A copy appears below.

Table 7—Questionnaire Data on 175 Cases in 28 Unions in Q Sample

Total Returns (26 unions)		123
Administered in person	46	
Given in person, returned by mail	30	
Mailed both ways	47	
Nonreturns (19 unions)		52
Total Cases		175
Extra Returns (from extra unions, or don't fit definition of expert)		39

Where personal contact was made, the questionnaire was handed to the respondent at the end of an interview and either filled out on the spot or picked up later. Questions covered in the interview were crossed out before being handed to the respondent, usually

1. James S. Plant, *Personality and the Cultural Pattern* (New York: The Commonwealth Fund, 1937), pp. 58-60. Cf. pp. 49-63.

leaving only questions on social characteristics, salary, etc.

Toward the end of the field work, when the list of Questionnaire Sample names was as complete as possible (several unions had not yet been visited), two waves of questionnaires were mailed, accompanied by several different kinds of letters:

1. First wave mailed from May 21, 1951 to June 13, 1951. First form letter for people not yet contacted. Second form letter for people contacted briefly or interviewed who had not yet filled out the questionnaire. Personal letters or personal postscripts on form letters were mailed July 11 to August 6 to several cases in the second category. These first wave letters were sent to 104 people in thirty unions.

2. Second wave mailed June 19 to July 6 with a form letter with no personal note added. Additional second-wave letters sent August 9 to August 20 with personal postscripts. The postscripts or personal letters mentioned that the respondent's boss or colleagues had given me his name when I'd talked with them, etc., and explained why his particular union was chosen. A few cases were asked to get a colleague to fill it out instead of themselves.

By the time I had visited all unions I had seventeen additional names which belonged in my Q Sample definition of expert. These are counted in Table 7 as among the fifty-two "nonreturns," though some of them received only one questionnaire or none at all.

The main aim here was to get social characteristics and job content for the Q Sample experts, and fill in gaps on Main Sample cases. Accordingly, the questionnaires were supplemented by secondary sources—authorized biographies in *Who's Who in Labor* (New York: The Dryden Press, 1946), as well as information from people who knew the backgrounds of the nonrespondents. These sources not only served as cross-checks on interview material from our staff experts, but also brought the information for some characteristics to 88 per cent of the Q Sample. Only two people of all those contacted in the Q Sample can be called "refusals," and in both cases secondary sources were adequate. Many of the nonrespondents for whom questionnaires are missing are Main Sample cases for whom interview and other data are most complete. A general suspicion of questionnaires and a disposition not to treat them seriously was apparent among many staff people. One fine two-and-one-half hour interview was concluded with a refusal to fill out the questionnaire on the grounds that quantification was ruining social science.

While it can be overcome through personal contact, such resistance to questionnaires does block the full use of this tool for the testing of insights and hypotheses derived from qualitative data. For this study, I could not depend on a mailed questionnaire constructed after interviews were completed and analyzed. Instead I had to use a questionnaire as an interview supplement—one constructed before major field work began for the limited purpose of gathering "objective" background information on each case.

Documents: Published and Unpublished

The house organs of ten unions in the Questionnaire Sample were read regularly throughout 1951; other samples of the labor press were read more sporadically, 1950-1953, as background for specific interviews or as general background. Reports on the doings and pronouncements of Labor's staff experts were excerpted from the Bureau of National Affairs' *Daily Labor Report*, the best commercial summary of labor relations news, from December 1, 1949, to September 4, 1952. This afforded a picture of them in their public roles. Further published sources used were convention proceedings, officers' reports to policy committees, speeches, press releases and the like.

Supplementing these sources were unpublished documents gathered in the course of field work: personal letters, internal memoranda, collective bargaining briefs and other unpublished examples of the staff experts' work, notes on meetings of labor lawyers, editors, workers' education specialists and researchers, and on groups of local line officials discussing services from the international. In two instances, brief autobiographical statements were written by the staff experts.

Other published and unpublished primary source documents are cited in footnotes in the text.

Observation

Sensitivity to the area of study and some sympathetic understanding of the problems of unionism were acquired through: two
staff jobs in the labor movement; two other jobs involving intensive
interviewing of union officials; three years with the Union Programs, Industrial Relations Center, University of Chicago (involving considerable contact with union leaders and staff experts); and
some previous research, in part a study of the operation of a local
union.

Participant and nonparticipant observation data specifically
pointed to this study, however, were gathered only in the course
of university work: notes on one conference of labor lawyers in
1950, two conferences of labor editors in 1951, and five conferences
of labor education specialists, 1948-50. I also participated as teacher
in many union-sponsored training institutes during this period, and
recorded relevant observations.

INTERVIEW GUIDE FOR ALL EXPERTS

August, 1950

[Memorized, but summarized on 4″ x 6″ card for occasional reference.]
1. What does your job consist of—what do you do?
   a) What are the (nonresearch, nonlegal, noneditorial, etc.) aspects
      of your work? Is your advice sought on matters outside (field)?
2. Who tells you what to do—gives you orders on what direction your
   work should follow? (or, defines your problems for you)
   or
   Is there anybody here who tells you what to do on the job—or do
   you have freedom pretty much to do what you want?
3. What are the main problems you run into in doing the job the way
   you think it should be done?
   and/or
   No job is perfect, and a union job like any other kind of job has its
   frustrations. Who or what gets in your hair around here?
   a) What's the dirty work on this job?
4. Has your work (the briefs you write, the studies you make, etc.)
   got much to do with the decisions made by the top officers of the
   union? When do they listen to you most?

5. When you have a good idea—one you think will help the operation of the union—how do you go about reaching the boss?
6. What contact do you have with the rank and file on this job?
7. Has the job changed much since you first came on? In what ways?
   a) When you first came on, how did your boss define your duties?
8. How did you get into this kind of work, anyway? (Get both the how and why.)
   a) What did you figure you were getting into when you first came on? Did things turn out any different from what you expected originally?
9. You certainly put in the hours (have a helluva lot to do)—it sounds like something of a rat-race. What satisfactions do you find in it, anyway?
   a) If a company offered you, say, 1½ to 2 times what you're getting now to do similar work for them, would you take the job? (Why or why not?)
   b) What are your chances for advancement in the union movement? What would be considered the next step up for you? or, What does this job lead to? What's the next step up?
10. Is there much communication between you and the rest of the staff—much interchange of opinion and information among department heads around here—do you have regular meetings, depend on informal contacts or what? Do you have much occasion to use other Depts.?
11. How about (experts) working for other unions—do you get together with them much?
12. How about the (nonlabor experts in same field)—do you have the chance to keep in touch with what they're doing and thinking? Does (name of union) ever go outside the staff for expert advice—use outside consultants? How come? Who chooses the outsider?
13. (For Dept. Heads) What do you look for in hiring staff for your Dept.?
14. What would the ideal (gen. couns., res. dir., ed. dir., etc.) be like? i.e., what personal qualities, skills, training do you need to make good on a job like yours? Or: If you were leaving and the boss asked you to advise on what kind of guy to get to replace you, what personal etc. . . . would you say are needed etc. In other words, what would the ideal etc.
15. You find among many union people a lot of feeling against the so-called intellectuals. Is there much of this anti-intellectualism in the (name union).
16. Some writers picture the union staff experts or technicians as a pretty frustrated lot. They're thwarted in their power strivings. From what you've said, I take it that you'd agree (disagree) with that picture.
17. (For unions with present or past factionalism in International): How

is your work affected by the factional struggle now going on? or Has your work ever been affected by factionalism in the union in the past?

or

(For unions with little factionalism): If there were a shakeup of top union officers after a bitter Convention battle, how would this affect your job tenure and security?

(*Also, pick out key decisions in major areas for each first priority union and ask, What part did you have in these?*)

ADDITIONAL INTERVIEW QUESTIONS FOR RESEARCH DIRECTORS AND ECONOMISTS

1. Union Researchers like yourself or _____, _____ work hard to prepare elaborate cases to buttress the union's demands. (Give example.) You go in there and present data. The company sits there and laughs up its sleeve and doesn't bother to answer. (Give example.) Why all the preparation? Isn't the outcome just a matter of bargaining strength? (or, Do you think the company is impressed?)
2. One Union Research Director (name) has written that even in unions with a big effect on the nation's economy there's been no real need for a serious review of the economic implications of specific policies. The main body of trade union policy has remained unaffected by social science. Agree?

ADDITIONAL INTERVIEW QUESTIONS FOR LAWYERS

1. A lot of people as they look over the range of staff experts hired by the labor movement tell me the lawyer is the only man who really has an important influence on policy. They say he's in a real power position. Hired as a specialist the lawyer soon moves into the whole broad range of union decisions. Do you think this is so? (If so, how do you account for it?) [Occasionally used for nonlawyers and officers, too.]
2. If you had the choice would you rather do this sort of work full-time in HQ of _____ or on a consultant basis with several union clients? Which is best from the union's viewpoint?

SAMPLE OF OCCASIONAL QUESTIONS FOR EXPERTS

1. (Where respondent was doing similar work elsewhere before the union job): How does this job compare with the one at _____?
   a) Which of the whole range of your job activities (list) is most satisfying to you?

2. When in your career do you have to decide that this is it—the labor job for life? Is it too late for you to change?

3. Like many competent (lawyers, etc.) working for unions, you could be making more money elsewhere. Why stay?

4. Moving-in process (see lawyer questions above). Does it occur
   a) at the international level; b) at the local level. To what extent and why?

5. List hypotheses on conditions maximizing expert influence. Ask for positive and negative instances from own experience.

6. What specific work that (experts in this union) do now do you think could be taken over eventually by line officers or other people from the rank and file?

September, 1950

INTERVIEW GUIDE FOR UNION OFFICERS

Introduction of study to officers: "Study of some problems in union administration. Focus on what some people say is an increasing need for technical knowledge and skill. They say that bargaining is becoming more complex—what with government intervention, new problems like pensions, job evaluation, etc. And that means the union leader has to become more of an expert himself on a wide range of subjects—that he has to hire more staff specialists to help him in his job —lawyers, economists, res. and ed. dirs., publicity men, etc. I'd like to explore this trend if it is one, find out what needs you've experienced for technical advice and what your union does about it. I've picked about a dozen unions to concentrate on; thought _____ should be one of them because _____."

1. What full-time staff experts does (name of union) use?

2. Why were they hired—what were the needs of the union and when were the needs realized?

3. What occasion do you as President (Sec.-Treas., etc.) have to use them?
   a) Do any of them have much say about union policy?
   b) Do they sit in on policy conferences?

4. How much, what kind of supervision of these departments is necessary? Do you spell out their duties or give them leeway to do what they think best?

5. What did you look for in hiring men to fill these jobs? Personal qualifications, skills, background. Where did you look for them?
   a) (For those officers who don't have power to hire the experts): If you were the man who hires and fires the staff experts to work for the International what would you look for?

b) You hear a lot about the feeling against outsiders who come to work for unions. Some unions have a definite policy of hiring all staff for service departments from the rank and file. What's your feeling on that?

c) Some people claim that these hired staff experts in some cases are taking over the union. They're making the decisions that only the elected officials should make. Is this really a problem? (Some also say that the use of specialists appointed from the outside is a threat to the internal vigor of the union—democracy is drained of its life when you have to depend on specialists for so much union work.)

6. Do you ever go outside the staff for expert advice? Is a man more valuable to the union as a full-time expert or as an independent consultant? (Take the lawyer, or the researcher.)

7. If you could finance expansion of the expert services available to you, where would you spend the money?

8. You're a bargainer and administrator of some years of experience. Was there ever a time in the course of that experience when you wished you knew more about any given subject—in other words when you'd have used expert knowledge if it were available?

SAMPLE OF OCCASIONAL QUESTIONS FOR OFFICERS

9. Some union people talk about the need for a kind of Civil Service for staff specialists. Is it inevitable that where there are political changes in a union, the staff technicians be changed—down to the last accountant?

10. Do you prepare for negotiations more than you used to? What do all the arguments and statistics have to do with the outcome?

11. Should lawyers be paid in relation to other members of the profession or other staff and line officials in the union?

12. I get the impression that lawyers (aren't as) (are more) important in your union than in other unions? How come?

[Other questions were designed especially for the individual interviews.]

INTERVIEW GUIDE FOR OUTSIDERS AND EX-EXPERTS

1. Name list of first-priority unions. Any variation in the use or recruitment of experts that these unions leave out?

2. Think of the three or four unions whose staff experts you know best. Who is in a power position and how did he get there?

or

Do you think any of these experts have much influence on union policy? Who, under what conditions?

3. Run over the master list of experts and of unions (for mailing). Do you know any others, or feel some shouldn't be included? Is top-priority list representative?
4. What's your impression of the general level of competency of the experts hired by unions. (Get examples, ask how come that's so.)
5. Many people say that unions, with some exceptions, don't hire their experts because they're really needed—they hire experts for window dressing, or just because everyone else is doing it. Agree?
6. What's it take to get a Labor job? What's it take to make good on a Labor job?
7. How about the outside specialist—the consultant. Is he in a better or worse spot to influence union decisions? (Examples.)
8. Many people look at the independent-minded intellectual who gets into unions and claims that in every case the union seems to shape him into a technician—a willing tool who goes down the line for union policy regardless of his social philosophy. Or if union fails to shape or convert him, he quits and is replaced by a technician type. Do you think that's so? How come? (Get case histories.)
9. How would you go about making a study like this?
10. Do you know of any cases—like the Helstein case—where a union technician moves into an elected position?

[*For ex-experts, get reasons for leaving, circumstances surrounding departure, and exit interview if any.*]

QUESTIONNAIRE ON THE WORK OF TRADE UNION STAFF MEMBERS

1. Name of organization you work for. Full-time. Part-time.
2. Description of your union job (include title, sort of work done, etc.). Are you elected? Or appointed? To whom are you immediately responsible (Give his title):
Is there someone else you're responsible to (someone with whom you work directly)? Yes. No. If yes, what is his title?
3. On what kinds of union decisions and problems are your services and opinions most used by the top union officers (give examples if you wish).
4. Do you sit in on meetings of any policy-making board of your union? Yes. No. (Specify on what occasions.)
5. What personal qualities, skills and training do you consider necessary to success on a job like yours?
6. Do you think your union is giving you a chance to do the best you possibly can? Yes. No. If no, why not (What are the main problems or obstacles)?
7. Have your duties changed on this job since you were first hired? Yes. No. How?

8. How many years has somebody been working full-time on the kind of work you now do for your union? When was the present title given to the job?
9. How many people held this job before you took it? What did they do when they left this job? What are they doing now? (Answer only for people you know about.)

Job when they first left: *Present Position:*

10. Other than yourself, what full-time staff experts or specialists (lawyers, economists, publicists, educators, researchers, etc.) does your union employ in the headquarters of the International? (Give each title. If there are more than 10 or 12, please note the fact and go on to the next question):
11. Does your union ever use any *outside* specialists (technicians or experts who are *not* full-time staff members)? Yes. No. If yes, what specialists for what kinds of work?
12. How many professional staff people are there in your Department beside yourself?
13. What is the range of salaries of professional staff people in your Department? (Do not include per diem or travel allowances) Lowest: $ per   . Highest (i.e., the Dept. head): $ per   . What other compensation is allowed (e.g., per diem, car allowance, expenses, etc.)?
14. Did your *first* full-time union job pay more or less (per year) than you were making on the job you had just before it? More. Less. The same.
15. Have you ever been offered a position outside the Labor movement since you have worked for a trade union? Yes. No. Indicate the type of business from which such offer(s) has (have) come:
16. *Occupational History.* What are the *main jobs* you've held *in or out of the Labor movement* since you first started to work. (Include any union office held, paid or unpaid):

			If union job, Elected or
Title of job (or brief job description)	*Type of business or Industry*	*Time Held* From To	*Appointed?* E A

17. Date of birth. Place of birth.
18. Education (circle only highest grade completed):
   a) Grammar or high school: 3 4 5 6 7 8 9 10 11 12.   College, technical institute: 1 2 3 4.
   b) Graduate work (number of years): 1 2 3 4 5 6. Institution(s):
   c) Degrees Received   Year   Institution   Field(s) of Specialization
19. List the names of associations to which you belong (professional, social, political, etc.):

20. Religion (Check one of the following): Protestant. Catholic. Jewish. None. Other.

21. Indicate the *principal* present or past occupation of your Father and your Father-in-Law (even if retired or deceased), your brothers and your sons (if you have any who are employed full-time). *Just check* the following list:

	Father	Father-in-law	Brothers	Sons
Laborer (unskilled or semiskilled)				
Skilled laborer (or mechanic)				
Clerk or Salesman				
Farmer Owner				
Tenant				
Small Businessman (Sales under $100,000				
Large Business (Sales over $100,000 Supervisor				
Executive				
Owner				
Other profession (specify):				

22. Here is a statement by one Labor staff expert about the way he sees his job:

> "My job takes me into a wide range of union decisions. Practically speaking, you can't separate 'policy-making' from the job of the adviser. In many informal ways I influence top-level decisions—though I'm careful to make clear that I don't think the final decision should rest with me. You can't push too hard or you defeat your effectiveness."

How close does this come to your idea of your own role in the union: Exactly. Pretty close. Not very close. Misses it completely.

THE SAMPLES

CHAPTER II contains information about the selection of unions and what kinds of experts are included in the total count, the Questionnaire Sample and the Main Sample.

Who Is Excluded

For a count of staff experts employed by unions in the Q Sample, I excluded the following:

1. *Experts employed in federation headquarters* (except in four cases where a large proportion of time was spent with one union), state, county, and city labor bodies. I interviewed a few of these, however, for data on experts in the member unions with which they deal. Experts working for *regional and local* units of national unions were also excluded, even if theoretically responsible to the top officers.

2. *Experts on the "housekeeping" side* of union operations (auditors, bookkeepers, accountants, comptrollers, etc.). These financial functionaries are typically viewed as a category separate from the Legal, Research, Education, Publicity, etc., groups. Reflecting this fact, one usually finds them in a different Headquarters location—a separate floor or room. The auditor is closer in function to the regular business agent, "International Rep." or organizer than to the technical staffs.[1] Some borderline technicians or "research

1. My interview data on this point confirm the conclusions of a study of

clerks" who perform only routine clerical-statistical services are also excluded from the count. In a few unions the test for exclusion is their membership in an office-workers' union (to which the staff experts do not belong).

(a) ADMINISTRATIVE ASSISTANTS. I did not include these in the count of "experts." However, if they have moved up from technical specialist positions or can reflect the boss' administrative viewpoint *vis-à-vis* our staff experts, I interviewed them.

3. *Subprofessional categories.* The work of the few librarians and office managers is close to the routine work of clerks and stenographers. Private secretaries, while they may play a role as a channel of expert influence (see Chapter XII) are also excluded from the count.

4. *Those who have the title, but in no way perform the function.* Some "Research Directors," "Editors," etc., are experts neither by function nor by experience and training. In those cases I looked for the acting director or assistant director of the department. The operating functionary is the one I count. Unfortunately this meant a few "wasted" interviews and questionnaire returns.

5. *Any elected official* whether he performs the function or not. In rare cases, the union constitution specifies that the lobbyist or the editor must be elected (e.g., the Washington representatives of some of the Railroad Brotherhoods not in the sample are elected officials, the editor of the IAM-AFL magazine is elected, etc.). I focus only on the appointed staff experts.

6. *Outside, independent, private consultants.* These are not counted, though many were interviewed and served as important sources of data. For the extent to which unions use them, see Chap-

---

the financial aspects of union administration based in part on field work. Most union officials in the national unions studied, says Kozmetsky, make little use of auditors or accountants in planning or evaluation; they see them instead as watchdogs for the honest handling of funds. Few unions have internal auditing departments with CPA's or college-trained accountants (the ILGWU-AFL is one exception). Most unions select auditors "for their knowledge of local union administration, rather than for their accounting ability," and train them on the job. George Kozmetsky, *Financial Reports of Labor Unions* (Andover: The Andover Press, Ltd., 1950). Dr. Kozmetsky kindly made his interviews available, and they were used as background for field work. Chapters VI and XII note some signs of changes in auditor recruitment methods and the fact that these functionaries occasionally appear in important political trouble-shooting roles.

ter II. Their special position of influence is discussed in Chapter XI.
Two borderline cases are included in the count; both are lawyers in
private practice who spend over half their time as General Counsel
for one union.

7. *Experts employed to run separately incorporated, or semi-
autonomous, union-owned enterprises*—e.g., banks, housing projects, health centers, office buildings, radio stations, etc.

8. *Full-time foreign affairs specialists.* Most of these are abroad;
the few in America are employed by the federations, the government, or the ILGWU.

The Questionnaire Sample.—This excludes all the functionaries
excluded from the count (above). It also *excludes the following:*

1. All those staff experts who have little or no direct contact with
line officials—e.g., most assistant directors of research, education,
publicity, etc.; all research assistants, editorial assistants, artists,
cartoonists, etc. I sought some homogeneity of position in the
union hierarchy. (In the rare cases where an assistant director of
some department has been able to by-pass the director and establish direct liaison with the top officer, I include him.)

2. Those staff experts who have been employed in the organization less than six months during the major field-work period.

3. Jobs temporarily vacant (experts on leave of absence with
government, etc.).

Compiling the Master List

To begin the study, a preliminary list of experts employed or
once employed by the unions of over fifty thousand was compiled
from these sources: (1) incomplete and outdated AFL and CIO
lists; (2) personal files of an ex-expert; (3) University of Chicago
lists of workers' education specialists; (4) a list of labor lawyers
attending two labor law conferences; (5) names mentioned in the
BNA *Daily Labor Report;* (6) a relatively complete BLS list of
officers, editors, research and education directors; (7) a list of
lobbyists supplied by a labor lobbyist; and (8) a list of economists
and education directors in the files of *Fortune.* These names were
arranged by union and by area.

The list was expanded as field work progressed. Names were gathered from interviews in each organization. People with wide labor contacts were shown the list and asked for names. The resultant master list was checked for possible additions from the *International Labor Directory* (not available earlier). My labor lawyer list was checked with a mailing list used in the Bar Association questionnaire study and was found to be more complete. The mailed questionnaire, Questions 9-12, was a final check on the completeness of my Q Sample count.

Explanation of Table 8

The column labeled "Number of people interviewed" refers to all types of respondents: officers, administrators, incumbent staff experts (including department heads, assistants, etc.), ex-experts, consultants and other outsiders—anyone who can be classified as having a primary job connection with the particular union.

The Membership/Expert Ratio was derived by dividing the membership by the count of all staff experts (including their professional assistants) working out of the national headquarters of the union. See Chapter II for details on the count.

To rate the characteristics of each union, I consulted the literature on union structure, the relevant interview comments on each union, the labor press, several histories of particular unions. The general works that were most helpful were: David Saposs and Sol Davison, "Structure of AFL Unions," *Labor Relations Reference Manual*, IV (Washington, D. C.: Bureau of National Affairs, March 1-August 31, 1939), pp. 1042-1048; and Florence Peterson, *Handbook of Labor Unions* (Washington, D. C.: American Council on Public Affairs, 1944).

Each characteristic was rated High, Medium, or Low as follows, to permit a test of the hypothesis that a high rating would predispose the union towards a low Membership/Expert Ratio (few members per expert):

1. *Industrial or multi-industrial structure.* If the union's membership is almost all in one craft, it is rated Low. If the union maintains some important structural units of craft, or amalgamated

Table 8—Distribution of Experts, Questionnaire Returns, Interviews, and Structural Characteristics by Union

Priority Number	Name of Union	Date Founded	No. of Experts in Count (incl. Prof. ass'ts)	No. Experts in Q Sample	No. People Interviewed	No. of repeat Interviews	No. Returns for Q Sample	Bkgnd. data other sources	Size Memb. in Thous.	M/E Ratio Thous. of memb. per expert	Indust. Struct.	Nat. and multi-employer barg.	Involvement with govt.	Central Control
1	UAW-CIO	1935	57	35	62	27	29	4	948	17	H	H	H	M
2	USA-CIO	1936	30	22	32	9	16	3	961	32	H	H	H	H
3	ILGWU	1900	37	18	29	5	11	5	423	11	M+	H−	M−	M
4	TWUA	1901	21	11	11	3	9	2	374	18	H	H+	M+	H−
5	Teamsters	1899	4	2	4	0	0	2	1103	266	M	M	M	L
6	Plumbers	1889	1	1	1	0	1		180	180	L	L	L	L
7	IBEW	1891	9	3	4	0	3		450	50	M	M	M−	L
8	Hotel and Rest.	1890	6	5	4	1	4	1	400	67	M	L	L	L
9	Maint. of Way	1896	5	2	1	0	2		171	34	L	H	H	H
10	Rlway Clerks	1898	8	6	5	0	5		350	44	M	H	H	H
11	Trainmen	1883	8	6	3	0	2	2	211	26	M	H	H	M
12	OWIU	1917	7	5	8	3	5		78	11	H	M	H	M
13	IAM	1889	12	6	5	1	2	2	600	50	M+	M	M+	H
14	UE	1936	8	6	2	0	4	1	250	31	H	H	H−	H
15	UMW	1890	7	5	4	1	2	1	600	86	H	H−	H	H
16	IUE	1948 (1st Conv. 50)	8	4	4	0	3		225	28	H	H	H−	H−
17	Paper-Makers	1893	3	3	1	1	2	1	59	20	M	M	L+	M+
18	Rubber-Workers	1935	9	8	4	0	2	5	150	17	H	H	M+	M−
19	ACWA	1914	18	7	5	0	6		375	21	H−	M+	L	M+

#	Union	Year										
20	Chemical	1940	4	3	1	0	130	33	M+	M	L	?
21	CWA	1949	9	6	4	0	240	27	M	M	H	L
22	AFT	1916	4	1	0	0	50	13	L	L	H	L
23	ITU	1852	1	1	1	0	96	96	L	M	L	M−
24	Musicians	1896	4	2	1	0	237	59	H−	H−	L+	L+
25	NMU	1937	5	2	2	0	46	9	M	M	H	M
26	Pulp-Sulphite	1906	3	1	1	0	120	40	M	M	L	M−
27	Amalg. Butchers	1897	4	2	2	1	175	44	H−	M	M−	M+
28	Packing-House	1937	6	4	1	0	84	14	M	H	M	M+
	Priority Totals		298	175	202	52	123	31				

Non-Users

29	Longshore AFL	0	0	1	0	55	
30	Transport	0	0	1	1	95	
31	Letter Carriers	0	0	1	0	90	
32	Bricklayers	0	0	1	0	65	
33	Carpenters	0	0	1	0	735	
34	RR Signalmen	0	0	1	0	13	

"Extras"

35	Longshore Bridges	0	1	0	30
36	AFL Textile	0	1	0	78
37	Paper-Workers	1	1	1	39
38	Hosiery AFL	0	1	0	30
39	UAW-AFL	2	2	0	54
	Total Non-User and Extra	2	37	11	

Total not classified by union (experts,
ex-experts, officers in the federation
or state labor body, outsiders and
consultants with broad labor contacts).

craft character, others in semi-industrial, or industrial form, I rate Medium. If the union is predominantly industrial or multi-industrial, makes few wage-worker exclusions and maintains few units of craft or multiple craft character, I rate High.

2. *National and multi-employer bargaining.* Where bargaining is typically in a local product market, with small employers, or with single employers on a local level, I rate Low. Where the typical bargaining unit is multi-employer, multi-company, but local or area, not national or regional, I rate Medium. Where bargaining is typically company-wide, multi-plant, or multi-employer *and* national or regional, I rate High. Where the contracts are not national, but there is clear-cut co-ordination on a national scale—identical initial demands, bargaining strategies, etc.—I rate High.

3. *Involvement with government.* When labor disputes in the union's jurisdiction typically invite large-scale federal intervention, or when the union is heavily dependent on the action of federal agencies to maintain its economic position, I rate High. When some important segments of the union's jurisdiction provoke federal intervention but others do not, or when the intervention is of a local character only, I rate Medium. When involvement with government is confined to local liaison with city political machines, but labor disputes remain relatively free from local, state or federal intervention, and the union's dependence on government for economic gains is slight, I rate Low.

4. *Centralization of control* (i.e., degree of international control over local union's bargaining and administration). In part, I rely on aspects of the formal organization reported in Peterson's handbook (above): per capita to the international, frequency of Convention, the role of the international in discipline cases, approval of contracts and strikes, leeway in the dues the local can levy, limits to assessments by the international, etc. Since Peterson's data are outdated, and the union's constitution is a limited guide to the dynamics of union government, I rely, where available, on interview data and/or an examination of union publications and relevant literature. Note: a union may be rated Low on this factor because of the relative autonomy of its local or regional units. But within their own spheres of dominion, these units may maintain

highly centralized powers. I focus only on the control of the international union over its constituent units.

Any student of Labor can quickly see the complexities involved
in the application of the above criteria. All these ratings are, at
best, rough approximations. Where doubts existed, I attempted to
resolve them against the hypothesis of high rating→high use (i.e.,
low Membership/Expert Ratio).

ANALYSIS OF DECISION-MAKING
AND INFLUENCE

My ANALYSIS OF INFLUENCE in Part IV is based largely on specific decision-making material elicited in interviews and on influence ratings of experts in the Main Sample.

Working Hypothesis

A preliminary analysis of early interviews and literature led to the following working hypothesis (which was used as one interview device to elicit decision-making material):

The staff expert is likely to have maximum influence in the decision-making process when

1. *The Nature of the Problem* (a) Requires technical knowledge and skills (competence); (b) Lies close to the expert's specialty (defined narrowly, by occupation, not functional type); (c) Is far from the core functions of the union as seen by the top officers (i.e., the decision is peripheral to the job of bargaining with the employer on wages, hours and working conditions). Officer not vitally interested in the problem; (d) Is not directly concerned with internal political control of the union; (e) Does not directly involve the union's relations with rival unions.

2. *Competence and Skill of the Boss* (union officer) in each area of union decision *and the aggressiveness of his administrative*

style are low.

3. *Tenure Conditions of the Expert* (degree of dependence on boss for income, security, prestige) *are good:* (a) His skill and experience are not readily replaceable; (b) He has connections (a "base" either through contact with membership or through contact with some other category of important people. Could mobilize influence in support of continued service); (c) Suitable alternative employment is readily available (skills are transferable) and demand for services elsewhere is high.

4. *Access to Boss Is Easy:* (a) Has close personal relationship to officer; (b) Has easy physical accessibility.

About half the cases in the Main Sample were asked to react to these ideas, and give negative or positive evidence from their own experience in refutation or support. This elicited (1) instances for analysis of the interplay between technical-economic-legal knowledge and considerations and political-ideological considerations; (2) talk about informal channels for reaching the boss, the institutional pressures brought to bear on the respondent and the typical patterns of union administration.

Decision-Making Material

For the analysis in Chapter IX of the points of highest influence in the decision-making process, and the nature of the problem as a variable in expert influence, I used data on 167 problems arising in twenty-six unions, 1944-1951. (See Chapter IX for an account of the purpose and direction of my effort to get this information.) All descriptions from any source of experts' part in decision-making on specific problems were assembled by union and by problem. This material was in part elicited by direct question—e.g., the statement of the above working hypothesis about the conditions maximizing influence with a request for negative and positive instances, and the use in first-priority unions of questions about key policy decisions within each area of union decision. Much of it, however, came from indirect questions: in describing his work, job satisfactions and frustrations, the respondent would be encouraged to be specific, give illustrations, etc. Many interviews were designed solely to check information about the role of specific experts on a given problem.

Analysis was confined to the problems on which data were judged to be reasonably reliable and adequate: (1) information was cross-checked by several participants in the decision-making process; *or* (2) interview rapport was unusually good *and* the information was credible in terms of (a) the respondent's reliability in other areas where I could cross-check, (b) his position as observer (could he know what he reports as fact?), and (c) the consistency and fullness of detail in his account. Obviously, reliability here could be checked only by a researcher having a grasp of the position and perspective of all informants used for each problem, as well as the character of the particular union involved. No interpersonal verification could therefore be attempted, and it is within this limit that the data are reported.

Each problem analyzed was put in the form of a question initiating the decision-making process. The question was put on a card, and the problem indicated was classified as primarily in one of the five decision-making areas: (1) relations with employers (RE); (2) relations with government (RG); (3) internal control and organization (IUC & Org.); (4) relations with other unions (RRU); (5) public relations (PR).

1. Relations with employer and with government may overlap, as in the case of a company request that a union join a company petition for tariff relief in a hearing before a government tariff commission. The criterion of choice: who can determine the final resolution of the problem? Here the government agency decision determines the outcome, so the union's action is classified as in the area of RG.

2. When a problem posed in one area leads to decisions in many areas of union operation (as in a strike in which the employer mobilizes courts, police, officials, community groups, etc., against the strikers), I classify in terms of the agency that posed the original problem (in this case, RE).

I exclude (1) problems in which the international union is in no way involved; (2) problems in which outside consultants were relied upon.

The influence of any participating expert was considered at

each point in the decision-making process: origination, policy, means of implementation, and execution (see Chapter IX).

1. Where the expert is acting as full-fledged negotiator and/or administrator, I exclude him from this portion of the analysis. (E.g., where a Contact Man is conducting negotiations, and draws on technical-economic, publicity, or legal assistants as needed, my interest is in the latter's influence on the former.)

2. When more than one expert participated, I treat their influence as a group. If they give conflicting advice, I focus on the most influential of the experts.

Expert influence in the decision-making process with respect to each problem was coded in four categories according to the following rules:

1. High-OPME. Expert originates and has High influence on decisions relating to policy, means of implementation, and execution.

2. High-PME. Expert does not originate but has High influence on policy decisions, as well as decisions related to selection of means, and execution.

(a) A precondition for judging the expert's influence is the presence of actual or possible counter-pressures on the officer he is trying to persuade.

(b) If officer is indifferent, but opposing views are held by some line or staff group in the union, and the expert goes ahead on his own, I score High-OPME.

(c) When the expert merely reinforces a strong conviction of the officer, and no opposition exists, I exclude the problem from the analysis.

3. Influence Medium or Mixed: i.e., influence is High on policy, Low on means and execution; High on origination and policy, but Low on means and execution; Medium on policy or means or execution, whether originated or not.

(a) When the expert has High influence on a policy decision to drop a problem or stay out of some area, I code High on policy only. This stacks the cards against the hypothesis of increasing influence as we approach the end of the decision-making continuum (means and execution).

4. Little or No Influence: e.g., influence is Low on means and

308

execution, absent on origination and policy; High on execution but Low on everything else; Low on everything; absent.

(a) When the expert originates a policy suggestion and is ignored or turned down, I score Little or None along the whole continuum. When he wants to initiate a change in policy, but is for some reason afraid to pose the issue, I score LNI.

(b) I exclude from analysis those decisions in which expert is simply told to relay union policy to a local and the issue is clear-cut, with no chance for the exercise of discretion.

The problems were then classified, where possible, in three further categories: (1) instances in which technical-economic-legal considerations or craft skills were dominant and overrode political-ideological considerations or skills; (2) instances in which political-ideological considerations overrode technical-economic-legal considerations when the latter were relevant; (3) "political" and "technical" aspects impossible to unscramble.

My interest was in getting extremes of expert influence and extremes illustrating the interplay of different kinds of intelligence. Moreover, it is likely that the decision-making data are most reliable at the extremes.

Influence Ratings

The experts in the Main Sample were ranked by relative amount of influence on the basis of (1) self-reported participation in decision-making in each area of union decision (Q's 3 and 4 on the questionnaire supplemented interview data); (2) general self-estimates of influence; (3) comments of those having intimate contact with them (e.g., union executives); (4) "influence reputation" —derived from judgments of other experts, ex-experts and consultants.

To systematize the method of ranking, each case was scored High, Medium or Low (2, 1, or 0) in each area of decision (RE, IUC and Org., RRU, RG, PR). Thus, the top influence score was 10; the lowest, 0. The assumptions made and rules followed in scoring influence were these:

1. Since I wanted to examine the rank order of influence of all

experts with reference to functional type and role orientation, the scores are relative to all experts, not relative to the functional type or occupational group, or experts within the area of competence. Accordingly, criterion cases were chosen to represent each rank from 0 to 10, and each case was scored with reference to these benchmarks.

2. Because the cases representing different *functional types* are not unduly concentrated in particular unions, differences in the influence of the types are not due to the unique histories, traditions and leadership personalities of some few organizations. In analysis of the influence of *role-orientation types,* the organizations were examined one by one to explain negative cases (i.e., High Influence Missionaries).

3. Most ratings are focused on influence of department heads with respect to the problems and actions of the top officers. But where the expert is a subordinate (these were included in law, engineering and pensions and insurance), I rate influence with respect to those line officials and problems dealt with (e.g., middle leaders, local officers in negotiations, arbitration cases, etc.). Thus, experts of varying skills and orientations have an equal chance to score High—and the desired homogeneity of position in the formal organization is not destroyed.

4. There is no basis on which to weight the relative importance of each area of union decision. The importance of government action, negotiations, or rival union relations, for example, varies tremendously both from union to union and from time to time within one union. Each of the five areas was therefore arbitrarily given equal weight.

(a) If the union seldom has problems within the area (e.g., relations with rival unions), I rate the expert on whether he had influence the few times the union *did* face policy decisions in that area.

(b) The decision-making area is defined in terms of the analysis in Chapter I. Thus, relations with government (RG) includes courts and administrative agencies, as well as legislative bodies—federal, state or local. Foreign affairs is included in government relations (but is relevant in only one case).

(c) Where the expert has High influence in one narrow sphere within an area—e.g., policy and strategy on one type of legislative matter within the area of governmental relations—I score Medium (1), not High (2).

(d) A rating of High in any area indicates full participation with much discretion and leeway throughout the decision-making process, as well as in the initiation of policy proposals. E.g., High in RE means that the expert is a full-fledged negotiator in collective bargaining sessions.

(e) A rating of Low in any area means the expert does not get into this area at all or, if he does, he has little or no influence.

(f) Where the data permit no judgment of influence in the area, I score "+." There were nine cases with pluses added (most in the area of rival union relations): one 3++, three 4+, one 7+, four 8+. Even assuming the pluses are worth 2 (High influence in the area unscored), this would have no effect on my generalizations about functional type. Neither would it change the relative rankings of role-orientation types. It would, however, slightly increase the proportion of Rank-and-File Careerists and Professionals scoring Medium or High, and move one low FFM to Medium, one Low ICS to High.

The expert's influence rating is the sum of his ratings within each area. The above procedure was used not to arrive at the fine quantitative discriminations implied, but to get a rough relative ranking according to explicit criteria of High, Medium, and Low— with special focus on the extremes. Since the benchmark cases near the top of the scale were in very marked contrast to those with the median influence score of 3, I used a broad definition of High: 6-10. Medium was 4-5; Low, 0-3. Even then, only twenty-one of the 128 staff experts rated High. To be rated High a man has to score High in at least three decision-making areas; or High in one, Medium in four; etc. Throughout the analysis, the arbitrary nature of these definitions was kept in mind and alternative definitions applied (e.g., see my use of "very high" in Chapter XI, and the various combinations in Table 5).

Twenty-six of the cases rated in the middle range were considered doubtful by a point or two. These were listed separately in relation to the benchmark cases at each level from 3 to 8 and the data on them re-examined. Result: one case was changed two points up; six changed one point up; three, one point down. That meant the following shifts in overall rating (by functional type): one CM from Medium to Low, one CM from Low to Medium, one CM from Medium to High, one ICS from Medium to High, two FFM's from Low to Medium—a net change that works against my hypothesis of the importance of contact-making skills. Table 4 would have been strengthened slightly if the re-examination of doubtful cases had not been attempted.

What of the reliability of self-ratings of influence, and of "influence reputation"? It can be argued that if a staff expert has any influence he will be afraid to tell (because of the imperative of knowing-your-anonymous-place). On the other hand, it is also reasonable that if he does not have influence he will be reluctant to admit it (because of loss of face, desire to impress the interviewer, etc.). There is no reason for assuming exaggeration any more than low-rating of influence in the experts' descriptions of their participation in decision-making. Judgments must be made on the basis of all relevant data in the interview cross-checked by the judgments of others. For instance, we can assume that line officials, having formal authority, will tend to underrate their hired hands' influence. So when one of them concedes, "They [experts] did the negotiating. . . . We put our contract in their hands" (13-1,2), and this is confirmed by the comments of the nonparticipating as well as the participating experts, we can assume a reasonable reliability. A reliability check by an independent judge was not attempted: such a judge would have to be familiar with the trade unions and issues involved, recognize terminology, names, and allusions, go through all the relevant interviews and documents and be able to assess the comments of different informants in terms of their relationship to the case being judged. No student of labor who could do this also had the time to undertake such a check. It is within these limits that my influence analysis is reported.

There is one further limit to my analysis. When seen in a proper time perspective, there is an ebb and flow of expert influence; the picture is not static. There are many examples of how the following variables can change the relative influence of different types of experts at different times, as well as the relative importance of different areas of union decision:

1. Leadership succession or the factional state of the union. See Chapters IX, XI, and XIII.

2. Degree of expansionism of the union; and proportion of its jurisdiction organized. The jack-of-all-trades becomes a specialist in narrow sphere as the union "matures." See Chapter XII. Types with different role orientations are selected for High influence posts at different stages of union growth. See Part IV. This is related to expert career lines and officer competences, discussed in Chapter X.

3. Changes in the "external" environment—especially the state of the business cycle (as reflected in management policies and practices) and the state of world tension (proportion of national income spent on defense mobilization). An expert on the fringe of business unionism, performing routine clerical-statistical services, becomes more important as defense mobilization creates new problems of union functioning, demanding different sets of skills, etc. See Chapters IV and X. The fact that the study was done during a period of war preparations may thus introduce a time bias in *favor* of high Facts-and-Figures Man influence. Note, however, that mobilization also meant inflation—which probably introduces a bias *against* high Facts-and-Figures Man influence. A period of inflation presents ideal circumstances for maximizing the importance of political forces in union wage policies.[1]

---

1. See Albert Rees, "Union Wage Policies," in Brooks *et al.* (eds.), *op. cit.*

ROLE ORIENTATION AND
DEGREES OF BUREAUCRACY

THE FOLLOWING is a description of the operations involved in the construction of the typology of present and past role orientations presented in Part III.

Present Role Orientation

The typology was centered around the staff expert's primary job-relevant group identification.

1. When the field work was about half done, six types were blocked out on an impressionistic basis, using broad criteria derived from reading of early interviews and from theoretical considerations. These criteria were listed on a face sheet for each case.

2. When the field work was completed, all the interviews were read. Seventy cases were selected to represent the range of variation in functions and role orientation, in as many unions as possible from among the cases in which data were most adequate. Interviews and other data on these seventy cases were examined repeatedly in an effort to sort out (a) typical responses of the expert to patterns of union administration cross-cutting diverse unions—clues to institutional pressures hitting all experts; from (b) variations in response due to differences in role orientation.

3. On the basis of the seventy varied cases, a code was con-

313

structed for each criterion—job frustrations, job satisfactions, concept of ideal expert, enemy targets, view of hypothetical or actual company job offers, etc. Possible objective correlates of the types—e.g., salary, salary transition, occupational origin, associational memberships, etc.—were also coded.

4. All were then typed on a gestalt basis—keeping the eight criteria in mind, but not weighing their relative importance. All cases, grouped by role orientation, were then put on large summary sheets in rows, with code categories under each criterion in the columns. This permitted an overview of all data on role orientation, typical patterns of union administration, and possible correlates, as well as functional type and influence rating. The summary chart has the appearance of a Guttman scalogram—with cutting points ideally at the end of a group of cases, where an attribute belonging to one type ends and an attribute belonging to another type begins.

5. To bring into relief the reduction used implicitly in constructing the impressionistic typology, to discover the crucial criteria which guided the grouping of cases, I then analyzed the summary chart. The aim was to discover which attributes cross-cut all types, which distinguished a main type from all others, a subtype from another, which attributes could logically be combined, which cases could better fit elsewhere, as well as possible coding ambiguities, errors in coding, or new types. (Since there were only two cases of Religious-Ethico Missionary and the criteria here were different from the rest of the types, this type was excluded from the analysis.)

6. On the basis of this attribute analysis, clusters of attributes were selected as "sufficient," "necessary," or "contributing" for classification purposes.

7. Cases which did not fit were then re-examined. The chart was used to force analysis of inconsistencies and negative instances in the data, a consequent reformulation of the typology, and a reclassification of all cases. The re-examination of cases according to this attribute analysis led to:

(a) A regrouping of deviant cases which resulted in the delineation of a new type, the Union Politico. Job Satisfaction Code 12 (satisfaction in game of chance, etc.) became guiding here.

(b) Sharpening of three code categories:

(1) Frustration 8 (thwarted mobility striving, etc.). If the complaint is qualified by reference to an overriding satisfaction with intrinsic excitement and challenge of the work—e.g., "not enough money but the work is *far* more interesting than my previous job," etc.—then I do not score here (one case).

(2) Satisfaction 12. If satisfaction in "excitement of the game" appears in context of discussion of satisfaction in program promotion, I do not score here (five cases).

(3) Ideal expert Code 1 (firm labor movement dedication, etc.). I separated out Code 2a (loyalty to particular union).

(c) Changes were made in sixteen code numbers for thirteen cases.

(d) The following rules handled inconsistencies:

(1) Where a "sufficient" attribute is coded that fits two types, I go back to original data and judge which is dominant in the case —e.g., Frustration 6 or 7 (conflicts between prof. values and requirements of job, etc.) overrides Frustration 8 (thwarted mobility striving, etc.) or vice versa. This affected 25 cases.

(2) Where a "sufficient" attribute is missing for the case, or not designated for a subtype, the "necessary" attributes are used for classification where all other data are consistent. E.g., Satisfaction 13 (borrowing or lending prestige etc.) and/or 14 (mobility via union career, etc.) plus rank-and-file origin and consistent "contributing" attributes become sufficient for a Rank-and-File Careerist classification.

(3) Where there are not enough data to code "sufficient" attributes and "necessary" attributes are missing, but reliable, cross-checked reputation data are available, the latter become guiding (if the available questionnaire and interview data are consistent). This rule was applied in five cases (129, 130, 23, 89, 119).

(e) I reclassified on the basis of the attribute analysis, twenty-two cases. Twelve were shifted to Politico, four to Technician Professional, two to LLM, two to Program Professional; data on two were judged to be insufficient and they were excluded from further analysis.

8. Possible correlates of the types were then examined. These were not used in the construction of the types and can therefore be

seen as internal checks on the validity of the types. E.g., the criteria from which we get a picture of the Careerist's mobility strivings find support from the "objective" indices of social origin (largest proportion of manual worker fathers), religion (not one answers "none"), and associations (respectable, nonprofessional, middle-class, community-oriented). See Chapter VII.

9. As a limited reliability check, an independent judge then examined the fifteen most doubtful cases (e.g., cases whose original classification had been changed, cases of inconsistency, where the writer's decisions on which attributes were dominant were hesitant, etc.). The judge was familiar with the study, had discussed some of the unions and the cases, but knew nothing about the fifteen cases in question. The judge was given a written description of the types, with specification of the criteria used to distinguish them. Instructions were to place the case in the best-fitting type. The results: thirteen of the fifteen choices were identical. The fact that the two discrepancies involved a choice between Politico and something else may indicate that this type is the least reliable. The data for the two cases, however, were very limited. In Case 31, the interview was a group interview; in Case 119 the interview was inadequate (3 pp. single-spaced), and the original choice had been made on the basis of reputation data. Eliminating the two cases would not affect my conclusions on relation of role orientation to career theme (both entered as Missionaries) or to influence (Case 31 is Medium, 119 is low.) It would strengthen my conclusions on Functional Type by Influence.

This system of analysis yields a typology with utility for classifying all the cases, and operational criteria specific enough to permit replication of the study. Small samples, imperfectly "standardized" data, and the limits of time and money permitted only rudimentary forms of quantification and only limited checks of reliability and validity. While the conclusions must therefore be taken as hypothetical, it is believed that replication would yield similar results.

Past Role Orientation

To permit analysis of patterns of change and the genesis of each type, a typology of past role orientations (i.e., orientation at time of first entry into union work, or "career theme") was constructed. Genetic data were separated from data used for present role orientation. The former were of course more limited. Because of the problem of retrospective falsification, I relied more heavily on (1) objective indices of past role orientation—e.g., political affiliation at time of entry; (2) reputation data—e.g., recollections by close associates of the respondent's entering orientation. Reliable information on affiliations coupled with information on occupational history and social-political conditions were taken as sufficient to infer reasons for entry—with or without consistent verbalization.

In constructing the typology I also used interviews with several staff experts who had entered only a few months before, men whose entering orientations are more readily available for discussion. Moreover, I interviewed several cases literally on the day or in the week of departure—ex-experts whose advantages as informants are described in Appendix A. These data should strengthen the validity of the typology.

Codes for Past and Present Role Orientation and Guide to Attribute Analysis

The following data and methodological material can be obtained by writing the University of Chicago Library for a microfilm of H. L. Wilensky, "The Staff Expert: A Study of the Intelligence Function in American Trade Unions" (Unpublished Doctoral Dissertation, Department of Sociology, University of Chicago, 1955), esp. pp. 449-552: (1) a chart which makes explicit the criteria of judgment used in typing each case by present and past role orientation; (2) the complete codes for the attribute analysis on which Chapter VII is based; (3) tables not reported here (e.g., Recruitment Methods by Functional Type, Problems and Areas of Union Decision by Amount of Expert Influence, Components of "Ideal Expert" by Functional Type, Occupational Origin by Career Theme and by Functional Type, Salary Transition by Career Theme, etc., as well as background data—religion, specialization in college, associational affiliations, etc.).

ANALYSIS OF FUNCTIONAL TYPE

THE OPERATIONS in the construction of the types were these:

1. *All interviews were read twice.* All interviews with officers and administrators, all those with the ex-experts, consultants and outsiders, with broad and varied labor contacts, plus interviews with seventy incumbent staff experts were then analyzed. These seventy were chosen to represent all variations in work noted in preliminary reading, in as many and varied unions as possible. The seventy included the cases on which I had the most detailed and reliable data. All first-priority unions were represented.

2. *Main recurrent activities were classified.* Used here were: detailed job descriptions given by experts, their predecessors, and their assistants in interviews and questionnaires; documents describing the work of departments; samples of their work. In some cases I was able to observe the staff experts at work. In some, published material helped. (See bibliographical note below.) All relevant interview content was clipped, sorted and classified.

3. *Distinctive skills and knowledge required.* Here judgments were based on: what union leaders say they look for in hiring their experts and the troubles they say they have with them; what the experts say it takes to make out and what they look for in hiring assistants. Statistics on occupational and educational background were seen as clues to expert skills, but not in themselves criteria for construction of the types. After all cases on which I had adequate data were typed, however, I examined the types with

reference to these indices of skills and knowledge—as a control over the generalizations derived from qualitative data.

4. *Functions.* These were based on union executives' comments on uses of experts, contrasted with explanations of union executives who make little or no use of them; on experts' own assessments of the direction of their influence; and on my interpretation of the specific decision-making material reported in Chapter IX.

Through the above analysis, I emerged with the three main functional types. When the typology was written, I then went over all of the 129 cases on which adequate data were available. These represented all first-priority unions, all but five of the second-priority unions, plus two extras.[1] Each case was classified according to the type he best fitted. There were only fourteen cases of the 129 which could not be easily and clearly typed. I re-examined these cases (1) to see if they suggested other distinct types or simply overlapped existing categories, and (2) to seek explanation for the overlaps. All fourteen were judged to overlap existing types with one minor modification (eleven embodied aspects of two types, three, aspects of three types). All but three cases, however, clearly showed a concentration of their job activities (well over half their time) and of their skills in one type. They were therefore classified according to the central character of their work and skills; I ignored the minor aspects which fall in another category. The overlaps can be explained as follows:

1. In five cases, the employing union was either new and engaged in vigorous organizing drives or it was involved in an all-out factional war. All five cases, therefore, do some of the work of the Internal Communications Specialist, although the bulk of their work warrants classification elsewhere. See Chapter VI.

2. In one doubtful case the union was small and the expert embodied to some extent all three types; the concentration of his time in activities characteristic of one type, however, permitted classification.

3. Six cases were Facts and Figures Men or Contact Men of

1. Twenty-seven additional cases—including experts in the five missing unions on the second-priority list—could be typed by function from questionnaire job descriptions and secondary sources only, but less reliably. I therefore used these cases only for analysis of social characteristics and the like, and I specify where I introduce them.

rank-and-file origin, who because of talents acquired in and demanded of their previous work, occasionally fulfill the functions of
Internal Communication. See Chapter VI. One of these was also
in a factionalized union.

4. Three cases could not be classified. One (Case 97) led to a
slight modification of the category Facts and Figures Man. See
Chapter IV. The other two (Cases 19 and 107) split their time
about evenly between work characteristic of the Contact Man and
that of the Internal Communications Specialist. Because their skills
in both cases were closer to those of the CM than the ICS, I typed
them accordingly. In the analysis of Influence by Functional Type,
Table 4, I separate these dubious cases.

The utility of this functional typology for classifying all but
three cases can be seen as a rough partial validation of the typology.[2]

Bibliographical Note on the
Functional Typology

The following supplementary sources offer detailed job descriptions on the various occupational groups comprising the functional
types.

Facts and Figures Men. See the articles by Solomon Barkin, Lewis
Carliner, Broadus Mitchell, Katherine P. Ellickson, John M. Brumm,
Warren F. Draper, and Eric Peterson, in J. B. S. Hardman and Maurice
Neufeld, eds., *The House of Labor* (New York: Prentice-Hall, Inc.,
1951), pp. 229-308, 369-70, 500-3; Solomon Barkin, "Applied Social
Science in the American Trade-Union Movement," *Philosophy of Science,* 16 (July, 1949), pp. 193-97; ————, "The Technical Engineering Service of an American Trade Union," *International Labour
Review,* LXI (June, 1950), pp. 609-36; ————, "Labor Union Research Departments," *Personnel Journal,* 16 (February, 1941), pp. 290-
99; ————, "Statistical Procedures in Union Administration," *Indus-*

2. The main difficulty is that the fifty-nine cases not analyzed in the construction of the typology, like the seventy cases that were, had nevertheless
been interviewed and the interviews read. The fact that the fifty-nine fitted
so well may be due in part to the "halo" effect—they may have influenced
the description of the seventy.

trial and Labor Relations Review, 2 (April, 1949), pp. 406-10. See also the account of research and engineering activities which often appears in Officers Reports and Convention Proceedings and in the Labor press—e.g., Albert Epstein, "The Statistician and the Labor Union," *Machinists Monthly Journal,* 61 (March, 1949), pp. 108-9; ————, "Our Research Department," *Machinists Monthly Journal,* 60 (August, 1948), pp. 288-91.

Contact Men. See the articles by Ralph Beaumont and W. C. Hushing on the labor lobbyist, Henry C. Fleisher and Gordon H. Cole on press relations and public relations, Leo Perlis and Mathew Woll on community services, Joseph Kovner and W. P. Kennedy on the labor lawyer in Hardman and Neufeld, eds., *op. cit.,* pp. 134-44, 185-95, 205-8, 333-44, 394-400; two articles on the labor lawyer by Harold A. Katz in *Virginia Law Weekly DICTA,* III, No. 6 (1950), and III, No. 7 (1940); Lester Asher, "The Lawyer in the Field of Labor," *Labor Law Journal,* Commerce Clearing House, IV (January, 1950), pp. 302-4; Robert M. Segal, "Labor Lawyers," *Labor Law Journal,* Commerce Clearing House, I, No. 4 (November, 1950), pp. 1105-7; W. Willard Wirtz, "Collective Bargaining: Lawyers' Role in Negotiations and Arbitrations," *American Bar Association Journal,* XXXIV (July, 1948), pp. 547-52.

On lawyers, the draft report of "Lawyers and Organized Labor: Labor Lawyers," a study done in 1951 as part of the American Bar Association's Survey of the Legal Profession, was made available by its author, Robert M. Segal. For comparative purposes, the similar study on the business side, "Services in Business for Salary: General Counsel" (April, 1951), was made available by its author, Charles S. Maddock.

On lobbyists, two unpublished studies made available by John W. Edelman, Washington Representative of TWUA-CIO were helpful: David J. Farber, "The Labor Lobbyist: A Functional Study" (undated); and a job analysis by Edelman, dated 1/3/49. The article, "Lawyers and Lobbyists," in *Fortune,* XLV (February, 1952), pp. 127-30, 142-50, was useful for comparative purposes.

Internal Communications Specialists. See Part Seven on "Union Education Activity" and the articles by Joseph D. Keenan, Jack Kroll and George Wartenberg on labor political action and education, by M. H. Hedges, Henry C. Fleisher, Nora Piore and J. B. S. Hardman on the Labor press, and by Emanuel Muravchik on "Unions and Minority Discrimination," in Hardman and Neufeld, eds., *op. cit.,* pp. 419-82, 113-33, 171-204, 209-25. The activities of workers' education specialists are also described in Orlie Pell, "Jobs in Workers Education," *Adult Education Journal,* IX (April, 1950); U.S. Dept. of Labor, "Wartime Developments in Workers Education," *Monthly Labor Review,* 61 (August, 1945), pp. 301-18; G. W. Brooks and R. Allen, "Union Training Program of the AFL Paper Unions," *Monthly Labor Review,*

74 (April, 1952), pp. 395-99; A. A. Liveright, *Union Leadership Training* (New York: Harper and Bros., 1951). A series of articles and letters to the editor in *The New Leader* from December 18, 1948, to May 7, 1949, discussing issues raised by James T. Farrell's "A Note on Trade Union Education," December 18, 1948, p. 3, is useful for a grasp of the controversies in this field. The best historical and theoretical discussion of the workers' education movement remains Theodore Brameld, ed., *Workers Education in the United States* (New York: Harper and Bros., 1941).

The writer's participation as teacher or delegate in many labor institutes and education conferences, 1948-1950, and informal discussions with union education directors, as well as notes on conferences of lawyers, editors and labor education specialists supplemented the interview, questionnaire data and documentary sources.

Table 9—Distribution of 156 Cases by Amount of Formal Education and Functional Type (Q Sample)

FORMAL ED. (Highest Attainment)	FFM	ICS	CM	TOTAL N	%
12 grades or less (incl. corresp. courses equiv. to high school)	7	8	4	19	12.2
High school plus part-time study (extension, etc.), but no degree	5	4	3	12	7.7
1-3 yrs. college or "some college"	4	9	5	18	11.5
4 yrs. college (undergraduate degree)	10	10	7	27	17.3
Master's, LLB, or up to 2 yrs. grad. work	35	11	9	55	35.3
Ph.D. or 3 or more years' grad. work	13	4	3	20	12.8
No information	1	1	3	5	3.2
Total Cases	75	47	34	156	100.0

Table 10—Distribution of 122 Cases by Annual Salary* and Functional Type (Q Sample)

CODE NO.	Annual Salary	FUNCTIONAL TYPE Facts & Fig. Men	Int. Com. Specialists	Contact Men	TOTALS
2	$ 3,000- 3,999	0	2	0	2
3	4,000- 4,999	4	2	0	6
4	5,000- 5,999	7	6	2	15
5	6,000- 6,999	12	11	4	27
6	7,000- 7,999	7	10	1	18
7	8,000- 8,999	7	4	7	18
8	9,000- 9,999	5	2	4	11
9	10,000-11,999	12	1	5	18
10	12,000-14,999	0	0	3	3
11	15,000-17,499	0	0	1	1
12	17,500-19,999	0	0	0	0
13	20,000 and over	1	1	1	3
	Total Known	55	39	28	122
?	No. info. (no answer, not asked)	20	8	6	34

* Note: this salary figure *excludes* (1) out-of-town per diem, travel expenses, lodging, food, etc., and (2) in-town "entertainment" and taxi expenses where job calls for such activity. The salary figure, however, *includes* approximate annual amounts for in-town per diem and in-town car allowances where these are clearly considered a part of the annual income. This is computed from a reasonable guess on amount of time in town for the given case (based on respondent's job description) and on the amounts the given union allows. The median annual salary for 122 staff experts on whom I have data is $7,500. Median for all cases where I have both role orientation and salary is also $7,500. The time: 1950-51.

Index

Lazarsfeld, Paul, 113
leaders
access to, 245 ff., 305
administrative style, 201 ff.
background of, 198, 233, 260 ff.
career lines, 259 ff.
changing role of, 196 ff.
confidence of, 223 ff.
competence of, 198, 201 ff.
dependence on, 224 ff.
and educational programs, 85
and expert's influence, 183 ff.
hypotheses about, 305
identification with, 148
independence from, 223 ff., 231
interview guide for, 291f.
legal background of, 233
mobility of, 197
origins, 260 ff.
pressures on, 179f.
prestige of, 84, 146
and radical ideology, 122
and recreation programs, 84
recognition by, 136
religion of, 260
self-image, 74 ff., 201 ff.
social distance from, 260 ff.
leadership, 4 ff.
charismatic, 268 ff.
expert's rise to, 215f.
the "inner-circle," 209 ff.
integration, 101
lower levels, 81
patrimonial, 268f., 271
training for, 87
types, 268f.
(*see also* professionalization)
legislative affairs, 64, 90f.
Legislative-Liberal Missionary, 124 ff.,
167 ff.
Lenin, 18, 119
Lerner, Daniel, 16
Letter Carriers Union, 64, 202
Lewin, Kurt, 273
Lewis, John L., 73
liberals, contact with, 125
Liberal Party (N.Y.), 124
Lindquist, Mel B., 48, 56f.
line offcials (*see* leaders)
line experience (*see* background,
rank and file)

litigation, influence of expert in face
of, 187, 190
Little, Herbert, 82
lobbyists, 64
locals as training-grounds, 216f.
Low, J. L., 197
loyalty
ambivalence in, 133, 141f.
as "ideal" criterion, 270
to ideology, 271f.
of intellectuals, 111 ff.
and leader confidence, 224 ff.
and personal relationships, 211
and political identification, 156
publications' function in, 89
to a sponsor, 222
as survival imperative, 269
and tenure, 256
training for, 87
Lundberg, Ferdinand, 62, 67, 77, 234
Lynd, Robert S., 129

Machinists Union, 202
Macmahon, A. W., 209
"Main Sample," 24f.
malfeasances, expert's knowledge of,
217
Malinowski, Bronislaw, 264
management
fraternization with, 148f.
goals of, 6 ff.
hostility towards, 142
house organs, 82
human relations experts in, 97
influence in dealing with, 181f.
job alternatives in, 113f., 116, 133,
142f., 149, 198
relations with, 6, 191
rights of, 7
training programs in, 83
weapons of, 8
managerial revolution, 209, 237 ff.
Mandelbaum, D. G., 112
Mannheim, Karl, 15, 17, 103 ff.
marital problems, 118
martyrdom, sense of, 117 ff.
Marx, K., 167
Marxist ideology, 117 ff., 263
"mass" society, intellectual's role in,
19, 105 ff.
Massarik, F., 177

BOOKS PUBLISHED BY

The Free Press

Lord Acton, *Essays on Freedom and Power* $6.00

Franz Alexander, M.D. and Hugo Staub, *The Criminal, The Judge, and the Public,* revised and enlarged ed. 4.00

Aristides, *To Rome* 1.00

Aristotle, *Constitution of the Athenians* OP

Raymond Aron, *German Sociology* 4.00

Mikhail Bakunin, *The Political Philosophy of Bakunin* 6.00

Edward C. Banfield, *Government Project* 3.50

Bernard Barber, *Science and the Social Order* 4.50

Salo Baron, Ernest Nagel and Koppel S. Pinson, eds., *Freedom and Reason: Studies in Philosophy and Jewish Culture in Memory of Morris Raphael Cohen* 5.00

Karl Bednarik, *The Young Worker of Today* 3.00

Reinhard Bendix and Seymour M. Lipset, eds., *Class, Status and Power: A Reader in Social Stratification* 7.50

Bernard Berelson, *Content Analysis in Communications Research* 4.00

Bernard Berelson and Morris Janowitz, eds., *Reader in Public Opinion and Communication,* revised and enlarged ed. 6.00

Bruno Bettelheim, *Love Is Not Enough: The Treatment of Emotionally Disturbed Children* 4.50

Bruno Bettelheim, *Symbolic Wounds: Puberty Rites and the Envious Male* 5.00

Bruno Bettelheim, *Truants from Life: The Rehabilitation of Emotionally Disturbed Children* 6.00

Robert Blood, *Anticipating Your Marriage* 5.00

Eugene Burdick and Arthur J. Brodbeck, eds., *American Voting Behavior* 6.00

Herbert Butterfield and others, *The History of Science* OP

Richard Christie and Marie Jahoda, eds., *Studies in the Scope and Method of "The Authoritarian Personality"* 4.50

Albert Cohen, *Delinquent Boys* 3.50

Morris R. Cohen, *American Thought: A Critical Sketch* 5.00

Morris R. Cohen, *A Dreamer's Journey: An Autobiography* 4.50

Morris R. Cohen, *King Saul's Daughter* 3.00

Morris R. Cohen, *Reason and Law* 4.00

Morris R. Cohen, *Reason and Nature,* revised ed. 6.00

Morris R. Cohen, *Reflections of a Wondering Jew* 2.75

Commission on Educational Reconstruction, *Organizing the Teaching Profession* 4.50

Charles Horton Cooley, *The Two Major Works of Charles H. Cooley: Human Nature and the Social Order and Social Organization,* 2 vols. bound in one 7.50

Lewis Coser, *The Functions of Social Conflict* 3.50

Donald R. Cressey, *Other People's Money: The Social Psychology of Embezzlement* 3.00

Herbert Dinerstein and Leon Gouré, *Two Studies in Soviet Controls: Communism and the Russian Peasant* and *Moscow in Crisis* 4.50

Emile Durkheim, *The Division of Labor in Society* 5.00

Emil Durkheim, *Education and Sociology* 3.50

Emile Durkheim, *Elementary Forms of the Religious Life* 5.00

Emile Durkheim, *Rules of the Sociological Method* 3.00

Emile Durkheim, *Sociology and Philosophy* 3.00

Emile Durkheim, *Suicide: A Study in Sociology* 5.00

Joseph Eaton and Albert J. Mayer,
Man's Capacity to Reproduce   2.00
Joseph Eaton and Robert J.
Weil, M.D., Culture and Mental
Disorders   4.00
Abraham Edel, Ethical Judgment:
The Use of Science in Ethics   5.00
Paul Edwards, The Logic of Moral
Discourse   4.00
S. N. Eisenstadt, The Absorption of
Immigrants   6.00
S. N. Eisenstadt, From Generation
to Generation: Age Groups and
Social Structure   6.00
Heinz Eulau, Samuel Eldersveld
and Morris Janowitz, eds.,
Political Behavior: A Reader in
Theory and Research   7.50
E. E. Evans-Pritchard,
Social Anthropology   3.00
E. E. Evans-Pritchard and others,
The Institutions of Primitive
Society   3.00
E. K. Francis, In Search of Utopia   6.50
E. Franklin Frazier,
Black Bourgeoisie   4.00
Georges Friedmann, Industrial
Society: The Emergence of the
Human Problems of Automation   6.00
Lawrence Fuchs, The Political
Behavior of American Jews   4.00
Harlan W. Gilmore, Transportation
and the Growth of Cities   3.00
D. V. Glass, ed., Social Mobility
in Britain   OP
Max Gluckman, Custom and
Conflict in Africa   3.50
Max Gluckman, The Judicial
Process Among the Barotse of
Northern Rhodesia   6.75
Herbert Goldhamer and Andrew
Marshall, Psychosis and
Civilization: Two Studies in the
Frequency of Mental Disease   4.00
Walter Goldschmidt, As You Sow   3.50
Joseph Goldstein, The Government
of a British Trade Union   5.00
William J. Goode, After Divorce   6.00
William J. Goode, Religion Among
the Primitives   5.00
Alvin Gouldner, Patterns of
Industrial Bureaucracy   4.50
Charles M. Hardin, The Politics of
Agriculture: Soil Conservation
and the Struggle for Power in
Rural America   4.00
Charles Hartshorne, Reality as
Social Process   4.00
Paul K. Hatt and Albert J. Reiss,
Jr., eds., Reader in Urban
Sociology, revised ed.   6.50

Amos Hawley, The Changing Shape
of Metropolitan America   4.00
Frederick A. von Hayek,
The Counter-Revolution of Science   4.00
Andrew F. Henry and James
Short, Jr., Suicide and Homicide   4.00
Roger Hilsman, Strategic
Intelligence and National
Decisions   4.00
George Homans and David
Schneider, Marriage, Authority
and Final Causes   2.00
Everett C. Hughes and Helen M.
Hughes, Where Peoples Meet:
Racial and Ethnic Frontiers   3.50
W. H. Hutt, The Theory of
Collective Bargaining   3.00
Herbert Hyman, Survey Design and
Analysis   7.50
Morris Janowitz, The Community
Press in an Urban Setting   3.50
Elihu Katz and Paul Lazarsfeld,
Personal Influence: The Part
Played by People in the Flow of
of Mass Communications   6.00
Patricia Kendall, Conflict and Mood:
Factors Affecting the Stability of
Response   3.50
William Kroger, M.D. and
S. Charles Freed, M.D.,
Psychosomatic Gynecology   8.00
Harold D. Lasswell, Political
Writngs of Harold D. Lasswell:
Psychopathology and Politics;
Politics—Who Gets What, When,
How; Democratic Character,
3 vols. bound in one   5.00
Harold D. Lasswell, Charles E.
Merriam and T. V. Smith,
A Study of Power, 3 vols. bound
in one   6.00
Paul Lazarsfeld and Morris
Rosenberg, eds., The Language
of Social Research: A Reader in
the Methodology of the Social
Sciences   7.50
Paul Lazarsfeld, ed., Mathematical
Thinking in the Social Sciences   10.00
Nathan Leites, A Study of
Bolshevism   6.50
Nathan Leites and Elsa Bernaut,
Ritual of Liquidation:
Communists on Trial   6.50
Seymour M. Lipset, Martin Trow
and James Coleman, Union
Democracy: The Internal Politics
of the International Typographical
Union   7.50
Charles Loomis and others,
Turrialba: Social Systems and
the Introduction of Change   3.00

W. J. H. Sprott, *Science and Social Action* 3.50

Chalmers Stacey and Manfred DeMartino, eds., *Counseling and Psychotherapy with the Mentally Retarded: A Book of Readings* 7.50

Alfred Stanton and Stewart Perry, eds., *Personality and Political Crisis* 3.75

George Stern, Morris Stein and Benjamin Bloom, *Methods in Personality Assessment* 6.00

Eric Strauss, *Sir William Petty: Portrait of a Genuis* 5.00

Leo Strauss, *On Tyranny* 2.50

Leo Strauss, *Persecution and the Art of Writing* 4.00

Adolf Sturmthal, *Unity and Diversity in European Labor* 3.75

Sol Tax and others, *Heritage of Conquest: The Ethnology of Middle America* 5.00

Dinko Tomasic, *The Impact of Russian Culture on Soviet Communism* 4.50

Ernst Troeltsch, *The Social Teachings of the Christian Churches*, 2 vols. OP

Jacob Viner, *International Economics* 5.00

Jacob Viner, *International Trade and Economic Development* 2.75

W. Allen Wallis and Harry V. Roberts, *Statistics: A New Approach* 6.00

Max Weber, *Ancient Judaism* 6.00

Max Weber, *General Economic History* 4.50

Max Weber, *The Methodology of the Social Sciences* 3.50

Max Weber, *The Religion of China* 4.50

Henry N. Wieman, *The Directive in History* 2.50

Harold Wilensky, *Intellectuals in Labor Unions* 6.00

W. M. Williams, *Gosforth: The Sociology of an English Village* 5.00

Martha Wolfenstein, *Children's Humor: A Psychological Analysis* 3.75

Martha Wolfenstein and Nathan Leites, *Movies: A Psychological Study* 4.00